ABDUL⎯ ⎯⎯⎯
TO
KALIGHAT

Joe Roberts was born in Bath, where he now lives with his wife and two sons. For seven years he lived in America, working as a bookseller in Manhattan and as a baker in Austin, Texas. Returning to England in 1984, he cooked in restaurants and worked in Waterstone's. He started writing in 1990.

Joe Roberts' previous books are *Three-Quarters of a Footprint*, about South India, and *The House of Blue Lights*, about coastal Texas. He has written articles for *The Times*, *Sunday Times*, *Cond Nast Traveller* and *Harper's & Queen*. He is currently writing a novel about Bath.

Joe Roberts

ABDUL'S TAXI TO KALIGHAT

Impressions of Calcutta

P

PROFILE BOOKS

First published in Great Britain in 2000 by
Profile Books Ltd
58A Hatton Garden
London ECIN 8LX
www.profilebooks.co.uk

This paperback edition first published in 2001

1 3 5 7 9 10 8 6 4 2

Typeset in 11 on 14pt Baskerville
Design and page make-up by Peter Ward
Printed and bound in Great Britain by
Bookmarque Ltd, Croydon, Surrey

A CIP catalogue record for this book is available
from the British Library.

ISBN 1 86197 282 2

To Emma and Llewelyn, of course,
and in memory of my mother,
Angela Roberts (1921–1996)

BAT-TALA WOODCUTS

The pictures that decorate *Abdul's Taxi to Kalighat* are nineteenth-century woodcuts in the Bat-tala style. Bat-tala is the old name for the north Calcutta neighbourhood around Shobhabazar and refers to a pair of banyan trees that were a local landmark. The area was long associated with printing, originally with printed textiles but from the first quarter of the nineteenth century with illustrated books and pamphlets, cheaply produced and hugely popular. The artists who made the Bat-tala woodcuts were, like their contemporaries, the Kalighat painters in the south of the city, generally anonymous. In style, the woodcuts and the paintings are very similar. Both use line and composition in ways that seem to anticipate European modernism by half a century. The cover is a detail from a Kalighat painting depicting Shiva and Sati.

CONTENTS

FOREWORD

Mother Teresa died of old age in Calcutta just after the Princess of Wales was killed. The world's media had already started one display of bereavement, there hardly seemed room for another, and the old nun's peaceful death lacked the element of shock and tragedy that kept the crash and the floral tributes on front pages for weeks. Mother Teresa did not pass away unnoticed, her death and funeral were merely overshadowed by events in Paris and London.

It meant something to me because I had recently returned from Calcutta where, along with my wife and my baby son, I had spent several months. In that time Mother Teresa had been ailing. I have to confess that I took no particular interest in her, although I met some of her British and American volunteers who told me that Mother (as they called her) had attended Mass with them on Christmas Day and they felt honoured to have caught what was most certainly a final glimpse of the living saint.

I was more struck by the disdainful remarks of my Bengali friends; one of them had even said, 'I wish she would get on and die.'

Before we went to Calcutta, I read Christopher Hitchens' book *The Missionary Position* which I admired for its bold iconoclasm. What I hadn't realised until I arrived in Calcutta was that the book's sentiments were echoed by most educated Bengalis. Again and again I heard them complain that Mother Teresa made their city appear terrible and hopeless in the eyes of the world, that her saintly mystique depended on the western perception of Calcutta as more decayed and more desperate than any other city on earth. That was quite at odds with how they felt about their city.

Sure enough, with the coverage of Mother Teresa's demise, along came those well-worn phrases about 'the poorest of the poor and the lowest of the low' and the descriptions of Calcutta as a dreadful, godforsaken place.

It was just at the time I was starting my own book on Calcutta, a record of our time there and our discovery of it as a civilised and charismatic city. I resolved to show Calcutta in a positive light.

We have grown used to negative images of the city. Everyone is familiar with reports and photographs of its squalor, its beggars and pavement-dwellers. The truth is that many of those images date from the early 1970s, the time of the Bangladesh War. In all the major Indian cities I have witnessed terrible poverty and yet Madras or Delhi are not synonymous with destitution in the way that Calcutta is. Few tourists find their way there and those that do pass through so quickly that they don't have time to shed their preconceptions. I am not denying that Calcutta is poor and overcrowded, but there is much, much more to it than crowds and poverty.

This is not a book about India as a whole, for Bengal was always a place apart, with its own history and development, its own language and ethos. Ever since its founding in 1690, Calcutta has been the great urban expression of Bengali culture. Of course, it could be said that Calcutta was, initially, not an Indian city at all but a British city in India. Although the main thrust behind Calcutta's development was colonial, there was already an ancient and sophisticated civilisation in Bengal. It was the fusion of British and Bengali cultures that gave Calcutta its unique character. For the first time Indians were confronted with a European model of urban life. Some were able to profit from this encounter between East and West and to prosper in a way that allowed them to transcend the old limitations of caste. Many embraced western education. Bengalis came to see themselves as a new type of Indian, in tune with progress and technology. This awareness led, in the middle of the 19th century, to the great flowering of cultural and social activity known as the Bengal Renaissance which, in turn, produced the first stirrings of Indian nationalism. So the people of Calcutta can take pride in an intellectual heritage that pointed India towards Independence.

Really, what impressed me most about Calcutta was the way that it buzzed with conversation. The favourite Calcuttan pastime is talking. This has a name, *adda*. Everybody is talking in Bengali and English and in other overlapping languages; the pavements rattle with chat. Calcutta is a confusing city. Sometimes the incessant *adda* confuses one further. I learnt to enjoy the confusion as one enjoys a kaleidoscope.

Abdul's Taxi to Kalighat is based on one extensive visit to Calcutta and makes no claim to authority. The strongest impressions are generally the first ones. I always let Calcuttans themselves explain to me what needed explaining. Often I was recommended books to read. This book does not tell the history of Calcutta in any formal manner, rather it presents tributaries from the broader course. The historical information comes in the book much as it came in real life, when it was needed. There are already excellent histories composed by trained historians.

This book is not the story of the city but the story of how we found a home in the city. Calcutta is where my son Llewelyn first walked and, fittingly, first spoke. Perhaps he will remember Calcutta as a place where everybody spoke to him, all the time urging him to respond.

I have tried to describe a foreign newcomer's first encounter with Calcutta, its brio, its optimism and its graveyard humour in a way that is not condescending. For that reason I have denied myself rose-tinted spectacles; they would distort the vivid and sometimes clashing colours of the original.

CHAPTER ONE

'Oh, we danced all night,' said Violet, effervescent with gaiety.

The Smiths had been to a Christmas party at the British High Commission. A new Deputy High Commissioner had recently been appointed. By all accounts, he was an unorthodox character.

Violet leant forward. 'He's mad about dancing.'

Ted snorted. 'Never seen anything like it. Boom. Boom. Boom. Lights everywhere.'

'Christmas lights?' I asked.

'No, discotheque. Flash. Flash. Flash. All different colours.'

'Like a dance hall. Well, it broke the ice.' Violet made little swaying movements to indicate a jolly time.

Ted shook his head. 'He brought the equipment with him. Over from London. It's his hobby. Peculiar hobby if you ask me.'

'You never know. People like dancing,' said Violet, bursting into song, 'Roll out the barrel . . .'

'Last night's crowd . . . ' Ted began.

Violet hissed a stage whisper. 'Anglo-Indians . . .'

'Very few genuine British there,' said Ted.

'There must have been a mistake. I told them myself, I said there's a different list. We're not Anglo-Indians . . .' Violet was sometimes mistakenly described as Anglo-Indian which, I believe, wounded her.

Ted continued: 'Nothing against them, mind you. Damn fine nurses. Women more reliable than men on the whole . . .'

'The men, ha . . .'

'Of course, only the best of them get invited to the High Commission. Perfectly respectable people . . .'

'Nothing against them. He had us on the wrong list, that was all.'

The telephone rang. 'Fairlawn Otel.' Patrash listened for a moment then, cupping his hand over the mouthpiece, turned to whisper to his employers.

Violet swelled in her chair, steadying herself before rising. Her face reddened, then she raised her cane to shoulder height like a sword.

'My husband has dealt with the matter. How dare she telephone? The impertinence. Who does she think she is? *Ki shahosh*! *Ki bhebechey*! My husband is a military man, he gives orders, he doesn't take them . . .'

Ted nodded his agreement. He wasn't about to be bullied by Communists.

As Patrash, flustered, relayed the gist of her response in polite Bengali, Violet fanned herself with a folded cotton handkerchief. 'The impertinence . . .' She went on repeating the phrase for several minutes after Patrash had replaced the receiver.

I steered the conversation back to the Deputy High Commissioner.

Ted raised his eyebrows. 'Twenty-five years old . . .'

'No, darling, older. He's got grown-up children.'

'Looked young to me, tiny fellow . . .'

'Small for an Englishman. Mad about dancing.'

'Very good at it too . . .'

We had heard so many conflicting reports about the Fairlawn Hotel: that it was an oasis of order in the chaos and that it was itself an insane place; that it was the only clean hotel on Sudder Street and that rats scurried through the dining-room; that it was good value and that no sensible person would pay those prices; that it was a small eighteenth-century palace; that it was a 1950s seaside boarding house transported to downtown Calcutta; that it was a Noël Coward play; that it was a *danse macabre* . . .

In August I had written to make a tentative reservation and to make sure the hotel would welcome a baby of eleven months. A reply came on purple tissue paper (typed so forcefully that many of the letters had punched right through) from R.N. Pal (Acting Manager) stating that the Smiths were away for the summer. The letter said Llewelyn would be most welcome and that we would be allocated a Superior Room with new U-foam mattresses. Mr Pal suggested that once we had our exact dates, we send a fax. With the letter was a brochure designed so long ago that the guests were depicted with billowing flares and rose-tinted granny specs.

In November I sent the Fairlawn a fax with the dates. I sent my Visa card number and asked them to confirm the booking by return fax. Nothing came for two days. I sent the fax again. Nothing came for two more days. Eventually, on a Sunday morning, I telephoned. The noise of Sudder Street came flooding down the line. 'Fairlawn Otel.'

Patrash the reception clerk checked the bookings and told us we had been expected the previous week. I assured him we had always intended to stay in the second week of December, and that Pal had provisionally booked us in when I had written in August.

[3]

'Bookings is not Pal's business,' stated Patrash firmly. He managed to find us a room though, that more or less fitted our requirements. We would have to spend one night longer in Delhi, before flying to Calcutta.

And so we arrived, to discover we were not booked in at all. There was a moment of panic. Patrash claimed not to remember our telephone conversation.

Then Violet descended the stairs slowly and grandly, shifting her weight from the banister to her malacca cane with each step. She was dressed with formal elegance in a scarlet blazer with brass buttons, a white georgette blouse and a black bombazine skirt. The most arresting aspect of her appearance was that she appeared to be made up for the stage: a generous application of 'slap' to the cheekbones and a high chestnut wig from some Restoration Comedy. A room-bearer stood to one side and saluted her, 'Salaam, Memsahib.' She waved her free wrist at him in the abbreviated way old people have, then stood at the foot of the stairs and smiled at Llewelyn, 'You are a little treasure, aren't you?'

We introduced ourselves and Emma explained what had happened.

'Don't you worry, darling. Patrash, give them Sixteen. Quieter for the little one.'

'We'd like to stay over Christmas,' I said.

Emma specified, 'Until we find a flat. About two weeks . . .'

'Darlings, stay as long as you like. Treat this as your home.'

That settled everything. We learnt it was best to deal with Violet directly and that Patrash only acted with her approval. We had been granted Violet's approval so Patrash treated us amiably. Whenever he saw Llewelyn, he laughed and said, 'Baby's day out, *yaar*.'

[4]

'Hotel, Patrash, not otel. How many times have I told you? You must pronounce the haitch. *Eta pukka sahibder hotel . . .*'

Violet's accent, in both English and Bengali, was clipped and bore traces of Cockney, which was misleading as she was actually Armenian, born and raised in Calcutta. She sounded Edwardian to me, old and regal like a Pearly Queen or the Queen Mother. Violet was enthroned at the back of reception, a small cluttered area of ledgers and metal cabinets to the left of the stairs. Both hands rested on the handle of her cane and her large diamond ring caught the light, sending multiple reflections dancing across the Christmas cards.

Ted sat beside her, wearing a blazer (his handkerchief pushed up the sleeve) and cavalry twill trousers. Ted often looked startled. His eyebrows wavered constantly above his glasses and his handsome, bucolic face. A native of Northamptonshire, Ted had been a Chindit, a member of General Wingate's commando force in Burma. He was, recognisably, a gentleman in the foggy manner of the shires; not a bookish man, perhaps, but unswervingly decent.

The Smiths together were a theatrical performance based on the premise that Independence had not happened, the Raj had dragged on a further fifty years, the imperial sun had still not set and would not while Violet and Ted were in charge of the Fairlawn, as they had been since the end of the Second World War. The notion was saved from unpleasantness by the stagy, almost vaudevillian manner in which it was presented. Far from being resented – for Indians have always loved flamboyant individuals – the Smiths were granted much the same affection that ancient film stars receive in Hollywood. In fact, for some time the Fairlawn had been a smart address for visiting actors, ever since Shashi Kapoor and Jennifer Kendal had stayed there.

[5]

All kinds of medals and citations had come their way from governors and presidents; all had been accepted by the Smiths with good grace, but perhaps no honour was truly valid to them unless it was bestowed by Rani Elizabeth the Queen-Empress.

Behind the small of Ted's back, squeezed in like a woollen draught excluder, crouched Fifi, a white poodle bitch. Fifi was old too, and beneath the thin white curls her skin was pink and sore, and brown channels ran like tears from the corners of her eyes down the sides of her muzzle. Fifi had known her own moment of fame: she had appeared in the Patrick Swayze feature, *City of Joy*.

Patrash, a wiry man with a dark and scrofulous complexion, nodded, muttered '*Han, Memsahib*' reassuringly and dealt with the call in his customary abrupt manner, then busied himself hanging keys on hooks. Violet patted the sides of her wig, making low clucking noises in her throat like the passing of seconds on a digital clock.

Sudder Street, one of the busiest and noisiest cross streets in Calcutta, takes its name from an Arabic term, *sadr 'adalat*, that means 'the council of the chiefs'. This was anglicised in the Hobson-Jobson way to Sudder Adawlaut. Until 1862 the Chief Court of Appeal for the District Judges of the Bengal Civil Service was located on the street. Now it is where budget travellers stay in Calcutta. They drift in, looking shell-shocked, for a few days before heading northward to the Himalayas. Those that stay in Calcutta invariably discover a practical spirituality (it is really Christianity) and, when they are not working for Dr Jack or Mother Teresa, hang around the Sudder Street cafés, disseminating their beliefs in an under-

stated way. In many of the cafés lurk sophisticated young Bengalis who crave stimulating conversation with western students; they usually end up discussing God with earnest girls. One feels they are both short-changed.

'It is all about love, don't you think? Holding the dying in your arms and giving them love . . .'

'Yes, yes. And Oliver Stone? What is his new film about?'

There are bookstalls and STD/ISD telephone booths and places selling souvenirs from Rajasthan. There are a few high-speed tailors but the better tailors, the thorough craftsmen, are around the corner in Madge Lane. The food-stands and street kitchens on Sudder Street sell omelettes and Chinese food; the kiosks sell imported cigarettes and lots of chocolate. Families of beggars pitch camp there and the children learn superior conversational English. I was told that some of the beggar children had read *Captain Corelli's*

Mandolin, the most popular paperback among the backpackers that winter.

Sudder Street is also where canny salesmen do a nice line in dried dogshit from Manali. All kinds of low-life prowl the pavement. At night the area swarms with hookers; around the corner on Free School Street there are several brothels. These establishments do not, on the whole, cater to foreigners; their Indian patrons believe that all female backpackers are hippies and therefore drug addicts and that one day they will find lissome Ingrid from Dusseldorf available for their pleasure. One of the brothels masquerades as a hotel; it is possible, I suppose, that foreign girls might stay there by mistake.

Sudder Street is lined with dormitories and cheap hotels. The Fairlawn, although by no means expensive, is not one of them. It was there long before backpackers came to India.

Violet inherited the hotel from her mother, Mrs Sarkie. In a guidebook to Calcutta published in 1940 the Fairlawn is not listed among the hotels, but in another list, of boarding houses, I found Sarkie's Central Lodge. The street number did not quite tally but the street numbers for many establishments that still exist had also changed.

Ted once told me about a *gully-gully* man who entertained the guests; he opened his act by planting a mango seed in the ground and when the act was over, half an hour later, he took a trowel and dug the seed out again. It had grown roots several inches long. 'Just over there, where Jamal's standing.'

'But that's all concrete.'

'Now it is. Used to be a beautiful lawn.'

I think it was a palace once, a small one, in u...
were palaces all over Calcutta. There was no h...
building, just a row of Corinthian columns. Th...
style of the eighteenth-century merchants' palaces w...
chosen solely for the sake of pomp, it was practical in u...
climate: the openness allowed the air to circulate; shade and
privacy could be arranged by hanging sweet-smelling *khus-khus* grass screens, called *tatties*, between the columns. It was
perfectly reasonable to live in an Athenian temple.

Green walls and sturdy metal gates at the entrance to the yard
provided the Fairlawn with security. The gates were watched
over all day by Mr Bose, an ingratiating fellow with slicked-
back hair who greeted the guests extravagantly, bowing and
saluting and enquiring after one's health. Once he asked for my
card. In return he gave me his own, handwritten on a square of
cardboard cut from a Wills cigarette packet; under the words
M. Bose, Securitty were two telephone numbers. 'So you can
reach me at night,' he told me, with a sly wink.

Every day Mr Bose stood at the gates, picking his teeth
and watching the currency-changers, the drug-dealers and all
the other chancers who prey on gullible tourists, realising there
were commissions to be made. The big *durwans* at the grand
hotels, he had heard, feathered their nests with discreet recommendations. Too mindful of his position to confront the
guests outright, he might drop the hint that should they require
anything hush-hush, he was their man. In the meantime he
would find them an honest taxi driver.

Opposite the hotel gates stood a number of taxis. The
drivers were mainly Bihari Muslims, some of whom had

... Calcutta to work as stevedores. They were organised by a grizzled Sikh called Janwar Singh. Janwar Singh and Mr Bose acted as middlemen between the Fairlawn guests and the taxi drivers. The drivers plainly disliked them both.

After sunset Mr Bose was relieved of his duties by a young Nepali known only by his job description which was *chowkidar* (nightwatchman). Chowkidar, because he spoke comparatively little Bengali, was less involved with the goings-on on Sudder Street.

Chowkidar slept in the lean-to beside the gates that Mr Bose grandly described as his office. Most of the staff seemed to sleep on the premises, in the tiny rooms and cupboards around the servants' courtyard.

Everything was painted a glossy leaf green and there were so many potted palms that the hotel had an overgrown tropical feel. Above the reception counter there was a framed certificate from some environmental agency proclaiming the Fairlawn a 'green hotel'. Emma was amused by this, joking that it referred to the colour scheme. In fairness, I don't think that the hotel added to the pollution in any way. The pollution in that part of Calcutta was chronic; one inhaled dust and exhaust with every breath. 'Never smoked in my life,' declared Ted in partial explanation, 'and Violet gave up in the 1960s. Need strong lungs in this business . . .'

A banyan tree, all twisty and Arthur Rackhamish, grew in the yard; in the late afternoon its branches bristled with sparrows. The *gully-gully* man, who had sprouted the mango seed, had summoned birds from the air to perform tricks. Now he would have plenty of feathered assistants. At all times there were crows and pigeons, and a pair of sleek beige cats might be seen darting across the red oxide floor.

Thousands of fairy lights twinkled when the sun went

down and the yard, with its tables under bicoloured umbrellas, became a place to drink and chat.

On certain days of the week a man sold shawls and bedspreads from one of the tables in the courtyard. He was quiet and not at all pushy, and at first I assumed he was just a guest who had bought the items himself and wanted to inspect them in daylight. The shawls were beautiful, covered with delicate embroidery. I asked where they came from and he said that some were from Murshidabad, others were old and had been restored by especially trained seamstresses.

In front of the reception was a small lounge with green loom chairs and white wrought-iron jardinières, a coffee table with a stack of ancient magazines and unclaimed mail.

Sometimes Ted issued bulletins that were typed out on headed paper and pinned on a board to the side of reception. These were to draw the guests' attention to some religious occasion (Id ul-Fitr, perhaps, or Saraswati Puja) that might affect their arrangements or to remind them that the room-bearers did not bring tea in the morning (there were kettles, milk and tea-bags provided in the rooms). Ted's bulletins were old-fashioned in their composition (he used words like 'presently' and 'inasmuch') and usually ended with the cryptic envoi: *Jehu, Our Chariot.*

The rest of the ground floor was taken up with the dining-room and the kitchen, and a passage around the side of the hotel led to the servants' courtyard.

The dining-room walls were decorated with Royal Family souvenirs, printed tea towels and Himalayan panoramas, old posters from the Soviet Union and Spanish bullfights, all muddled in with prints of Calcutta by Solvyns, the Daniells and Sir Charles D'Oyly.

This was the domain of the dreaded Burra Bearer. The Burra Bearer had neither a chin nor a sense of humour, but managed to cut a considerable dash in his puggaree and cummerbund and his immaculate white gloves, taking great pride in his position while regarding the guests, at whom he scowled menacingly, as an unwelcome interference. At our first lunch Emma asked the Burra Bearer if we might have some butter for the melba toast. 'Butter at breakfast only,' he snarled.

The guests were encouraged to share tables, to ease the work of the waiting staff and to minimise the washing of table-cloths. Most of the tables seated six or eight but there were a couple of smaller tables. There was no high chair available so we took it in turns to hold Llewelyn, a slapstick arrangement that often resulted in strewn food or upturned glasses. We would try to get a small table so as not to ruin other people's meals. In this the Burra Bearer constantly opposed us, shaking his head solemnly while I gave our reasons for dining apart from the other guests. Eventually we just parked ourselves at a smaller table anyway, ignoring his frowns and sighs. Our defiance resulted in slow and surly service.

The Burra Bearer was assisted by a younger man named Jamal. I believe the two were related. Jamal was more agree-able although we learnt that the Smiths mistrusted him for being a Communist.

Ted and Violet took their lunch in the dining-room, but they sat at their own table and their food was set before them in orange Le Creuset oven-dishes from which they served themselves, as if eating at the kitchen table.

The food itself consisted of Edwardian English recipes subtly transformed by generations of Indian chefs. A typical lunch ran like this: thin peppery soup served with dry melba toast, then fried *bekti* fillets with 'tartare sauce' (actually plain mayonnaise) and crisps, then perhaps a mild curry of diced mutton, or roast chicken (carved, I suspect, with a cleaver) with mashed potatoes and cabbage. For pudding there might be 'soufflé' (blancmange) or stewed fruit with custard or rice pudding. The rice pudding was really a Bengali dish, *payesh*, and consequently the best of the Fairlawn puddings, the cook being on familiar territory.

At dinner there would be a savoury as a last course (this was known, in the Raj period, as 'second toast'). This might be spiced chicken liver or even a crushed sardine on toast. It paid to read the typewritten menu pinned up in reception, just to be able to identify this final offering, usually placed on the side of a plate next to the bowl of pudding in a somewhat misleading way. Several times we watched as some hapless guest bit into his savoury after a mouthful of blancmange, supposing it to be some kind of wafer.

We found this type of cooking at clubs and old hotels across northern India. It is a legacy of the Raj that the Indian élite strives to preserve, a distorted memory of British food. I suppose it serves two purposes: it allows nostalgists to reminisce about nursery food, and it gives sophisticates something to sneer at. Actually, in the context of Indian food in general, it is an extraordinary introduction; far more alien in character than, say, the Persian food of the Mughals.

I was intrigued by the condiments: sour mustard, Maggi ketchup that tasted thin and sweet, and the smaller bottles of Tom-Chi, better but still tasting like a sweetened Bloody Mary, and best of all, an unnamed brown sauce, its consistency some-where between HP Sauce and Worcester, which, with its piquant flavour of tamarind, mango, vinegar and anchovies, improved the grey soups considerably.

The high point of this cuisine, surprisingly, is confectionery. We found various bakers in Calcutta producing extraordinarily old-fashioned cakes, plum cakes and pound cakes, based on English originals but cunningly Indianised with spices like cardamom and fennel seed; often brilliant mixtures of shredded peels and candied fruits (including *karamcha*, a sort of sour cherry, and *petha*, strands of white pumpkin) were substituted for raisins, so that a slice of fruit cake became a bejewelled wedge. Bengalis have their own notions about sweet things and feel they have improved the cakes. The best bakery of this kind was said to be Kathleen's, around the corner on Free School Street. We found the shop but it was closed, due to industrial action, and big handwritten posters were plastered on the iron shutters: *We Say No More Hitlary Treatmant Of Staff.*

Up the stairs were countless framed press clippings about the hotel, not all of them favourable. The 'notices' were a fitting show-business touch. The Smiths were so like veteran performers that I could imagine them in the theatrical retirement home in Norwood. We had been told Violet possessed a wonderful, deep singing voice. I don't know if Ted accompanied her on the piano, but it would have been charming if he did. I asked Ted if there had been music halls in Calcutta.

'Indian ones, yes, I think. But the international entertainers were in the cabarets, places along Park Street.' He mentioned several singers unknown to me. 'All the latest songs you'd heard on the gramophone records. Very good at it.'

In the old days, he said, he would wear a dinner jacket if he was 'going on anywhere'; most of the nightclubs had a dress code.

At the top of the staircase, to the right, were the Smiths' private quarters, which included the balcony above the columns. Two cabinets displayed family photographs. Their daughter's wedding. Their grandchildren. Ted as a young officer, looking bedazzled (perhaps by the idea of sitting for a portrait) and radiant with decency. No pictures of Violet as a young woman. It was difficult to imagine her young at all. Her age was part of her authority. She knew the score because she had been around a long time.

Upstairs the chintz set in. There were rose patterns everywhere, and small fresh roses in vases. To the left was a card-table used for typing by a woman known as Mrs A, who was Anglo-Indian. She typed on purple tissue paper.

Mrs A was tall and gentle and dressed in the artistic manner of the late 1950s: bold patterned skirts, colourful sweaters and ear-rings made of twisted wire. Her hair was in a loose bun. I could see her dressed like that in an art school refectory in Liverpool. Emma thought Mrs A was religious; she overheard her one day muttering Hail Marys. I suggested that some Catholics use prayers to time things: two Our Fathers and one Hail Mary to poach an egg, for instance. Emma said she looked serious about it.

Then a dark lounge with bedrooms leading off it, each door draped with a chintz curtain. One of the doors had a brass plaque, the Eric and Wanda Newby Suite. In the dark lounge were more cabinets, full of tribal carvings and model elephants. Nobody really used this room except the hotel electrician who tuned the television for hours at a time, especially during cricket matches. He sometimes required a second or third opinion on these occasions; his colleagues sat with him, judging the reception.

The next room was the office, where the various administrators of the hotel, including R.N. Pal, worked around a large square table with a globe on it. Pal was in his late thirties, plump and usually dressed in the style that Americans call 'Friday casual', chino trousers and a button-down shirt. His accent and manner implied that he had spent a considerable time in the West. Pal always seemed to be arguing with his colleagues, spinning the globe to make a point, as if he were a terrible god venting his fury on the world. Every now and then Mrs A would walk through to calm everyone down.

Beyond the office a walkway led to the annexe, the upper floor of which was a row of bedrooms. The annexe was painted a darker green than the front of the hotel and had a functional military look.

Room Sixteen was at the far end of the row. It was small and cubic (decorated with Chinese scrolls and a framed photograph of Andrew and Fergie) and it had a rickety bath-room plumbed with lengths of hosepipe.

The rooms were attended by a bearer called Osman who came from a village near Cuttack in Orissa. When he was not on duty Osman would sit on the balcony of the annexe tying a fishing-net. It was skilful work, a sort of macramé. He told us that he was a fisherman (a *jeley*) with his own boat. But times were hard, he had debts to clear, and so he had left his wife in charge of the boat (she rented it out to other *jeleys*) and come to the city to find work. He would return home in February, in time for the festival of Id ul-Fitr. He missed his three children; the youngest, a girl, was the same age as Llewelyn.

We also became friendly with Laxmi the ayah. Laxmi was not a Bengali, she came from Gaya in Bihar. She was really Violet's personal maid but she did various jobs around the hotel as well.

It was hard to guess her age; she had grey hair but her face was girlishly pretty and her complexion was dark which disguised the wrinkles. Ayahs tend to dress in a rural manner, still tying their saris in the traditional style of their native villages after years in the city, and Laxmi always wore a pale cotton sari that floated like chiffon, whose original colour had faded into something so muted there was no word to describe it. Its colour changed with the light.

'I like those bunchy saris,' said Emma, 'they're so biblical.'

Llewelyn adored Laxmi and she would take him off our hands for hours at a time. We would hear them laughing together in the servants' courtyard. Other staff would gather and clap along while Laxmi sang snatches of Bihari folk songs. She would take him to see the model elephants in the dark lounge and try to make him say *hathi*, their name in Hindi and Bengali.

CHAPTER TWO

Llewelyn was born in January 1996. We were living in a flat in Bath. The people who lived below us were nudists who kept their own flat so warm that the heat rose up through the floor. We never turned radiators on from winter to winter, we were not even sure that they worked properly. That summer the nudists moved out. We thought about going abroad for the winter months, and what, at first, seemed unrealistic became a possibility, a matter of juggling funds and commitments.

When I first met Emma in November 1990, at a beach café near Benaulim in Goa, it was her enthusiasm for Calcutta (a city I had never visited) that caught my attention. She described it as her favourite city in India; despite its poverty and overcrowding, it was, she told me, grand, battered and soulful. She praised the humour and tenacity of the people. Of all the Indians she had encountered, she had found the Calcuttans to have the gentlest manners.

The winter temperature in Calcutta is that of a mild summer's day in Britain. Of course, it is all comparative. The Bengalis regarded it as extremely cold indeed. People shuffled about in long, old-fashioned tweed coats, taxi drivers wore scarves around their heads, over the crown and under the chin as if they had toothache, and at night beggars set tyres alight to make reeking bonfires in the gutters.

The major Indian cities tend to be ancient; Delhi is at least 3,000 years old, Patna existed in Alexander's time, Varanasi is said to be the oldest living city in the world. Calcutta, on the other hand, is younger than New York. Walk through the city and, despite the frantic bustle, you will see the past everywhere. The present city exists on top of the earlier versions, scrawled over them like a palimpsest. Like most Indian cities, Calcutta appears chaotic; it also appears to be collapsing. To my mind, Calcutta has the fascination of an overgrown garden; I imagine the remaining Georgian and Victorian buildings as sturdy introductions, unkempt but clinging on, overtaken by the indigenous flora, some of which have produced vivid, flamboyant blossoms.

The magnates of the East India Company perceived Calcutta as the grandest of headquarters; a Georgian contemporary of Bath or Edinburgh, their city was composed of wide streets and classical palaces. The Victorians recreated Calcutta as a great port, an Indian Liverpool; they built shipyards, railway stations and mills, vast administrative buildings. And, all the while, alongside these colonial plans, there was a Bengali city developing; a looser, more improvisatory concept, taking what it needed from its own architectural tradition and borrowing freely from the British models.

Until 1911 Calcutta was the second city of the British Empire, more important than Hong Kong or Sydney. Now Calcutta's imperial buildings have taken on the grandeur of much older remains, as if its golden age was not just one human lifetime ago but several centuries.

Calcutta can change from grand and monumental to dark and squalid, very quickly – ruined warehouses, their walls reeking of urine, and heaps of stinking food debris (eggshells, chicken bones) picked over by crows, small black pigs and old women.

Although there is dust everywhere, there is not much litter in the western sense. That is because everything has a price. If you collect enough waste paper, you can sell it, the same with tin cans or broken bottles. What cannot be sold can be used to patch a hole in a roof, or burnt. So it is a paradox: the wretchedness of poverty actually maintains the city. There is no need to tell Calcuttans about recycling, everything you can think of has a secondary life: waste paper, broken bicycles, cow dung – there is someone who can use it. Of course, when this system fails, it fails catastrophically and the streets are haunted by starvation.

On a corner of Chowringhee, a limbless man slithered towards us. The cheapest amputations are performed along the railway tracks, with illicit liquor (if you can afford it) as the anaesthetic. 'Think about that,' said the look in his eyes, 'just think about that.' The traffic clanged and screamed all around us.

Inevitably we were shocked by the beggars of Calcutta. They play across one's vision like a grotesque procession, horrible but horribly theatrical as well. The apparent disorder contains intricate patterns of order and there are just as many classifications of beggar as Mayhew described in nineteenth-century London.

The children especially work on the pest principle, but the really desperate beggars of whatever age just sprawl on their mats groaning and passers-by toss them change.

Figures from the imagination of Grunewald or Francis Bacon: many with missing limbs – tiny stumps like starfish growing from their armpits, as if hands were trying to break through – others with contorted spines, writhing like bony seals.

It was horrifying to witness their misery and degradation, especially the look in their eyes, both pleading and sour with resentment and loathing. My reaction, and Emma's, was not to look, we knew we would be upset. Llewelyn's reaction was quite the opposite; he took it in unblinkingly, as the Calcuttans do.

In London, the worst suffering is hidden away. What you see is dispossession, addiction, mental illness. In Calcutta that's all on display, and worse is what follows – the suffering you would only see in hospital in London. You look down and feel vertigo. It's difficult and frightening to relate to the misery, so you throw your coin and walk on.

Often the most distressing beggars have agents who deliver them to the same spot each morning and gather up the coins at the end of the day; in return the beggar gets food and shelter. An agent might handle several beggars and, if they are sufficiently shocking, make a lot of money.

Yet often the city seemed to us a rackety, vibrant place – brightly painted houses with wrought-iron balconies, boys playing cricket and women with chains of jasmine and *mogra* plaited in their hair.

My eye would catch unlikely classical details: an architrave peeping out from behind iron shutters or a tangled mass of electric wires clinging like ivy to a fluted column.

The older buildings were of brick, covered over with *chunam*, a rough stucco made from lime and ground seashells; the iridiscent effect, in its day, must have been delightful. Often large oblongs of *chunam* had fallen away, as if the walls had withstood cannonade.

I kept thinking of an architectural draughtsman called Greeves, who made fantastic drawings, in the manner of Piranesi, of imaginary cities, often in ruins and all composed of

High Victorian buildings; I wonder if Greeves ever saw Calcutta.

Sometimes there were odd allusions. The office of the East India Railway is modelled on the Farnese Palace in Rome, its corner pavilions all engrimed and covered with what appear to be grey bandages. On the corner of the pavement below we saw a man selling twigs to use as toothbrushes.

We were curious about little shrines we found on the street, that might contain the image of a deity but often no more than a smooth pebble with a hole in it, surrounded by offerings of flowers and incense-sticks. A woman, noticing our interest in the shrines, explained that the pebbles are called *shalagrams* and regarded as very holy indeed; black ones are associated with Shiva, white ones with Vishnu and other colours with Mahadevi the Great Goddess. *Shalagrams*, she told us, are formed naturally and most are found in a tributary of the Ganges called the Gandaki. They are sometimes called 'worship stones'; Hindu families keep them in their household shrines.

After a while I stopped trying to make sense of Calcutta and let the whole thing roll by like images in a dream. Cable spools, like gigantic cotton reels, blocking a side street. Hundreds of identical taxis, all battered and snarling, careering like a stock-car race in slow motion. A red bus nearly squashing us, its conductor reciting the streets and neighbourhoods on its route. Ancient lopsided doubledeckers, trucks painted like gypsy caravans and a red jalopy with blue fish painted on the side. Irritable traffic police in jodhpurs and jackboots. Scuttling clerks in white nylon shirts and polyester trousers. Spry old men in starched *dhotis*. Muslim labourers in prayer-caps and checked lunghis. Hindu pilgrims in dusty orange. Saris, pyjamas, all the bright colours against the grey walls and cement-coloured air. People walking in all directions through the screaming traffic; bicycles, rickshaws, handcarts, headloads. Carbon monoxide, rust, fruit peelings. Advertisements for Limca, NBR Hawaii, Banthool Tooth Powder, Olympic Circus, Kingko's. Posters for soft-porn films at the Metro Cinema (*World of Passions, Night Eyes, Call-Girls In Vegas Vice*). Shoe repair stands, second-hand books and cassettes displayed on tarpaulins. Patent medicines (for indigestion, impotence, low self-esteem) provided by *pansaris*; stalls selling cutlets, omelettes, samosas, fruit salad with tomato, *jhal moori, bhel puri*, green coconuts, sugar cane water, *chai* . . .

We stopped for *chai*, dispensed in little earthenware pots. I was carrying Llewelyn in the Dream Rider, a rucksack for transporting infants, more practical than a pushchair in a city of crowded bazaars and teeming pavements. I usually wore the Dream Rider because Emma found that the straps caused her bosoms to jut out in a way that attracted unwelcome attention; it had occurred to her that girl backpackers complain about sexual harrassment ('eve-teasing', as it's called in India) because the weight of a backpack throws the female form into a position that emphasises a comic-book sexuality. Male onlookers simply cannot believe that a woman who sticks her bottom and breasts out like that is not sexually available. Indian women tend to carry loads on their heads, which allows them more dignity. The women we saw working on building sites had the elegance of figures in a classical frieze.

Emma walks faster than me anyway (and has a better sense of direction) so we must have made a rum family group:

me following Emma like a packhorse, Llewelyn on my back.

This relatively new paternal rôle often made me think of my own father, who died in 1989. He was an architect. He didn't travel much in his life. I doubt he would have enjoyed Calcutta. He liked order, proportion, harmony; he had no time for chaos and detested squalor. He would have liked the civic buildings and the churches best, I think – functional, classical structures designed by military architects. Whereas I was drawn to the untidy, the bizarre hybrids and the grotesqueries: Whiteaway and Laidlaw's, for example, formerly a mammoth Edwardian department store, all crumbling away, only partially occupied, its upper storeys like ragged battlements, patrolled by birds of prey.

We were standing outside Esplanade Mansions, on the corner of Government Place and Esplanade Row. Around the turn of this century, the Mansions were the smartest in town. Still impressive but neglected, the curved belle-époque façades are encrusted with grime and guano, most of the windows glassless.

The upper storeys must have a fine view south over the Maidan, beyond Curzon Park (laid out, it is said, in the form of the Union Jack) and the monument to Sir David Ochterlony (a weird structure, an attenuated Greek column standing on an Egyptian base, crowned with a Turkish cupola).

It was disappointing to find the Curzon Park rat colony had been destroyed, we thought Llewelyn would have enjoyed seeing it. The rats had been fed by the administration staff from Raj Bhavan. 'Over several generations, they grew as big as cats,' we were assured by one such administrator, who happened also to be drinking chai. He evidently missed the rats. 'So gentle, like deers. They would take rice from hand. Their fur was soft and clean, like women's hair,' he murmured, then coughed as if he had embarrassed himself. 'Proteinous diet had boosted their fertility, their numbers had increased so much. We feared their tunnels would undermine the road.' The administrator sighed philosophically. 'It is one of those things . . .'

'Pity,' I said, 'our son loves animals.'

Emma said, 'He's asleep anyway.'

The administrator, a grey-haired, sprucely anonymous figure with an air of suppressed grief (we guessed he was a widower, but it is possible that he missed the rats more than he could say), put a cigarette in his mouth, then discovered he had no matches left. I couldn't help him. A man selling flip-flops (Indians call them 'Hawaiis') obliged with a metal lighter, its jet of flame at least a foot long, which allowed him to remain seated on the ground while the administrator leant forward.

Beside the flip-flop man sat a fortune-teller, a bare-chested staring-eyed man with peculiarly mobile pectoral and abdominal muscles. He sat on a tarpaulin with one chart showing the organs of a human body and another marked out in squares, some of which contained astrological symbols. I asked the administrator if people with medical problems consulted the fortune-teller.

'Not only such people, all kinds come. You see, this man has a bird flying inside his body. He points to chart and shows you where it alights. Each body part has its own department of enquiry, traditional. The bird speaks to him.'

'What kind of bird is it?'

'It is a parrot, but very small.'

'A budgie?' asked Emma.

'It has the power of speech . . .' The administrator puffed a few times. Then he told us he was actually working a half-day and on his way home. When we announced that we were heading south, he offered to cross the Maidan with us. As we headed off, the man with the parrot inside him called after us, 'OK, baby's day out!'

'We will benefit from the fresh air,' said the administrator, but we felt that we would have to venture a long way from the city to find any fresh air at all.

What we did get on the Maidan was space (the word is Persian; it means 'open space') and it is vast, some 1,400 acres in the heart of the city, bounded on the north by Esplanade and Raj Bhavan, on the south by the Lower Circular Road, on the east by Chowringhee and to the west by the river Hugli. It is to Calcutta what Central Park is to New York. The Maidan, the administrator emphasised, was not designed as a park, its origins were military. It was established in 1758 by Lord Clive so that the guns of Fort William could fire freely in all directions.

At the time, explained the administrator, defence was a priority. The city had recently been sacked. Siraj-ud-daula, the Nawab of Bengal, had felt his authority threatened by the East India Company. He could not understand why a group of merchants, officially under his protection, needed a fortress at all, nor was he pleased that his own disaffected subjects took refuge in Calcutta where they generally prospered, encouraging others to cast their lot with the English instead of their native rulers. In the summer of 1756 Siraj's army beseiged the city.

I remarked that it was the time of the Black Hole incident. It turned out to be a contentious remark, for the administrator, like many Bengalis, believed the number of the suffocated to have been exaggerated for propaganda reasons. Whatever the body-count was, it was a gruesome massacre.

(The Poste Restante department of the General Post Office in BBD Bagh now stands on the site of the Black Hole. I liked to joke that our postal address was Black Hole, Calcutta.) For nearly a year Siraj controlled Calcutta, until Clive was sent north from Madras to reclaim the city for the East India Company. Siraj-ud-daula was overcome in a series of battles. With the victory at Plassey, the East India Company found itself in full control of Bengal. New opportunities to make vast profits arose and Calcutta entered its triumphal stage.

The administrator explained that the old fort that had so enraged the Nawab was deemed inadequate, so a new one, large enough to contain the entire British population should another siege take place, was built, clearing tracts of jungle and the village of Gobindapur to form the Maidan.

As the city burgeoned, the Maidan gradually took on civilian status. Statues of kings and viceroys were erected. The statues have gone now but the Anglican cathedral, Saint Paul's, and the Victoria Memorial still stand on its southern stretches, as do the Race Course and the Polo Ground, and across the whole thing runs Red Road (now officially Indira Gandhi Road) which was used, and is still used, for ceremonial parades. The Ochterlony Monument has been renamed Shahid Minar, 'the Martyrs' Monument'.

When we had met the administrator, his grey hair had been brushed and parted tidily. Now the wind on the Maidan had tousled it and, as we scuffed through the dusty topsoil, his stride became loose and lolloping to match his hairstyle. The space was as exhilirating to him as a beach and, although the sadness remained in his eyes, he seemed to kick up his heels with freedom.

The Maidan was like a giant playground where adults became children again. We would see men in office clothes break suddenly into a sprint; not in the virtuous manner of Central Park joggers but, like schoolboys, for the hell of it. We crossed the Maidan often. There were hundreds of little pavilions, each one the headquarters of some sports club, for Calcuttans love to be affiliated almost as much as they love games. Cricket, hockey, *kabaadi* and football are played on pitches all over the Maidan, many games at once on weekend afternoons, attracting crowds of spectators as well as peanut-sellers, acrobats, fortune-tellers with green parakeets, snake-charmers, wrestlers, and men wielding spindly hooked implements to remove the wax from one's ears.

At times it presented a rural picture. We would see boys

tending flocks of goats and, early in the morning, Muslim drovers herding cattle southwards, to the abbatoirs in Kidderpore, and coolies pulling handcarts northwards, laden with goods for Barabazar. Beneath the trees solitary figures did yoga exercises, standing on their heads or arching backwards as if their spines were made of rubber.

From his comments on the Black Hole, I suspected the administrator of anti-British leanings, so I was surprised when he grabbed my arm and asked if I had ever seen a more beautiful building than the Victoria Memorial. 'The most perfect example of classical architecture in Asia. I say it is perfect.'

As a matter of fact, it did not strike me as a particularly good building but it would have been rude to say so because the administrator was so rapturous about its perfection.

The Memorial was Lord Curzon's idea. Its foundation stone was laid by the Prince of Wales in 1906, although the building was not completed until 1921. Funds for this vast project were raised entirely by public subscription.

It was designed by Sir William Emerson, then President of the RIBA. Its admirers (the administrator included) compare the building to the Taj Mahal; indeed the marble used for its facing came from the same quarry, Makrana in Rajasthan.

In fact, it looks like Belfast City Hall. It has a distinctly 'municipal', stodgy look. Emerson made a few nods towards Indian architecture: the domes at the corners have a vaguely Mughal appearance and the whole thing stands between two square ornamental ponds or tanks. The overall effect however is second rate.

Inside, as we later discovered to our delight, the collection is anything but second rate. There are Mughal and Rajput

[29]

miniatures, Persian manuscripts, medieval Indian armour. There are some good portraits by Zoffany and Tilly Kettle as well as Burne-Jones' portrait of Kipling. There is a large collection of landscapes by William Hodges, Sir Charles D'Oyly and the Daniells. Only Queen Victoria's desk looks ragged and in need of repair.

We left the Maidan at Outram Road and found ourselves at the junction of Chowringee Road and Park Street. There we said goodbye to the administrator who, flattening his wild hair with his palms, headed for Lansdowne Road. As we watched him merge into the crowd, Emma remarked on the friendliness of Calcuttans towards complete strangers. We came to recognise this as the urge Calcuttans have to explain themselves and their surroundings to outsiders. Perhaps this is because they feel Calcutta has been misreported so often by foreign observers.

Park Street, with its smart shops and restaurants and mansion blocks, always reminded me of London. In those days before Christmas, it even had illuminations to complete the effect.

It was surprising what a big deal Christmas was in Calcutta although (as in the West) the imagery was more to do with Father Christmas and his sleigh than the Nativity, and the shops were selling Christmas decorations and cards rather than general goods as presents. There were lots of references to the *Burra Din*, which means the Big Day.

On Free School Street, Chinese merchants sold paper lanterns, crackers and paper chains. On Park Street we saw a midget dressed as Santa at the door of a restaurant, employed as a grotesque living ornament.

People queued at Flury's for chocolate cakes decorated

with tinsel bands and paper Santas. I liked the tearoom at Flury's, the brown and orange formica, even the aquarium, reminded me of cafés in my childhood. They even served baked beans on toast there. After some weeks in Calcutta I tried them; the beans were as hard as pebbles. Flury's tearoom was such an institution that the food and drink did not matter; it was a romantic place, its tables occupied by young lovers and newly-weds. Outside, Flury's sign was decorated with dozens of small stars to give it a cinematic glamour and, to many of the customers, holding hands across the formica tabletop was like dropping coins in the Trevi fountain.

Outside, by the doorway of A.N. John the hairdresser's, a man sold me a long cylindrical balloon, printed with a peculiar assortment of imagery: a leprechaun juggled balls that said 'well come', 'happy x-mass' and 'happy birthday'; below the leprechaun, three brontosauruses wallowed in a swamp under the legend 'Dangerous animals: Jurassic'. Llewelyn was pleased with it. I was reminded of travelling fairs in Britain where the rides, especially those for younger children, are decorated with a comparable jumble of references: Michael Jackson, racing cars and extraterrestrials. Perhaps a lifelong love of fairgrounds (the colour and the noise as much as the rides themselves) prepared me for Indian cities: the primitive hand-painted artwork everywhere (trucks, film posters, advertisements in general), the constant hullabaloo and the decorative use of hundreds of small light bulbs.

Walking back toward Sudder Street, we were followed by a group of schoolgirls, all cooing over our ginger-haired baby, exclaiming 'So sweet!' (pronounced in baby-talk as 'Cho chweet!') and imploring us to stop and unstrap Llewelyn so they could hold him. They kept saying, 'Baby's day out, baby's day out.'

'What do you mean, 'Baby's day out'?' asked Emma.

'It's the name of a movie, very popular this year. The baby in it looks like this one . . .' Neither of us had heard of this film before.

Llewelyn soon got used to such attention. At times it was inconvenient: 'Cute baby' was a useful opening gambit for all kinds of hustlers. And sometimes we would be shooing off some exceptionally insistent beggar-child, only to discover that Llewelyn was smiling his encouragement.

The Indian Museum stands on the corner of Sudder Street and Chowringhee; a large Victorian institution, the building was originally a private school. Now its long dark chambers are full of skulls and meteorites and stuffed jackals, but everything dusty and ill lit.

There was usually more excitement on the pavement outside: card sharps, numismatists with displays of ancient brass coins like flattened buttons, booksellers and demonstrators of miraculous household gadgets, such as a skewer with a rotating blade attached – you spike the potato, then turn the blade around and, hey presto, wafer thin slices to fry as crisps. These sold well, and, after each demonstration, beggar-children snatched the raw slices away for their mothers' cooking-pots.

There, one afternoon, we came across a pavement dentist who extracted teeth and, to our horror, replaced missing teeth with those he had pulled from other mouths. He kept a clear plastic box of polished fangs in front of him as well as some crudely fashioned metal ones like small steel tent pegs. His tools were essentially a blacksmith's in miniature: little tongs, pliers and dainty hammers. One would have to be in terrible pain to seek such treatment.

CHAPTER THREE

The room next to ours was occupied by a couple from York called Harry and Rosemary Dent. We were introduced by Laxmi, who had already introduced them to Llewelyn.

Harry was a native Calcuttan, Anglo-Indian, somewhat older and shorter than his English wife; he had retired and Rosemary was approaching that age.

Rosemary was from Yorkshire; she had a tall girl's self-deprecating wit. She worked in a university library. A series of minor disasters (flooded kitchens, wheelclamps) attended their domestic life and these she worked up into comic turns, short enough to throw into conversation.

Rosemary told us they visited Calcutta most years for the Christmas holidays. Usually they stayed with Harry's relatives, but this year there was a wedding in the family so they were staying at the Fairlawn, so as not to get in the way of the preparations that sounded exceedingly involved.

Every day Rosemary filled us in on the proceedings. The bride was Harry's niece, Ursula. The groom, Barty, had been married before and had custody of a young daughter called Emerald. In the days leading up to the wedding, Emerald moved in with Ursula's family. Someone had been dispatched to find an ayah. Rosemary was aghast at how carelessly this was undertaken; an unknown woman with no references whatsoever was brought to live in the house. The ayah turned out to be a thief, making off with the television set as well as several wedding presents. 'That cast a bit of a pall over things,' said Rosemary, turning her mouth down at the corners.

The plot darkened further when Barty's first wife found out where Emerald was living. To try and sweeten the situation Harry's brother, Patrick, invited her to the wedding. Barty and Ursula were aghast, especially when she accepted.

Worse, the first wife – whose name was Daphne – came to stay with an aunt in the neighbourhood, so that she could look after Emerald. This meant that Daphne and her aunt were constantly in the house, upsetting the poor bride.

Daphne was engaged to a man called Findley, who shared Barty's passion for general knowledge quizzes. In fact, they both led quiz teams. So intense was their rivalry that they loathed one another, and had done so long before Daphne came into the equation. Daphne intended to bring Findley to the wedding, to meet Ursula's parents.

And all the while, room by room, the furniture was being taken outside, so that the house could be repainted for the big day. Rosemary told us that many important family discussions took place on a sofa and two kitchen chairs out on the street.

Emma asked Rosemary how she was accepted by Harry's family.

'Well, they don't regard me as foreign because they regard themselves as English. But they do think I'm too soft on the Indians. Among themselves, they constantly vilify the Indians. Indians this, Indians that. I want to say, look in the mirror, you are Indians. Whenever Harry and I get in a taxi, someone makes a note of its number, in case our throats are slit . . .'

Were such attacks common?

'Not at all,' said Rosemary, 'it's just prejudice.'

One morning Rosemary wore, with an otherwise drab outfit, a beautiful shawl of white lawn cotton embroidered with white flowers and leaves. Emma asked her about it and she replied that it was *chikan* work from Lucknow. The shawl was very old, it had belonged to Harry's mother. There used to be itinerant salesmen of embroidered goods, known affectionately as 'chickenwallas'.

Harry was a sweet-natured man but he was rather deaf and spoke quietly which made conversation difficult: he couldn't hear me and, half the time, I couldn't hear him.

But when we did understand one another, I could ask him questions about the Anglo-Indian community that it would have been difficult to ask Mrs A.

Harry was the right person to talk to for he was eloquent and scholarly on the subject. He had written essays on Anglo-Indian history. He explained that Anglo-Indians, or more accurately Eurasians, have existed in India since Alexander's time. The community prefers the name Anglo-Indian (employed for the full range of European-Indian mixtures: Franco-Tamil, Luso-Gujerati, Graeco-Punjabi, Hiberno-Bengali and so on), based on the notion that all Europeans were Sahibs in India, and therefore Anglo. To add to the confusion, all British residents in nineteenth-century India used to be called Anglo-Indians. Anglo-Indians have been called East Indian, half-caste, Mustee, Indo-British and Britasian but it is as Anglo-Indians that they are accepted in the Constitution of India.

It was Harry's guess that the majority are still to be found in Calcutta which is virtually where the community was born.

To begin with, they were not regarded as a separate

community. Many Europeans took native mistresses (these 'sleeping dictionaries' were considered the most effective way of learning Hindustani or Bengali) and often they would marry them.

Although the children of such unions were raised as Christians, when native wives died, they were usually buried apart from their husbands, the Church being 'sniffy', as Harry put it, about such unions. He told me a story about Arabella, the beloved of General Pater of Masulipatam in Orissa, who was denied a Christian burial. The General buried his Arabella in a plot of land beside the small cemetery and then built a brand new church over her grave.

Many leading figures of the Company period, including Colonel James Skinner of Skinner's Horse, had Indian mothers. Colonel William Gardner of Gardner's Irregular Horse married a Mughal princess, as in turn did his son. The Victorian repugnance at 'going native' was not really a consideration in the preceding century.

Anglo-Indians proved immensely loyal – because, in most cases, their Indian mothers had both lost caste and been rejected by their families, their interests lay entirely with the British – and they were invaluable as soldiers, better able to cope with the climate and its attendant illnesses, better at communicating with the native sepoys, better suited to subterfuge and espionage than their British colleagues. But as soon as there were more Anglo-Indians than Britons in India, the situation started to change. Anglo-Indians were promptly barred from the higher military and civil positions. Their children were prevented from going to England to receive the education that would qualify them for such posts. The orphaned sons of Englishmen were forbidden to settle in their fathers' country lest they contaminate the native race.

It was as a result of this that the Indian public schools,

modelled directly on their British counterparts, came into being, and even now the schools have Anglo-Indians on their staff, often old boys themselves. These schools still strive quixotically for a lost ideal. Harry smiled when he told me that his own school (where Lawrence Durrell had studied) had prepared him splendidly for life in the nineteenth century.

The mutiny of 1857 was a watershed in Anglo-Indian history. The establishment of the Raj and the building of cantonments further separated the two communities. The memsahibs arrived in India and mixed marriages became a thing of the past. However, the presence of British army regiments in India (alongside the Indian Army with its native sepoys) brought inevitable encounters between white soldiers and prostitutes and, birth control being at best primitive, at worst nonexistent, the size of the Anglo-Indian community increased as it slipped further from respectability.

The mutiny had given Anglo-Indians the chance to prove their loyalty and, with the inauguration of the railways, the telegraph and the postal systems, they were rewarded with middle-management positions. The railways were an Anglo-Indian stronghold all through the Raj.

Socially, however, they inhabited no-man's-land. Derided by the British as *chee-chees*, it was not unusual for a memsahib, suspecting a younger woman to be Anglo-Indian, to lift the girl's upper lip to check for blueness in the gums just as one might inspect the teeth of a horse. Such treatment led to shame and self-deceit: light-skinned women would pretend their singsong accents were Welsh. It is an odd thing, but the Anglo-Indians of Calcutta actually do sound Welsh. Bad impersonations of both the Indian and the Welsh accents sound broadly similar, I know, but to my ears Indians in general do not really sound Welsh at all – except the Anglo-Indians of Calcutta who speak just like the citizens of Swansea.

Perhaps some have a smattering of Welsh ancestry (the surnames would imply that Irish is more prevalent), perhaps it was the influence of Welsh missionaries and teachers. Whatever the case, a Welsh-sounding accent did nobody any favours; at the time, the English (and the Welsh gentry) found the Welsh accent common. So the Anglo-Indians, who looked like natives and sounded like socially inferior Britons, were certainly not welcome at parties.

At the same time the Anglo-Indians were resented by the Indians as lackeys and favourites. When Independence was granted, many Anglo-Indians felt betrayed and vulnerable to the nationalist forces they had helped the British suppress. Those that could left for Britain, others went to Canada and Australia. Those that remained, especially those in Calcutta, did their best to fit in.

To most Anglo-Indians, Harry felt, this meant carrying on exactly as they always had done. The city itself, the part they inhabited, between Bowbazar and Park Street and especially the streets around New Market, cradled a convergence of European and Indian ideas, aesthetics, histories; the Anglo-Indians felt themselves to be more truly Calcuttan than their Bengali fellow-citizens.

Harry told me that most of the star performers in Calcutta's dance-bands and cabarets of the 1940s and 1950s had been Anglo-Indian. They had a natural feeling for western music and, because they usually had English names, it was possible to promote them as 'international' artistes. Some Anglo-Indian singers went on to bigger things: Engelbert Humperdinck started out as Gerald Dorsey in Madras and Peter Sarstedt who crooned *Where Do You Go To, My Lovely* was from Delhi. I had always assumed Cliff Richard to be Anglo-Indian (his father was a railwayman from Lucknow). Emma had reviewed a biography of him where he denied having any Indian blood at all.

'What nonsense,' said Harry, and I said it puzzled me that he should make such a denial when his extraordinary success, indeed his knighthood, ought to be a source of pride to the Anglo-Indian community.

'People used to be ashamed,' explained Harry, 'and I suppose if you were light-skinned enough, you kept your mouth shut about your origins. It's understandable, really.'

Physically Anglo-Indians look much the same as any other Indians; some are noticeably light-complexioned but most are dark. Harry, for instance, was far darker than both Jamal and the Burra Bearer.

The older generation is more visible than the younger. They can be distinguished by their outdated western clothes. They resemble suburbanites from the 1950s: the women in twin-sets, the men in grey flannels and blazers. Many Anglo-Indians are desperately poor, which makes their effort to keep up appearances all the more poignant. Harry, being a foreign resident, transgressed the dress code, and in his soft shoes, casual shirt and zip-up jacket looked positively bohemian.

Within the hotel, Harry was a mischievous presence, in cahoots with the staff, to whom he chatted in Bengali. He gave me some riveting information. For instance, Patrash's telephone voice was an imitation of a French *maître d'hôtel* employed at the Grand in the 1970s whose urbane manner and Continental accent remained the model for senior hotel workers across the city. This explained the *Otel* pronunciation. Violet clearly had not recognised the Gallic nuances and probably would not have been impressed if she had.

Harry pointed out that the Anglo-Indian food served at the Fairlawn was quite different from the food Anglo-Indians ate at home. In order to preserve their social status, many Anglo-Indian households employed cooks and, in most cases, the cooks were unable to cook anything except simple 'non-vegetarian' Indian food. 'We eat a lot of mutton curry,' he told me. But just as other Bengali fathers brought sweets home, so the Anglo-Indian father brought cakes from Kathleen's, Flury's, D'Gama's or Nahoum's. Hence the survival of the confectioners.

CHAPTER FOUR

Madge Lane, connecting Sudder Street to Lindsay Street and the entrance to New Market, is a narrow, crowded thorough-fare, lined with Muslim tailors – some the equal of any in London, at a tenth of the price – and shoe shops selling brittle, unfashionable shoes, *chappals* and slippers, jewellers specialising in yellow gold, Punjabi *dhabas* exuding wonderful garlic aromas, and a profusion of street kitchens, *pau bhaji* stands, men frying *singharas* (the Bengali name for samosas) and selling cold drinks (Limca, Thums Up, Pepsi).

It was always noisy – taxis, rickshaws and motorbikes pressed through the queues outside the Globe Cinema – and, like Sudder Street, but worse because it was more compressed, it was a place where European tourists found themselves defenceless, without guides or minders, prey to the beggars, con-men and pickpockets, as well as wayward hands on breasts and bottoms.

Lindsay Street is wider and venerable businesses, like Dey's Pharmacy, are set on its arcaded pavement. Some of the garment shops used ancient mannequins, patched up and repainted so that they resembled the victims of unsuccessful plastic surgery: arched eyebrows, rosebud lips and a protrusion, like a small cauliflower, erupting from the forehead. Many of these mannequins were of white people and reminded me inexplicably of *A Clockwork Orange*.

New Market is also known as Hogg Market, after its founder, Sir Stuart Hogg. Nobody calls it Hogg Market however, perhaps because of its many *halal* butchers, although it is possible to buy pork or any other meat there. Just about anything that can be sold is on sale there.

It is a weird red-brick Gothic monstrosity with its clocktower, fretwork bargeboards and corrugated iron roofs. The Lindsay Street entrance resembles a Victorian railway station. Calcuttans have used the clocktower as an assignation point for the last century.

The idea, I'm sure, was to recreate the British notion of a covered market but the Indian bazaar mentality took over and transformed it into a surreal *opéra bouffe* of its own.

Sometimes, around the clocktower, we saw wedding cars entirely covered with roses or decorated with painted wooden feathers to resemble swans or peacocks. The pavement fruit-sellers arranged their wares with remarkable artistry; pyramids of guavas and green bananas, apricots and fresh dates. All this seemed to anticipate the garish selection of goods inside the market.

All around the entrance swarm porters, generally Muslims, whose job is to guide one from stall to stall and carry one's purchases in shallow dish-shaped baskets on their heads. Each porter wears a badge with a number on it. At first, we found the porters annoyingly persistent, but after a few visits we realised how helpful they could be. New Market really was a labyrinth and the assistance of a good porter saved a considerable amount of time. It was only necessary to choose one once; he would recognise us on all our subsequent visits.

We became the charges of an old man called Number Two. His real name was Amjad but he preferred the numerical designation and seemed oblivious to its infantile scatological connotations. What Number Two liked best of all was to be presented with a long and eclectic shopping list. If the list contained some relatively arcane requirements (loudspeakers for a Walkman, say, or disposable nappies) Number Two rose to the challenge with pride. I think he knew exactly what every tradesmen stocked, above and under the counter.

As it happened, Number Two did take an interest in bowels: he often enquired discreetly about my digestion by rubbing his stomach and making a grimace to indicate discomfort. At first, I thought he was telling me that his own stomach was troubling him. He was a great believer in liver salts.

My 1940 guidebook gave a plan of the market; it was still applicable 56 years later. The basic design seemed to be one of radial corridors, each given to their own speciality: china, hardware, drapery, hosiery and so on.

Beyond the flower stalls selling wreaths and stiff bouquets, small tight roses and sickly scented lilies, were the dark nightmarish butchers' halls where goats and chickens forlornly awaited their execution and the stone floors were sticky with blood, and white cats prowled for scraps, and nesting in the walls and under sacks there were (Number Two informed us) large and ferocious bandicoots.

Pigeons and crows flew everywhere, crapping on everything.

There were ancient, creaking electric fans and some parts of the market were still gas-lit. Quite recently a fire had destroyed the northern end of the market, which has been rebuilt in an angular, unsympathetic style.

Rosemary told us she had bought a petticoat in New Market. It was not clear which was the back and which was the front of the garment. The shopkeeper had told her, 'Madam, it is a real bargain, two fronts and two backs, all for the price of one.'

There were many shops providing hideous curios for tourists. There was no need to seek these places out; lupine hustlers approached one every few yards, hungry for commission.

Sheets of dried fruit and Kalimpong cheese (kept moist in banana leaves), barley sugar and hot peanuts were on sale, as well as pellets of peppermint fudge called Green Peas.

The market contained numerous places to eat: the porters themselves dined at a café in the butchers' hall; they ate brains and spleen and every kind of offal served up in pungent red sauces. The chief nutritional benefit of this food, Number Two informed us, was its freshness. All the porters had strong hearts and military digestive systems.

There was a little six-note refrain that we heard all the market workers singing and whistling and sometimes so many joined in that the passageway resembled a musical number from *My Fair Lady*. The words of the refrain were '*Pardesi, pardesi . . .*'

When we learnt that *pardesi* means 'foreigners' we had a paranoid frisson that all the stallholders were alerting one another to our presence, that the song was a kind of signal to raise prices.

It was a relief to learn that it was a popular film song. 'Everyone is singing it. This is the song on our minds,' Number Two reassured us.

At Nahoum's Confectionery we would buy brown bread and Anglo-Indian cakes. They baked cheesecakes, very old-fashioned, like Maids of Honour.

Nahoum Nahoum (known as Mr Norman), a stout, elderly Jew, yellow in the face, always sat at one side of the store, dabbing his forehead with a handkerchief. The first Nahoums arrived in Calcutta as bakers; initially they made the same halva-like confections they had made in Baghdad and sold them to their Iraqi compatriots, but when they opened in New

Market in 1912 they were producing cakes to please Englishmen: walnut cakes and lemon sponges, plum cakes and seed cakes. The shop was still using its original display cabinets.

By the 1920s (according to an old price list I was shown) they were baking a few Armenian pastries (*nazooks* and *goozumgamis*) as well, for they recognised the distinctly cosmopolitan ambiance of the Grey Town. They sold boiled sweets in a staggering variety of fruit flavours.

At the same time the shop remained at the heart of Jewish life and Nahoums sent hampers to Jewish families in far-flung parts of India and Burma. Their kosher cheese was especially popular. Nahoum's wedding cakes were sent as far as China, dispatched with an assistant to repair any damage done to the icing in the transit and to guard the silver stand and knife.

Mr Norman said most of Calcutta's Jewish community descended from Middle Eastern immigrants who arrived in India from cities like Aleppo and Baghdad throughout the nineteenth century, attracted by the stability of the British Raj. There were still two synagogues in the Canning Street neighbourhood.

There had been schools, a hospital, a club and even a weekly newspaper in Hebrew. And there was a resort, Madhupur in the Deoghar Uplands of Bihar, where the Jews relaxed in the winter holidays. In the summer, they went to Darjeeling.

The main hurdle the Jews faced was that, no matter how rich they became, the government refused to classify them as Domiciled Europeans, which of course they were not.

In the early 1940s there were 4,000 Jews in Calcutta. By the end of that decade most had left for Israel. There is no longer a rabbi in town; the faithful must conduct their own services. Mr Norman reckoned the community numbers less than sixty now.

Other minorities were evident: occasionally in New Market we would see groups of women in long chintzy dresses, their heads covered in peculiar frilled bonnets of a matching fabric, so that they resembled Victorian lady bee-keepers. They were Bohra Muslims from a Shi'ite sect, with their own mosque on Lansdowne Road. Emma imagined the mosque had Laura Ashley wallpaper. Bohra Muslims are far more numerous in Bombay than Calcutta. Their ancestors were Yemenis who came to India in the sixteenth century, after the Turkish invasion of their homeland.

I held a special regard for the music shop, Symphony. Because of limited space they displayed mainly cassettes of film music and western pop, but the assistants really loved Indian classical music. They kept the classical cassettes in wooden cases under the counter and brought them out with great reverence, as if they only stocked the work of masters. One assistant, if my eye fell on a particular cassette, would clap quietly; then he would describe to me how Amjad Ali Khan weaves folk melodies into his improvisations on the *sarod*, or V.G. Jog's violin trembles above the rhythm.

He recommended an album of *ghazals* by Begum Akhtar. He informed me that she was the singer in Satyajit Ray's film, *The Music Room*. *Ghazals* are love songs, Persian or Urdu couplets set to music. Translated on the page, *ghazals* are like Imagist poetry.

The Begum has a plaintive voice – she sounds as if she is singing under a dome and, as the notes rise, they float around her – but very stately; it is courtly music. Begum Akhtar died in 1974. She was celebrated as a singer of *thumris*, light classical ballads, in the Punjabi manner.

There were bookstalls inside New Market but their stock was arranged behind the counter in such a way that it was impossible to browse. A few times I was seduced by a promising title, only to find that I had bought a second rate, unattractive book. In any case there were other bookshops that we frequented, some that sold new books and some that sold good second-hand ones.

The most civilised bookshop was the Ritika, inside the Grand Hotel. Certainly their stock was aimed at foreign visitors but it was good stock and, taken as a whole, formed a thorough introduction to Indian culture. The manageress, Mrs Bhandari, encouraged her customers to read current Indian novels; not only would they learn how Indians saw contemporary life, she felt that as writers they manipulated the English language more skilfully than anyone else.

Mrs Bhandari was beautiful in a long El Greco way. Her height was due to her Punjabi blood, and like many high-caste Sikhs, both male and female, she dressed with great elegance. We never saw her in a sari, she preferred the *salwar kameez*, made of rich cotton or heavy silk, always in subtle artistic colours and worn with a well-chosen *dupatta* or scarf that accentuated her ivory complexion and limpid eyes. She should have been painted by Sargent.

Mrs Bhandari (who bore the traditionally masculine first name of Deepak, which reminded me of American girls called Robin) had travelled in Europe and North America. Her husband Anil, a bonsai enthusiast, sailed the world as an officer in the merchant navy. Her son was studying finance in Chicago. To avoid loneliness, she read broadly and critically.

She attended literary discussion groups and, once a week, conversed in French with a circle of sophisticated friends. Sometimes she described the homes of her elegant acquaintances for *House & Garden*.

Mrs Bhandari would emphasise that she was an urban North Indian rather than a Bengali but she had a thorough and discerning knowledge of Calcutta and its culture. She would encourage us to visit the old palaces in the north of the city. 'It will be a surprise for you.' Often we would drop in on her, after some exploration, to ask her about an historical figure or an unexpected community.

For example, we learnt from Mrs Bhandari that there had been a Venetian architect working for the East India Company. This architect, Eduardo Tiretta, was supposed to have been a contemporary of Casanova, exiled in India after a scandal. He made enough money to buy a bazaar that still bears his name, just off the Chitpur Road.

CHAPTER FIVE

Violet was keen for us to meet Shashi Kapoor's son – 'the handsomest boy in India' – who was staying at the Fairlawn. I asked Emma if she found Shashi Kapoor handsome. She said, 'His face, yes, but his body reminds me of a great big door.' I knew what she meant. Violet said his son Karan (whom she called 'Tom') was making a fortune as a male model. All the starlets of Bombay were in love with him.

Shortly afterwards, he came down the stairs. He was undeniably handsome, not at all door-shaped, and everything about his appearance, from his well-combed light brown hair to his shiny black loafers, was immaculate. Violet said, 'Let me introduce you to Felicity Kendal's nephew.'

This unexpected reference to his aunt seemed to throw him. When I shook his hand, it darted from mine like a fish. He said he was on his way to a meeting at the Tollygunge Club. 'Always busy,' said Violet and, after he had gone, she nudged Emma and winked, 'rather an Adonis, don't you think?'

'I'm never sure about vain men,' said Emma.

'Tom? Vain?' Violet insisted that he wasn't vain at all.

'Well turned out, that's all,' said Ted, 'we all looked like that in my day.'

We had noticed a gothic figure, a tall gaunt old man who crept around in the shadows, who always sat in the same chair at the same table in the dining-room and who spoke seldom and quietly in a soft Irish accent. He had a solemn manner and looked down at his food sadly. He always wore tight high-waisted jeans and gym shoes.

I said to Emma, 'I bet he's a defrocked priest.'

He reminded Emma of James Joyce. 'That's not how Joyce looked,' I told her. Emma said it was something to do with the gym shoes.

Eventually Harry Dent introduced us. The gothic man's name was Andy Devane. He was an architect, a widower who had lived at the Fairlawn for several years. I presumed he had retired but he told me he still practised, drawing his designs on sheets of A4 and faxing them over to Dublin.

Why had he moved to Calcutta?

'It's a good place to think about buildings, it puts me thoughts into perspective. Of course, it's hard work at times. That keeps me on me toes.'

Andy advised us not to upset the Burra Bearer. 'Terrible things might happen, I wouldn't put anything past him . . .'

Andy's conversation was peppered with stray bits of information, recommendations and advice: he looked at Emma's feet for instance and announced that she would find sandals the best footwear for Calcutta; the best kind were called *kolhapuris* and he told her the name of a shop that sold them in Ballygunge. The Government Tourist Office on Shakespeare Sarani, he told us, held a list of recommended paying-guest accommodation. Most people took these places for a week but there was no reason at all why one shouldn't stay longer. 'Decent places, some of them, so I've heard.'

[51]

The staff at the Tourist Office turned out to be most helpful, printing us out several sheets of addresses and ticking off the ones they recommended. Many of the landladies offered dinner, bed and breakfast and the rates were reasonable – the most expensive places on the list were still cheaper than the worst backpacker hotels and, as I had been a paying guest before in India, I had a fair idea of what to expect. We decided, once we had found one we liked, we would pay the rent in advance so that we could keep our belongings locked up and come back to our own place after a journey.

That evening we telephoned the first of the recommended places, down at Lake Gardens, a middle-class residential area south of the Dhakuria Lakes. The house belonged to a widow called Mrs Lahiri. I spoke to her son and we arranged to look at the room.

CHAPTER SIX

We shared a breakfast table with a silver-haired American clergyman ('Andy Warhol,' said Emma, *sotto voce*) who professed a great affection for the British Raj (clearly he was delighted by the Fairlawn) and a middle-aged Londoner who was complaining that the English no longer produce or appreciate poetry. The clergyman shook his head sadly, politely declining to comment, except to say that, in his opinion, Flora Annie Steel was an underrated talent. Neither was paying much attention to the other. The Londoner (small, slim; round glasses; long Semitic face; frizzy gingery hair, pink cheeks, soft red mouth; fluttering hands) said that most writers were more concerned with money than literature. The Thatcher years, he remarked to the clergyman, had bred a morbid preoccupation with material success. Emma glanced at me, we had heard this platitude so many times. He spent a few moments tearing into Julie Burchill, whom he regarded as 'a demon of cynicism', then held up his newspaper, to indicate the conversation was closed.

The rest of us contemplated the scrambled eggs that had been set before us. 'Aha,' chuckled the clergyman, 'the legendary 'scandal dogs',' then asked if he was right in assuming Chitpur Road to be a continuation of Chowringhee. Emma told him it was a continuation of Bentinck Street but the three ran in a straight line northwards. The clergyman pronounced it Chow-Ring-Ghee, with pauses between the syllables as if it were a Chinese word. It was an unusual name: later I learnt the road was named after a hermit called Chourangi Giri who lived in the area when it was still jungle.

The newspaper came down again. 'What about Tagore?' asked the Londoner, pushing his glasses back up the bridge of his nose, 'Tagore was a real writer, a genius, and well above the racket of publishing.'

The Londoner introduced himself. He was Albert Lyon, a retired schoolteacher from Greenwich, writing a cultural history of Bengal, from Henry DeRozio to Subhas Chandra Bose. He stated that Tagore's own translations were unsatisfactory (Bertrand Russell's verdict was that the poetry 'does not, in fact, mean anything at all') and one had to read them in Bengali to appreciate them. Albert found the poems to be fantastically crafted, full of complicated lyrical twists and turns, allusions, even puns. All things considered, he said, Tagore was a figure of Shakespearean magnitude, one of the greatest Indian artists of all time.

Albert Lyon was not staying at the hotel. He had his own flat just off Park Street. He came to the Fairlawn for breakfast when he felt homesick for English food and conversation. He did not seem to be on good terms with Violet, who suspected him of Communist sympathies and spoke to him abruptly, if at all. '*Agey holey okey ami tariye ditam, Patrash.* In the old days we'd have slung him out.' Albert was, to his credit, thick-skinned and treated Violet politely. I interpreted Violet's disdain as theatrical: his presence spoiled their act, he was from a different England and, although he would have been acceptable in a walk-on part, he was a strain as a permanent character.

'Are you planning to visit Shantiniketan?' Albert asked.

I said we hoped to. I especially wanted to hear the Bauls perform.

'You do know it's Poush Mela on the 23rd? If you're interested in the Bauls, that's just about their biggest gathering. It's early this winter. Sometimes it falls in January . . .'

He was spending the Christmas holidays at Shantini-ketan.

Later the same day I ran into Albert again. We were both browsing at the Oxford Bookshop on Park Street. I was looking for a book about the Bauls and he was able to recommend Professor Bandopadhyay's study.

The manager of the bookshop greeted Albert warmly and told me, jokingly, that nobody knew more about Bengal than Albert. 'Even we ourselves turn to him for clarification . . .'

I asked how near to completion his book was.

'About half way,' said Albert. But he had not found a publisher. It was most likely, he told me, to be published privately. 'It is a difficult concept, really.'

'I don't see why. A book about Bengal might, at least, be popular with Bengalis.'

'True, true, but the form presents problems . . .' Albert revealed that the book was composed of rhyming couplets, most in English, some in Bengali. In other words, I said, it was a 150,000-word poem.

'Yes. But the point is that it enfolds so much.' He made a cradling gesture with his hands. 'I'm hoping some publisher will be bold enough to take the risk.'

'Why did you decide to write it in verse?'

'There is a tradition, you know . . .'

Mrs Bhandari at the Ritika bookshop knew many writers and spoke of them tactfully. Asked about Albert Lyon, she said, 'He is an unusual poet, he is angry about not being Indian . . .'

Harry Dent knew Albert was a poet and that was enough to put him off. 'The one invalid literary viewpoint on India is that of a foreign poet,' he declared with a fierce look on his face.

CHAPTER SEVEN

We spent some time contacting the friends of friends whose numbers we had been given.

Manish Chakraborty had been the most enthusiastic, arriving at the Fairlawn within two hours of our telephone conversation. We met outside in the illuminated jungle garden.

Manish had a 1920s walk, a shuffling glide, clumsy and graceful at the same time, and, in its way, the perfect gait for a flâneur with architectural interests, although the evidence was that he worked hard, publishing articles and instigating projects. In Calcutta's small world of conservation, Manish was a force to be reckoned with. On many subsequent occasions we were to accompany him: he would stop mid-shuffle to draw one's attention to a wrought-iron balcony or a gingerbread barge-board, speak a few informed and pertinent sentences, all the while drawing his feet slowly together before increasing the speed of the glide towards the next curiosity. Although he took small steps, it was difficult to keep up with him.

Manish was in his late twenties, but heavy smoking and an air of mild anxiety had aged his appearance. Sitting down, he stiffened his neck and kept his head high and cocked, like a cormorant.

He had considerate ways, which he expressed with elaborate courtesy. This courtesy had been put to the test when he had been in England; he had made a point of studying and emulating the manners of everyone he met, but what was appropriate in academic circles had appeared stilted in the nightclubs of Leeds, and the table manners of fellow students were unsuitable for dinner parties.

We laughed. 'You should have just been yourself.'

'But it is important to fit in always, don't you think?'

Manish had studied conservation at York. Calcutta, in fact all of Bengal, he told us, was studded with fine buildings. The problem was that they fell into disrepair and the standard expression of corporate or social prestige was to erect new buildings. It was a matter of persuading people that conservation was worthwhile.

The other drawback was that the people who did approve of conservation only considered very old, pre-colonial buildings worth saving, and the buildings of Bengal were often of European design and less pleasing to patriotic taste.

'That is, of course, claptrap. I have a hell of a job.'

Manish made a great fuss of Llewelyn. 'You must have seen *Baby's Day Out* already . . .'

'To tell the truth, I think that film was more popular in India than it was in the West. We'd never heard of it until we came here.'

'It is fun for all the family,' declared Manish without a trace of irony.

We all went to Nizam's on Hogg Street for dinner, in the Muslim enclave directly north of New Market. To get there we walked straight through the market just as it was closing for the night. I mentioned to Manish that the market porters all seemed to be Muslim. He told me there was actually a mosque inside the market.

Hogg Street was chockablock with people. All along the pavements were stalls selling tinselly bangles, prayer caps and cassettes of *qawwali* musicians from Delhi and Lahore.

There are several cinemas in the area, and many restaurants to catch the post-cinema crowd, serving Muslim specialities like *halim* (a hearty, porridgy stew of mutton, pulses and cereals, traditionally eaten to break the day's fasting during Ramadan), *biryani* and *chaap* (chicken breasts or mutton chops, stewed in a spicy gravy in a huge cooking vessel called a *kadai* which is placed on hot coals at the entrance of the restaurants, so that the pungent aromas entice prospective customers).

Nizam's, Manish insisted, was the best of these establishments. It was a simple, clean place on a street corner, with two dining-rooms, wooden tables and mirrors, and little private booths with curtains, like swimming-pool changing cubicles, where groups of women or families with small children eat. We chose one of the booths.

Manish asked how Llewelyn was pronounced. 'I am always thrown by that double L. Flewelyn, Clewelyn? How is it, please?'

'We say it with an underemphasised H, if anything,' said Emma, 'but you can just say it as if it's one L.'

'And why did you choose this name? Are you Welsh, in fact?'

I said that my father's family originated in Anglesey and that Llewelyn was a family name.

Emma asked how Hindu names were chosen. Weren't most the names of gods?

'Many are, yes. Most mean something or another at least. Manish means 'Lord of the Mind', for instance.' That sounded very grand.

Manish told us that astrologers usually come up with auspicious names for a newborn infant. There might be a choice of five or six and, in a special name-giving ceremony conducted by a priest, each one is written on a banana leaf. Beside the leaves are placed little oil lamps and the one with the strongest flame indicates the right name.

I had heard about another ceremony where as soon as the child can sit up, a book, a gold coin and a pile of earth are set before him. Whichever he chooses is supposed to indicate the career he will eventually follow. Manish said that among Bengalis that ceremony usually accompanies the first taste of solid food which is traditionally *payesh*, the Bengali rice pudding. 'That is why we have the sweet tooth . . .'

Manish leant forward. 'May I ask you a question I ask of all foreign visitors? Why do you come here?'

I let Emma answer that India is 'like visiting a different universe . . .'

'So it's a luxury?'

Emma reddened, saying it made her sound self-indulgent.

'And why not?' asked Manish. 'Tell me, do you regard yourselves as travellers or tourists?'

'Tourists,' I answered, not to be caught out, 'in that travellers are fully nomadic. We may not travel on tour buses but we are making a tour, of our own devising. When it's over, we'll go home again. Students call themselves travellers because they do it on a budget, but they're still here on holiday.'

Manish smiled, 'What's wrong with a Grand Tour of Bengal? People should do this. Don't you agree? In your position, I would choose to be a tourist. But do you travel from boredom?'

'It certainly stimulates my imagination. That stops me getting bored.'

'Oh ho,' said Manish, 'Kierkegaard regarded travel as insufficient to tackle boredom. External changes are not enough. One must make constant inner changes of direction, without committing oneself in any way to a vocation and its responsibility. This approach, which resembles that of a dilettante, steers one towards a higher level of awareness, and that is a reward in itself.'

'The problem is that dilettantes need money,' said Emma.

'I was talking philosophically only.' Manish was quiet for a while, as if unsure that we understood this. 'You are different from many tourists in the sense that you would settle some-where else.'

'If we found the right place,' said Emma.

'Then we would be immigrants,' I said.

The waiter recognised Manish, who often dined at Nizam's. Manish ordered some *kathi* rolls (pieces of mutton, cooked on skewers with onions, wrapped in rotis that had been dipped in beaten egg and fried like French toast), a dish of *murg rezalla* (a chicken curry with hard-boiled eggs, tomatoes and potatoes) and some *roomali roti* (handkerchief bread) to mop it up with. We ended the meal with *firni*, a pudding made of milk, semolina and rose water. Llewelyn particularly enjoyed the *firni*. It was all good and we managed not to over-order for once, to finish the meal satisfied by all the different flavours without feeling stuffed.

Emma said, 'I really liked that, it's working-man's Mughlai cuisine.'

Manish nodded, 'I think that's a fair description. One day we'll go to the Royal Indian Hotel, up by the Nakhoda Mosque. There you'll like.'

I told him we had passed hundreds of restaurants as we had walked around the city, serving Mughlai food, South

Indian food, Punjabi food, Chinese food and European food, but apart from the sweetshops, none of them at all served Bengali food. And yet I had read so much about Bengali food, how it was the most sophisticated cuisine in India, with infinite care taken in the selection and preparation of the ingredients.

Manish lit a cigarette. 'You see, Bengali food is home food, it is not taken in restaurants. It wouldn't be so good. Actually, there are one or two Bengali food restaurants. Aaheli, for instance, is nearby. But when we go out to eat, this food we take. You must visit my home. My mother will cook Bengali food.'

We had already learnt that Manish was a Brahmin. Bengali Brahmins differ from those in other parts of India (who are at least supposed to be vegetarian) in that they eat fish. What about meat? He had certainly eaten mutton and chicken with enthusiasm in front of us. Would his mother cook meat?

'No, no. We take meat outside the house, that's all. At home, we observe the dietary restrictions, within reason that is. Outside, you see, it is up to each one of us.' I asked Manish if he had ever eaten beef. 'I have taken beef once or twice, yes, but I found it unpleasant, like eating slices of leather . . .'

'You seem quite liberal . . .'

'Of course, we are liberal Hindus. That is the style in Calcutta. You have to look at the Brahmos, that is our culture.' We had mentioned to Manish that we were going up to Shantiniketan for Poush Mela. He said, 'Well, that is a Brahmo celebration. It commemorates the initiation of the Maharshi, Rabindranath Tagore's father, into the movement.'

'What does Poush Mela mean?' I asked. Manish said that Poush or Paush was the ninth month of the Bengali year – it meant the Winter Fair.

Manish told us about the Brahmo movement. The impact of western ideas, during the eighteenth and early nineteenth centuries, resulted in an Anglicised Bengali upper class, the *bhadralok* or 'good people', many of whom were attracted to Christianity, which they associated with cultural progress. In the hope of preventing mass conversion, Hindu leaders were forced to carry out considerable reforms as well as to revive certain spiritual aspects long neglected in most branches of their religion.

The most important reformer was Rammohan Roy, who was born in 1772, the son of an impoverished *zamindar*. Throughout his early life he combined filial responsibility with the quest for spiritual wisdom and, as well as restoring his family's wealth in the new commercial atmosphere of Bengal, went on extensive pilgrimages and learnt Sanskrit and Persian. In 1814, at the age of 42, Roy moved to Calcutta where he led the dandified life of a rich *babu* while simultaneously indulging his passion for scholarship. He learnt Arabic, Hebrew, Greek and Latin, and he read many great religious texts in their original language. He published a work on monotheism in Persian and started to seek the basic truths common to all religions; some of Roy's early pamphlets were published by the Unitarian Church. In 1828, Roy founded the Brahmo Sabha, a back-to-basics approach to Hinduism that stressed monotheism and refuted such hallowed institutions as the caste system. Socially, the movement was uncompromisingly progressive. Roy argued eloquently for more widespread English education, principally as a vehicle for mathematical and scientific studies. He ran several newspapers and championed the freedom of the press. In his newspapers Roy campaigned for the abolition of *sati* (widow-burning) that, through his formidable erudition, he proved was without any scriptural sanction. Issues such as child-marriage, Brahmin polygamy and the supposed sinfulness of sea-voyages were also called into question. In 1831 he was awarded the title of Raja and sent to London as the emissary of the Mughal Emperor. There, seated among other foreign ambassadors, he attended the coronation of William IV. He befriended social visionaries like Robert Owen and visited factories in Lancashire where he was taken for 'the King of India'. After two years in England Rammohan Roy died suddenly of meningitis, in Bristol. He is buried there in the Arnos Vale cemetery, in a fine mausoleum commissioned by Dwarkanath Tagore, grandfather of Rabindranath.

Manish asked if we had seen this grave and we confessed that we had not. 'But Bristol is near Bath? You must go upon your return.' He understood that it resembled a miniature Bengali temple.

After Roy's death, he told us, the Brahmo Sabha floundered. Disagreement about the rights of women split the movement, as did the acceptance of inter-caste marriages, and one faction even gravitated away from Hinduism towards Christianity. Eventually the movement split. The original Brahmo Sabha withered away while the ideals of Rammohan Roy were upheld by a new faction calling themselves the Brahmo Samaj. The movement was led by Tagore's father.

The liberal culture of the Brahmo Samaj, Manish believed, had influenced the education system and the civic values of Calcutta. 'This is a very free city. There is not a lot of interference . . .'

'Maybe there should be more interference, to help the poorest people.'

'That there is. I meant on a different level . . .'

'What level?'

Manish said that tourists miss the vitality of Calcutta by focusing on the chaos. 'When it was first our city, we would say when order is injustice, disorder is the beginning of justice

[64]

and, in a way, chaos is still a political badge. It says Calcutta is turning into something else.'

'Into what?'

'I can't say. I can only say this we can use, this we can use. These must be kept.'

'Don't Brahmos recognise the caste system?' asked Emma.

'Yes, as family history.'

It seemed to Manish that Calcutta was one place in India where caste considerations were secondary to the acquisition of wealth. A bourgeoisie of the occidental kind had evolved, encouraged by the British presence and the opportunities it presented. From the beginning, the British merchants were reliant on Bengali intermediaries who subsequently prospered and whose families became the *banedi*, the leading native citizens.

I had read about a British ship, sailing into Calcutta in the early eighteenth century, sending a message ashore that they required an interpreter. The word for interpreter was *dobhashi* but, mutated through a series of Chinese whispers, this turned into *dhobi* or washerman. A *dhobi* went aboard and found himself engaged as a middleman between the East India Company and various native suppliers. He rose to the challenge and ended up one of the wealthiest men in Calcutta. Yet *dhobis* are considered a lowly caste among Hindus.

Manish agreed there were such cases, but insisted that the majority of the *banedi* families were Kayasthas or hereditary scribes, who were undermining the caste system long before the Europeans arrived. The Kayasthas had established themselves in all the secular literate occupations that were Brahmin preserves across the rest of India. They were less conservative, more flexible than the Brahmins. Just as they had learnt Persian to gain employment under the Nawabs, they quickly learnt

English to work with the East India Company and grabbed all the social advantages that came their way.

We said good night to Manish and carried our sleeping baby back to the Fairlawn. He had eaten well and, apart from a slight cough, his cold seemed to have improved. Emma put him in bed beside her. We had found this the easiest thing to do when travelling.

I lay awake listening to a cassette of *Raga Mian Ki Malhar*, performed on the sitar by Ravi Shankar. It was composed by Tansen, the court musician to the Emperor Akbar. Tansen was said to have magical powers: once he performed a night-time raga at noon and the sun immediately set, and whenever he performed *Raga Megh* (another composition associated with rain) clouds would gather over Fatehpur Sikri.

CHAPTER EIGHT

Just after two in the morning, Emma woke me. She said Llewelyn felt hot and she was going to take his temperature.

I had a look at him. He was peaceful enough, but she was right, his little body was baking. Emma put a thermometer strip on his forehead. His temperature was 102.

We both looked at one another in horror. This was the situation we had dreaded most.

Many people had advised us against taking a baby to India, especially Calcutta. But every time we had taken Llewelyn abroad there had been people who thought us crazy and they were usually people who would wrap a baby in cotton wool and keep it in a nursery until it went to school. Our attitude was that life, from the word go, should be an adventure. Nevertheless, we had had some qualms about India. But we had decided it would be feasible if we took the right equipment and had sufficient insurance to fly home if necessary. Now, we felt scared and guilty; we had taken the risk and it had gone wrong in less than a week. For a futile minute or so my brain raced with a new set of challenges, how to get a sick baby out of India. Then I breathed deeply, took control of my panic, resolved to do things a step at a time. The first thing was to see a doctor, as quickly as possible, in case the temperature went on rising.

We woke Llewelyn. He was unusually passive, almost serene. Emma gave him a spoonful of Calpol. I went downstairs to see if anyone was about who could contact a doctor for us, but in vain. We decided to take Llewelyn to the Bellevue Clinic. It was supposed to be the best private hospital in Calcutta; they were bound to have doctors on duty around the clock. We went down to wake Chowkidar.

Sudder Street was eerily quiet, moonlit, the sky full of stars, no traffic at all, the drivers sleeping in their cabs, the dogs sleeping in the gutter, and the beggars sleeping in little ragged encampments along the pavement, under sacks and tattered sleeping-bags and coarse grime-coloured blankets.

A few wakeful men huddled around miniature bonfires, smoking the butt-ends of other people's cigarettes. God, I wanted a cigarette. Nobody said a word, there was no sound at all but our footsteps.

The driver of car 507 was lying on the back seat, swathed in a blanket, a shawl and a headscarf that must have muffled the sound of my knocks on the window, but eventually he woke up and agreed to take us.

As we drove south I thought how quiet this part of Calcutta was at night. There was nothing to distract us, to stop us imagining awful diagnoses. I said, 'It's not malaria. We'd know if he'd been bitten. There's not a mark on him.'

'I never considered malaria. It's meningitis I'm worried about.'

I asked the driver if meningitis was prevalent in Calcutta.

'*Yaar*, melongirus. Anyways, many people this here with melongirus.'

Llewelyn was lying passively in my arms, awake and bewildered. I felt scared, powerless. There were monsters out there I couldn't fend off. Emma was quietly panicking. 'You don't think the Burra Bearer put something in his food, do you? You know, like in that documentary about Rumer Godden?'

'No. We'd all be ill. We were feeding him from our plates.'

We arrived at the gates of the Bellevue Clinic. I leapt out and explained our predicament to the gatekeeper.

He shook his head, not in the wagging manner that implies consent, but firmly and steadily, a definite negative. 'Gates locked, sir.'

'We can see that. Could you open them, please?'

'No, sir.'

The taxi driver spoke to him in Bengali. The gatekeeper went on shaking his head. There was a telephone in his office. I asked if we could speak to a doctor. He refused to allow this, saying, 'This is a private hospital only.'

'We appreciate that. We're prepared to pay. Please could you be more helpful?'

'No, sir.'

We got back into the taxi. Another possibility, I suggested, was to go to one of the five-star hotels, the Taj or the Grand, where there is generally a doctor on call. The driver, who was taking more and more interest in the situation, turned around and said, 'Anyways, children's hospital near this place, *yaar*.'

'Okay, take us there please.'

Hanging from the rear-view mirror was what appeared to be a voodoo talisman: two dried limes and three chillies on a thread, a combination supposed to purify the air and repel flies. I had noticed the same device in many taxis.

The children's hospital was somewhere near Park Circus; it was a small scruffy building, a converted private house. It looked as if it was low on funds, the glass in the windows was dirty and broken. The driver quietly greeted the nightwatchman, who went inside for a few minutes, then opened the gates so that we could drive into the courtyard.

We then walked through a side entrance, past various figures sleeping on wooden benches, to a door that was unbolted by a nurse in a habit-like uniform. We stood in a corridor outside a smelly bathroom while she went to wake the doctor.

The driver asked if he could hold Llewelyn; he took him carefully from Emma and after rocking him for a while held him at arm's length, tilted him gently from side to side. 'Anyways, *yaar*, is hot. No melongirus, mem.'

Perhaps he really knew, perhaps he had seen it before; we were grasping at any sign of hope.

In the light we could see that the driver was a small thin man, around thirty-five, as wiry as a tree, with dark skin and an upright shock of hair. A black line ran straight down the middle of his face, more of a brand than a scar, and when he smiled his teeth were long and pointed and, as a result of the *zarda* he chewed habitually, nicotine yellow. Llewelyn gave him a lazy smile.

'I will take him please.' The doctor, wearing white pyjamas and a shawl, sounded impatient. He felt Llewelyn's stomach and took his temperature (causing him to cry) which had descended to 101. He told us to give him Calpol.

'I have,' said Emma.

'That is why his fever is coming down,' said the doctor. 'Wash him with a cold flannel. Tomorrow morning you may bring him for a blood test, if you wish.'

'What's wrong with him?' I asked.

'Maybe nothing at all. Meningitis I don't think . . .'

He then wrote a receipt for the consultation, twenty-five rupees.

As I handed him the money, he glanced disapprovingly at the driver and muttered, 'You must be careful with such a young one. If all and sundry handle him, the risk of infection is there.'

All the way back to the hotel, Llewelyn suckled. Emma said he felt cooler by the minute. I spoke more to the driver. His name was Abdul. He came from a village near Muzaffurpur in northern Bihar, not far from the Nepalese border; he had a wife and two children there. Several of the Sudder Street drivers came from the same village. Twice a year he went home and worked in the fields with his father. He had lived in Calcutta for twenty years.

We paid Abdul and knocked on the gates of the hotel. Back in our room, Emma checked Llewelyn's temperature again. It was still around 100.

We turned the ceiling fan and the air-conditioning on, sponged our son with cool water and got back into bed.

At 7.30 we woke up again, freezing and exhausted. Llewelyn was cool and composed, as if it had all been our own nightmare, nothing to do with him.

I looked him in the eyes, 'Enough, already! Don't do this to us . . .'

His temperature was 98.4.

'He was teething,' said Emma.

'I thought we had decided he wasn't teething.'

'No, we'd decided that we couldn't risk putting it down to teething, in case it was something else.'

[71]

'I can't remember, I was so freaked out.'

'We'll find the name of a really good doctor and take him there,' said Emma.

I told Violet what had happened and asked who her doctor was. She told us to see Dr Wats on Short Street, 'a smooth operator'.

We shared a breakfast table with Albert Lyon again. He was kind and helpful, having suffered various maladies himself over his time in Calcutta. 'Yes, Dr Wats. Definitely. Very professional. You'd be in good hands there.'

Llewelyn had just finished a slice of papaya and had started on a chipolata.

Violet said, 'Little ones can get a temperature like that. No reason at all. He looks all right to me.'

We said we'd feel happier taking him to a doctor.

Ted had come downstairs. He agreed, 'Rajeen Wats? Everyone swears by him. Treats all kinds of problems. Very good at it.'

Llewelyn beamed at Fifi, who blinked distractedly then snarled at him.

'Steady, old girl.' Ted patted her small white head.

'Shall we telephone and make an appointment?'

'No need to,' said Ted.

A little later, as we were leaving the dining-room, Ted waved me over. 'There is something, um, I wanted to ask you.' He leant forward in his chair. 'Have you been cautious?'

It was such a cryptic question. I guessed he was referring to insurance, and that he had some aversion to discussing personal affairs.

'We're insured to the hilt,' I assured him. 'It's a really comprehensive policy, no cutting corners.'

'Aha! I thought so, I thought so.' My answer plainly satisfied him. He sat back as if he had scored a point. 'We must talk further one day. Not now, though . . .'

CHAPTER NINE

We had an appointment to meet Mr Biswajit Lahiri at his mother's house at Lake Gardens, to look at the room, so we decided to drive down there with Abdul and then visit Dr Wats on the way back.

Out on the street the night's events were known to every-one; the other drivers, even some of the beggars, asked after Llewelyn's health. Abdul took him from Emma and paraded him along the pavement. Wahlen, he called him, buzzing the first syllable, Wahlen Bachha.

'Lake Gardens is very nice place,' said Abdul, 'anyways is lakes and gardens.'

Mr Bose opened the taxi door for us. 'Lake Gardens? Rabindra Sarobar metro district, *han*, nice place. Clean air. Only first you see Alipore.' Alipore is the smartest district in Calcutta.

Just as we were getting into Abdul's taxi, a tall shaven-headed German approached us. A surprising number of back-packers have their heads shaved; perhaps it is easier to cope with intermittent and unreliable showers that way, or perhaps it is some misguided attempt to look spiritual like a monk or a *sanyassin*.

The German asked where we were going and we answered Lake Gardens, which meant nothing to him. Nevertheless he asked if he could come with us.

'No,' said Abdul, 'this is a crazy man.'

'I am not crazy,' said the German, 'I am being hunted.'

He then told us a garbled account of how he had escaped from the International Society for Krishna Consciousness; he knew certain secrets about the movement, and Krishna devotees were attempting to murder him.

'Please, no listen, this a crazy,' insisted Abdul and we drove off.

For weeks after that, I would see the German button-holing European visitors on Sudder Street or Park Street. If he was a fugitive, he was certainly not keeping a low profile. My suspicions were raised when I heard him being discussed by a group of new arrivals in the Fairlawn courtyard; one had agreed to deliver a parcel of clothes to some friends of the German in London, so that they would have proof he was still alive.

I told Abdul about that. He shrugged his shoulders. 'This man anyways very bad and these peoples also crazy . . .'

In the taxi Emma and I realised we were still shell-shocked. I began to feel a peculiar anxiety, a panic attack caused by spelling mistakes. Every notice or sign I read contained a mistake. I saw an *Untied* Bank of India, a general *manger* called Mr Singh. I saw a lorry carrying *highley inflemmable* chemicals. My head was spinning. I wanted to stop reading but I couldn't.

At first I thought my eyes were failing, then I wondered if my eyes were sending false signals to my brain. It was a short step to hypochondriac paranoia.

At a traffic light I saw a little boy with *Sports Are Xeciting* on his T-shirt. I told Emma. 'It doesn't bother me,' she said, 'just think what it means . . .'

It means, I thought, we are all at sea here.

Soon we were driving past Southern Avenue and the bridge over the Dhakuria Lakes, a soothing Japanese waterscape with paths running along the water's edge and trees with leaves the colour of rust.

Across the lakes in the newer, but somehow more chaotic world of the neighbourhoods or *paras*, the traffic lessened; there were more pedestrians on the roads, fewer taxis, more autorickshaws, and there were more cows than in the relatively cow-free city centre.

The air in the narrow streets was cleaner; the smells were of cooking and drains instead of carbon monoxide. The saris drying on clothes-lines rippled like prayer-flags.

The *paras* were self-contained, like small Bengali towns; each one's personality quite individual, something that emanated from its bazaar and wafted on through its squares and playgrounds and its residential streets. Many of the traders were rural people, women selling vegetables and flowers, and old men (called *mirshikars*) selling birds they had trapped in the jungle.

The houses changed too; gone were the classical European details and sharp corners, to be replaced by concrete and cement applied like mud, all slapped on, giving some houses the look of cartoons with windows for eyes and doors for mouths; or else you found the futurist *art deco* style that has lasted longer in Indian architecture than anywhere else in the world, imparting a 1950s science-fiction look to so many developments, colonies and extensions.

There was always a lot of construction going on, in a scurrying termite way; no heavy machinery but gangs of men, women and children tearing down buildings and replacing them. Such labour meant there would be tall mounds of sand in the middle of the street, where children and pariah dogs played King of the Castle.

A miniature railway line, long since abandoned, ran along the southern edge of the lakes, and a small white goat was tethered to a sleeper, like the heroine of a silent melodrama. And just south of that sprawled a real branch line out of Sealdah, with a level crossing, on either side of which there were little shrines to Mahadevi; the deities standing behind mesh doors and, on one of them, a little bell on a chain with which to wake the goddess.

The tracks themselves became a bazaar; small produce like chillies, balls of tamarind pulp and cones of incense, laid out on banana leaves and madras cloths, to be gathered up whenever a train was approaching.

The real bazaar was an area of clapboard Wild West shopfronts and painted signs. There was a toyshop (selling balls, kites and cheap plastic toys, the dolls always representing white children), a tea merchant (who scooped the tea directly from the chest), several pharmacies and an optician's studio. There was a barber shop (displaying photographs of desirable hair-styles) and various kiosks selling everything from light bulbs to biscuits. There was a butcher's shop (a gruesome flyblown place where the carcass of a goat hung from a hook and the butcher hacked off pieces to sell to his customers, first come first served), a shoe shop, a Chinese beauty parlour, photographic suppliers, an ironmonger, two 'Banarasi' *paan* stalls, two laundries (one that repaired shawls), a branch of the Milan Sangha fraternal organisation and a sweetshop. Beside the permanent shops, a plethora of small traders pitched in every available space.

It took Abdul some time to locate Mrs Lahiri's house because Lake Gardens is a peculiarly amorphous district, its streets curving off in all directions and, as often as not, running back on themselves. It was certainly quiet, compared to Sudder Street.

Abdul was enthusiastic. 'Look there, is park for Wahlen,' he pointed to a patch of yellow grass, surrounded by a concrete wall. At one end of the park, some ayahs queued with steel pots outside a government dairy. Abdul said, 'Mother Dairy, *yaar*, very nice milk.'

There were several doctor's surgeries and chemists, which were indicative of a middle-class district. The house numbers were not in any sequence.

Eventually we stopped the car and asked a stroller if he knew where Mrs Lahiri lived. 'Mrs Lahiri who has a son called Biswajit,' I added, to be more specific.

The stroller asked, 'Mr Biswajit, qualified travel agent, as yet not married?'

'That I couldn't say . . .'

He then gave Abdul some directions in Bengali and, minutes later, we found Mrs Lahiri's house, on the same street as the Adhunika Housing Colony. It was a four-storey modernist affair, all concrete and aluminium, painted cinnamon pink. A doorman opened the gate, we followed him along a passage to a sliding screen that was also locked. Abdul remarked on how safe it all was.

Mr Lahiri, a bearded man with glasses that magnified his eyes, giving him an owlish appearance, stepped out of an office on the first floor and complained that we were fifteen minutes late. We apologised, explaining that we had had some difficulty finding the house. 'I am busy just now,' said Mr Lahiri, 'will you have tea?'

The room, on the second floor, struck us as perfectly suitable. It ran the full length of the house with windows on three sides. The walls were white streaked with blue (Indian whitewash often seems to have blue in it) and the floor was dark linoleum.

At one end there was a balcony and a small bathroom. There were two ceiling fans, a lockable cupboard called an *almyrah*, a table and chair, two folding picnic chairs and a large square bed, high off the ground with a thin hard mattress.

Abdul pointed out some holes in the mosquito screens. 'Those will be mended,' said Mr Lahiri.

I was prepared to take it, and so was Emma. We agreed the terms with Mr Lahiri and arranged to move in on the 26th of December.

As we were leaving the room, a figure appeared on the stairs, Mrs Lahiri. She was small, elderly and austere, dressed in the plain borderless sari, called a *thaan*, that widows wear in Bengal. She greeted us by pressing her palms together into a *namaskaar* and asked if we would take *sandesh* with our tea.

We explained that we could not stay, we were on our way to the doctor.

'They will come on the 26th, three days hence,' said her son, and she gave us a saintly smile.

By day, with the Chowringhee traffic in full throng, Abdul's driving turned into charioteering. He could squeeze his battered cab through the narrowest gap, cut across a rival's path or hurtle down an alley if the traffic moved too slowly. Whenever we stopped at a light he would roll his window down and crack jokes with the other drivers. Once we were moving again, if anyone crossed him, he let rip with a volley of insults:

'*Bhenchod*!' '*Kukurer bachha*!' '*Ulook*!'

The last of these, *ulook*, is the Bengali word for an owl, which wouldn't be much of an insult in English. The other two are more obscene.

CHAPTER TEN

Abdul knew exactly where Dr Wats' surgery was. We walked into a crowded waiting-room. As we gave our name to the receptionist, I asked if it would be a long wait, suggesting we make an appointment and return later. She said the doctor would see us within ten minutes. 'What about all these people?' asked Emma.

'They are always here,' she told us, 'the doctor treats if there is time. Where should they wait, outside in the dust?'

So we took our place among the anxious people. I wondered if we were wasting the doctor's time; Llewelyn seemed completely well, but Emma wanted to be sure.

Dr Wats called us into his consulting room. He was a courteous man with an Islamic beard and purple shadows under his eyes. He reminded me of some character from nineteenth-century Lucknow, a cleric with worldly tastes. According to Ted, he was actually a Parsee from a wealthy family.

Dr Wats was assisted by a nurse with a manner as brusque as his was polite. She told us to undress Llewelyn and lay him on the 'mackintosh' (a rubber sheet she had spread across the bed).

'British, huh? Have you met the new Deputy High Commissioner?' Dr Wats asked us, allaying our worries with social chat. Emma told him we had not although we had heard him mentioned by the Smiths.

'Yes, of course. And do the Smiths approve?'

'I think so. Mrs Smith mentioned his dancing . . .'

'Dancing, huh? Well I never . . .' Dr Wats shook his head with amusement. 'I can tell he takes regular exercise. He's a fit man. Perhaps this dancing is the reason. I would never have guessed . . .'

'I don't know if it's all that regular . . .'

'Well, he will find many opportunities to dance in Calcutta,' said Dr Wats. 'You don't mean ballet dancing, huh?'

'No, disco.' I pointed out that we were basing this on one conversation with the Smiths and we did not want to spread misleading information about a man we hadn't met.

'Still,' he chuckled, 'a disco British High Commissioner. That is, in my opinion, a rare and marvellous thing . . .'

Dr Wats pressed Llewelyn's stomach, then opened his mouth to look at the teeth pressing against the red gums, about to burst through.

'Those are the blighters,' he told us.

All he suggested was what we had already done. Dr Wats said, 'He is your first child, huh? Everything worries you. Just relax. Some of my patients have eight or nine children . . .' and burst out laughing as if he had told the most hilarious joke. The peevish nurse laughed as well, and we started laughing too, with glorious relief.

Outside, Abdul exclaimed, 'Wahlen Bachha! Is not ill!' and burst out laughing himself, causing Llewelyn to do the same.

For the rest of our time in Calcutta, we used Abdul's taxi whenever possible. When he wasn't driving, he parked on

Sudder Street and passed his time in conversation with the other drivers.

Abdul had a brother who worked in the area, not as a taxi driver but as a rickshaw-puller. Abdul's brother Faisal looked very like him, except that he was paler and, whereas Abdul wore a grey military-style uniform, Faisal wore a checked *lunghi* and an old white shirt. We never saw Faisal with a passenger, he just seemed to use his rickshaw as his own portable armchair. I was surprised to find that Faisal spoke good English. He always approached us if Abdul was not around, to say what time he would return or to recommend another taxi. Both Abdul and Faisal would greet us with what I initially took to be a salute; I later recognised this gesture (touching the brow with the right hand) as a *salaam*; more ingratiating Muslims would bow as well.

I doubt that Sudder Street was much of a pitch for rickshaw-pullers. There is something ugly about beefy white folk being carted around by thin (and often ancient) Indians. It never appealed to us and I doubt that many of the backpackers would want to be seen in such a politically incorrect conveyance. Rickshaws seemed to be most popular with Chinese women; we would often see them trundling up from Free School Street. A Chinese manicurist came once a week to do Violet's nails, and always arrived by rickshaw. Rickshaws are in fact a comparatively recent introduction; they first appeared in Calcutta around 1910. At first the pullers were exclusively Chinese. Nowadays you never see a Chinese rickshaw-puller.

Rickshaws are used to take groups of small children back and forth from school. Ted told us that they really come into their own during the monsoon months when, with their high chassis, rickshaws can negotiate flooded streets better than cars can.

CHAPTER ELEVEN

We had a late lunch at How Hua, a Chinese restaurant on Free School Street. It was recommended to us by Andy Devane. Chinese food is never one of my favourites; I feel I ought to like it, the ingredients (pork, duck, seafood, ginger, crunchy water-chestnuts and greens) are appealing to me but I usually end up bored by the 'brown' fried taste of everything. Emma, who has been to Hong Kong, insists that the street food there is superb. I admit I have only ever tasted Chinese food prepared for non-Chinese palates. At How Hua the speciality was a Steamer, a bubbling cauldron of soy-flavoured broth in which one boiled various ingredients. We also tried *jiaozi*, little parcels that resembled won-ton or ravioli. Llewelyn seemed to enjoy it all. He showed no evidence of the night's trauma. Emma said she was shattered. I felt listless and not at all hungry.

Calcutta has the largest Chinese community in India and the oldest; there have been Chinese in the city for two centuries. Many Chinese still follow traditional occupations: the leather trade, laundrywork, restaurants, beauty parlours. Chinese dentists are renowned in Calcutta (Andy Devane sang their praises) and I discovered that the Chinese ran piggeries that provided hotels like the Fairlawn with ham and bacon.

Andy admired the Chinese immensely. There was once a proper Chinatown around Bentinck Street and Bowbazar; he told us about the surviving Sea Ip Temple in Chatawala Lane where porcelain fish stand, tail up, on the roof. Although there is still a row of Chinese shoemakers on Bentinck Street (their names have been anglicised from Huan Li to Wanley's, Fo Li to Foley's) most of the Chinese now live in Tangra, a tannery district to the northeast of the city. We would pass the tanneries on the way to the airport, recoiling at the stench of curing fluids. Tangra is supposed to have the best Chinese restaurants in Calcutta.

From the restaurant we walked over to the Park Street Cemetery. The cemetery is at the eastern end of Park Street, occupying a large square of land between Rawdon Street and the Lower Circular Road. It was opened in 1767. For nearly a century British men and women were buried there and in its way it is the grandest and most melancholy monument the British have left in Bengal, far more moving than the Victoria Memorial. A city of the dead: pyramids, obelisks, catafalques, urns and pavilions, many on a colossal scale, all jammed tightly together. I was reminded of Highgate Cemetery but Park Street was more claustrophobic, the tombs were so large and so tightly packed you could not walk between them.

A friend who had known Calcutta in the sixties told us that the cemetery was hopelessly run down and that dogs and tribes of beggars inhabited the ruined mausoleums. When I had mentioned this to Manish, he had insisted that the cemetery was in excellent repair. Sure enough, we found it all shipshape and tidy, the trees and flowers well tended. The maintenance, we learnt, was not paid for by the city but by a

[85]

charity called BACSA (the British Association for Cemeteries in South Asia). Where there were spaces, boys played cricket and others sat on the tombs to watch, or dozed in the shadows cast by the hulking edifices. Near the entrance we noticed a number of potted plants; part of the cemetery was used as a nursery. The Park Street Cemetery is in all the guidebooks; it is plainly a monument that Calcutta values. We were surprised to find ourselves the only foreigners there, in fact the only people to be looking around at all, for all the Indian visitors were playing or relaxing.

We were walking around, reading inscriptions, when a student resting against a headstone asked what we thought of the place and I told him that, at first, we were almost disappointed it wasn't spookier, more desolate. But soon we had attuned to the strange ambiance of the place: elegance overblown into muddle, and what might look grand and monumental in a Kentish churchyard looked like so much outsize masonry in a salvage yard when every other tomb was massive.

The student said that many of the earlier stone memorials came from England but supply had failed to meet demand, which led to local manufacture. The stones were sometimes lifted from ruined Hindu temples in long-abandoned cities such as Gaur in Bengal.

Then he told us that he often came to the cemetery to meditate on historical processes; he had been comparing the East India Company to Walt Disney. 'It is what happens when a business turns into a culture . . .'

Emma felt that the sheer quantity of graves reflected the dreadful mortality rate of the time. Many of the inscriptions had been worn away by two centuries of heat and monsoon rain. The carved symbols, broken columns and hour-glasses, crossed swords and scythes were blurred and blunted. What could be read revealed how perilous life had been for people transplanted from a gentler climate, with little knowledge of tropical medicine. They died in their droves of dysentery, malaria, cholera; other sturdier ones would survive half a lifetime in Calcutta only to die at sea on their way home.

The British in eighteenth-century India must have been accustomed to sudden death; there was a dying season, heralded by the monsoon. Manish had been full of macabre details. He told us that Calcutta's first undertaker, Mr Oldham, who is also buried in the cemetery, made a fortune. He had an office near the cemetery. If there was no chaplain available Oldham conducted the service himself and rented black clothes to the mourners as well. 'There were queues even . . .'

The worst cholera epidemic was during the monsoon of 1817, which killed one tenth of the city's population, claiming 200 lives each day. Often the sufferers were killed not by the disease but by desperate and futile 'cures'. One doctor, noticing that the Indians were less prone to tropical diseases than the British, had proposed complete blood transfusion, pint by pint by venesection.

Funerals (held at night by torchlight, with drums and fifes) became social events. With death all around them, the British lived extravagantly, gambled and duelled, dined and drank heavily, and were carried through the streets lying on their backs in covered palanquins. The nabobs wore exquisite clothes. Naturally, they preferred ostentatious graves.

Manish took some delight in recounting their Hooray Henry behaviour to us. 'Many of these Britishers would flick bread pellets at dinner parties. There was a certain Captain Morrison who announced that he would not tolerate such behaviour. No sooner had he spoken than a bread pellet struck him in the face. In terrible rage, this captain threw a cold leg of mutton at the offender, knocking him off his chair. So a duel ensued. Captain Morrison won the day. That kind of thing was typical, actually . . .'

Many Bengalis, especially the Muslim courtiers of Murshidabad, regarded such loutish conduct with disdain. The nabobs seemed to them pork-eating gluttons, who handled one another's wives and called it dancing; who drank quantities of alcohol and pretended not to be drunk. The feeling was mutual. When Englishmen were entertained by Bengali hosts, they complained about the unfamiliar food and booed at the 'caterwauling' of the musicians. Sometimes, to amuse the foreign guests, clowns with white-painted faces and flaxen wigs performed grotesque imitations of western dances.

Turning a corner, we saw another foreigner, a tall old man, we guessed in his eighties, walking with a black stick, and looking patrician in a broad-brimmed straw hat, a linen suit and a flowing blue chiffon tie. He resembled Cecil Beaton. He was accompanied by an elegant Indian woman, in her sixties, with a Modigliani face and a petrol-blue sari. Emma guessed they were married. My instinct was that she was his hostess in Calcutta.

They were looking at the tomb of Sir William Jones. As we drew closer, we heard the old man speaking in an upper-class Boston accent, that accent that at first sounds English until you realise it isn't and then it sounds very American indeed. The woman spoke sophisticated Indian English with a slight American inflection. He addressed her as Kitty. My guess was that the old man was a history professor at some Ivy League college.

In actual fact, to our surprise, the man, whose name was Foot (he mentioned no other name), was a retired general from Vermont. He was more like a general in the War of

Independence than the cigar-chewing crew-cut stereotype of an American general, and the more he spoke, the less effete he seemed and the clothes, rather than the outfit of an aging exquisite, became those of an eighteenth-century colonial gentleman.

His companion was called Mrs Chellaram. Mrs Chellaram asked how old Llewelyn was. Then she told Emma she had twenty grandchildren. 'Well, I have seven daughters. No sons.' She made a horizontal gesture with her right hand.

General Foot told us that he had an ancestor buried in India, not in Calcutta but in Madras. It was not uncommon in the eighteenth century for a man to make a fortune in India then set himself up in America. Two Foot brothers from Deptford had worked for the Company; only one had survived.

General Foot knew a great deal about the occupants of the cemetery. He had visited it many times and made notes for further research. He told us about Sir William Jones, who served as a judge in the Supreme Court from 1784 until 1790, and made the first step towards an official recognition of Indian philosophy by learning Sanskrit and studying the Vedic laws observed by the Brahmins. Sir William instigated a new spirit of enquiry and he made the study of ancient India as dynamic as the study of ancient Greece. He was a friend of Dr Johnson; Edward Gibbon had declared him a genius. As soon as he arrived in Calcutta he founded the Asiatic Society ('for enquiring into the History, Civil and Natural, the Antiquities, Arts, Sciences and Literature of Asia').

Sir William ascertained that Sanskrit shared a common source with many European languages and the vast corpus of Sanskrit literature began to emerge. He found that the Hindu gods and the classical gods were strikingly similar. He discovered that chess and algebra had Indian origins, as did the heptatonic scale. He established an accurate chronology of

Indian history. Sir William's most riveting assertion was that the people of northern India and their British rulers were, in fact, distant cousins.

Apparently, Jones' reputation as a scholar spread across the civilised world like a legend. Louis XVI was told Sir William spoke every language in the world except that of his own country. General Foot told the anecdote with enthusiasm:

'Now, let me see. The King questioned this, "*Mais, sans aucun doute, il parle Anglais?*" To which the reply came "*Monseigneur, c'est un gallois . . .*" I think that was it . . .'

Mrs Chellaram burst out laughing.

The General smiled at her. 'Kitty dear, you speak such good French. I'm sure you're laughing at me.'

'Not at all, not at all.'

The General said that after his retirement, Sir William and Lady Jones remained in Bengal. They lived in a bungalow beside the Hugli at Garden Reach where Sir William devoted all his time to study. He kept a giant turtle as a pet and seems to have adopted, privately, many ideas from Hinduism, especially the doctrine of reincarnation.

The problem is that now I cannot separate my image of Sir William Jones from my image of General Foot.

The General was staying at the Bengal Club which had reciprocal arrangements with several of his American clubs. He knew about the Fairlawn because a Vermont neighbour, the Reverend James Cleveland, was staying there. 'We met him,' said Emma, remembering Andy Warhol. I was actually thinking in terms of an elderly black man because there is a famous gospel star with exactly the same name.

General Foot showed us another tomb, dated 1828, a model of a Hindu temple. Beneath it lies Major-General Charles 'Hindoo' Stuart, an Irishman who 'went native' with such enthusiasm that he bathed in the river every morning uttering Hindu prayers, and, when he visited Europe in 1804, carried the full complement of household gods with him. Stuart built a Hindu temple at Saugor. It seems odd that he was buried at all, not cremated on the banks of the Hugli.

Mrs Chellaram said, 'I'm afraid we will be late, my dear, if we don't leave immediately. I don't like to hold Ayesha up . . .'

General Foot turned in a sprightly way and said, 'We are off to see the Maharani of Jaipur,' but with an absolutely dead-pan expression, as if to avoid any imputation of self-satisfaction in the announcement.

Then they bade us farewell and we watched them trotting away together, past the tombs and the cricketers and through shafts of sunlight, looking like a drawing by Edward Ardizzone.

Only one of the graves, on the eastern side of the cemetery, had flowers upon it, that of Henry DeRozio, the poet and rad-ical. That flowers were still laid upon his grave suggested that he was a significant figure to contemporary Bengalis.

I wanted to know more so I asked Harry Dent. DeRozio turned out to be a hero of his, whom he described as the Shelley of Bengal. All I knew about him was that he was Anglo-Indian and that his clothes were so foppish he stood out at any gathering. A contemporary portrait I came across shows a round-faced, alert boy; he reminds me of the young Disraeli. DeRozio's heart reeled to political events in Europe; he felt the frustration that rebels have always felt, standing on the touchline, so he wrote poems that howled with rebellion. He published a radical newspaper called *The East Indian*. The paper's message was that Bengalis of whatever colour were a new people capable of governing themselves.

In the early nineteenth century western education was blossoming in Calcutta. Wealthy Bengalis used their money to found schools that would teach a new rationalist curriculum.

DeRozio was engaged to teach senior boys at the newly established Hindu College; he must have impressed the governors
because he was still a teenager himself. The dandified DeRozio
proved immensely popular with his pupils, he was a mixture of
Miss Jean Brodie and Lord Byron. He proclaimed his own
atheism and urged the boys to question their religion, to free
themselves from the strictures of caste. He encouraged
Brahmin boys to discard their sacred threads and to eat beef.

I learnt from Harry that DeRozio's followers called themselves 'Young Bengal'; they saw themselves as a new species of
Indian, liberated by education, and they were probably the first
Indians to speak English amongst themselves. DeRozio taught
them about the French Revolution and the Rights of Man;
some of his students even draped the French tricolour over the
Ochterlony Monument.

Reports of this firebrand teacher scandalised both the
British and the orthodox Hindu establishments and DeRozio
was sacked from the Hindu College. Shortly afterwards, in
1831, he died of cholera, only twenty-three years old. The
'Young Bengal' movement soon fizzled out, based as it was
on youthful enthusiasm, but it set the pattern for any number
of radical groups in nineteenth-century Calcutta. DeRozio's
career is almost too brief for serious consideration, but he
asked questions that Bengalis would go on asking.

That evening we all went to bed early. At some point in the
night I got up and had a bout of diarrhoea. I found that I had
passed a length of parcel string about ten inches long. I reckoned it was from one of the bundles of ingredients boiled in the
Steamer. In my lack of enthusiasm I had not looked at what I
was putting into my mouth, nor had I discerned the taste of

jute amongst the other salty flavours. I felt just like the cows I had seen eating newspapers and damp sacks.

I felt so disturbed by the string that the anxiety I had suffered over the mis-spellings returned. I lay in bed wishing we had stayed in England. But I knew from experience that such torments dissolve in the light of day.

CHAPTER TWELVE

The following day we took the Metro uptown to Girish Park. We expected the Metro to be something horrific; for some time we were loth to venture beneath the surface of the streets. We imagined being pursued along echoing corridors by hordes of lepers. Also, knowing that the city is built on swampland, it struck me that an underground railway could not be very safe. In fact the trains run through a tube that has been sunk into a ditch – the 'cut and cover' method – and there was no tunnelling involved in its creation. The Metro took twelve years to build and opened in 1984. Immediately it became Calcutta's pride and joy, a symbol of its rebirth as a city. Today it is the cleanest underground railway I have seen anywhere. It is a little grim though, with government posters and Tagore poems done in calligraphy, and everything is battleship grey; the Indian grey of railway carriages. Most fares are no more than two rupees, but I suppose that it is too expensive for many people. The Metro was rarely crowded.

Manish was waiting for us on the pavement. He was eager to show us what used to be called the Black Town, the quarters Mrs Bhandari had recommended. I already knew something about the Black Town from the drawings of Baltazard Solvyns.

A number of European artists travelled to India towards the end of the eighteenth century: some, like Tilly Kettle or Zoffany, to paint portraits of the Company grandees and the native princes; others, like the Daniells (uncle and nephew), captured the landscape and the picturesque buildings in prints that proved immensely popular both in India and back in Britain.

Solvyns was an unsuccessful marine artist from Antwerp. He arrived in Calcutta in 1791, almost penniless, eager to make a fresh start. With no particular gift for portraiture or for landscape, Solvyns made a living cleaning and restoring paintings, providing decorative backdrops for balls and entertainments, giving art lessons to children and, when times were really hard, painting coats of arms and insignia on coaches and palanquins.

All this changed when, in 1794, Solvyns met Sir William Jones. Fired by Sir William's intellectual zeal, Solvyns announced his intention to prepare '250 coloured etchings descriptive of the manners, customs, character, dress, and religious customs of the Hindoos'. Sir William agreed that the purpose of the work should be ethnographic, to record with accuracy a more or less neglected subject. Solvyns gathered enough subscribers to make his project possible and, five years later, published the drawings.

The collection was divided into several sections: the first, consisting of sixty-six prints, was entitled 'The Hindoo Castes with their respective professions'; others portrayed servants, holy men, costumes, musical instruments, means of transportation, leisure and festivals.

The project was not a success. The etchings failed to satisfy the popular taste for the picturesque; had they been romanticised they could have found the same audience as Beckford's *Vathek* or Coleridge's *Kubla Khan*, but instead the drawings were repetitive and the colours drab.

Partly, this was because etchings made in India were not up to the quality of European prints. In fact, a London publisher had sixty of the prints redrawn and recoloured and produced a pirate volume, *Costumes of Hindoostan*, that far out-sold Solvyns' original. There were evident limitations to Solvyns' draughtsmanship; his people all looked the same with their long melancholy faces.

In the meantime Solvyns had married a widow with private means and in 1804 they left Calcutta for Paris. There, with financial stability, he tackled the project again, and four volumes, entitled *Les Hindous*, appeared between 1808 and 1812. Solvyns reworked the drawings, adding several more from memory.

The drawings are an extraordinary document of life in the native quarter. The distance from the original (the scenes recreated through the artist's memory and understanding, rather than drawn directly from life) sharpens the work. Even Solvyns' misunderstandings are fascinating.

Solvyns showed a new world being built, the rural Bengalis adapting to an urban environment, the new European-style buildings going up beside the traditional temples. In particular he captured bazaar life: he showed the tradesmen under their wicker canopies, their wares displayed on the ground; he drew the weavers, *tantis*, whose products had been the original economic base of the community, but he also drew the bankers and middlemen whose influence emerged in the bazaars and grew to affect the whole economy of the city.

He showed how the security, wealth and culture of Calcutta attracted the landed aristocracy of old Bengal who built mansions in the Black Town and he drew the entertainments, with dancing girls and musicians, the wealthy inhabitants gave.

He drew religious ceremonies, such as the submersion of

the images at the end of Durga Puja, and Charak Puja, the eve of the Bengali New Year, when devotees attached themselves to giant rotating swings and flew through the air to expiate their sins (in Solvyns' time, the devotees attached themselves with sharp hooks through their ribcage, but nowadays they use straps).

All in all, it was a side of Indian life that no European artist had previously depicted.

Manish felt the area was overlooked: all the guidebooks mentioned the famous landmarks – St Paul's Cathedral or the Victoria Memorial – but, with the exception of the Marble Palace, little was written about North Calcutta. He felt that, in many ways, the buildings up there were more impressive, not transplanted British buildings but a genuine fusion of two distinct traditions. Clearly they were worth preserving.

Many of the merchants' palaces, he said, were too far gone to save, but the smaller houses, still inhabited and hardly changed since they were built in the eighteenth century, could be preserved, and without any need to appeal to government agencies. It was just a matter of making the inhabitants proud of their surroundings.

Sutanuti, he told us, was one of the villages that existed, along with Kalikata and Gobindapur, before Calcutta was built; there was a weekly market there for centuries and it was a centre of the textile trade. The market attracted ships passing through the estuary to and from the upriver ports. Before the Europeans arrived, goods travelled from place to place by river. The Nawabs of Bengal established Satgaon as their chief port. In the late fifteenth century the Portuguese settled at Hugli (the river itself was called the Bhagirathi in those days). Hugli was overtaken in the sixteenth century by the Dutch. To gain control of trade, the East India Company needed a base at the mouth of the river. In 1690 Job Charnock saw the commercial and strategic possibilities of Sutanuti. The city grew around it, transforming a small village into an urban neighbourhood. It remained an area of craftsmen, solvent self-employed families.

CRUTA (Conservation and Research of Urban Traditional Architecture) is an organisation whose mission is to protect the architectural heritage of Calcutta.

As we approached their offices on Beadon Street we heard music; a *shehnai*, a *tabla* and a harmonium. Three musicians were practising in the porch of the Chhatu Babu *thakur dalan* ('the gods' house'), the ceremonial courtyard of an urban estate, where flowers were being delivered for a wedding.

Manish led us in. 'Let me through please, I am an architectural historian.'

A fine early nineteenth-century quadrangle surrounded by galleries. All decorated for the festivities with ribbons and garlands. Classical columns gave way to Gothic arches around the image platform. Manish led us up some stairs (past a chamber where a bridal throne rested on a splendid carpet and two voluptuous women in brocade saris lay asleep on the floor) to a small room lined with portraits of Chhatu Babu, his descendants and adopted sons. Chhatu Babu and his brother Latu were themselves the sons of Ramdulal Dey, the eighteenth-century pioneer of trade with America, whose family mansions are dotted all around Beadon Street.

The CRUTA office is in one of the properties, set back in a little square behind a twin-domed Shiva temple. In the office I met Debashish Naik, the instigator of the organisation, and his colleague Akil Sarkar. Their enthusiasm and local knowledge seemed boundless, and, like Manish, they believed that a sense of its own history can instill more self-respect into a neighbourhood than any effort by politicians.

To demonstrate this they took us on a short tour of the Beadon Street area. 'This is where you can see Charak Puja,' said Manish, 'if you come in April.'

We walked through a maze of narrow streets that were cleaner and better preserved than many of their European counterparts. It was a revelation. I was reminded of some Italian city, Venice or Rome, alleyways and piazzas, the grand beside the mundane.

The architecture (most of it eighteenth century) was quite beautiful, displaying the meeting of European and Indian aesthetics so characteristic of Calcutta itself, and because, by and large, the thoroughfares were too narrow to be penetrated by traffic, the air was light and fresh and the only noise was the murmur of conversation and the sound of children playing.

We were shown a plaque on one wall that commemorated the lyric poet Ramprasad. Ramprasad was not born in Sutanuti, but he worked in the area as a *munshi* while he composed the mystical hymns to the goddess Kali that made him famous; hymns that were sung by all Bengalis, the eighteenth-century precursor to Tagore's *Rabindra Sangeet*. Not long ago the plaque was obscured by a garbage mound. Behind the wall was another small *thakur dalan*. This had been a squalid ruin where alcoholics gathered but now it was cleaned up and evidently well looked after.

I mentioned the glimpse we had had inside the Chhatu Babu *thakur dalan* and soon we were discussing the 'urban rajas', the great *babus*, the late eighteenth-century Calcuttan élite who profited as middlemen between the East India Company and the Bengali merchants, amassing enormous wealth and building themselves opulent palaces in the Black Town.

There is some confusion about the word *babu*: it is, first and foremost, a term of respect – to a Bengali speaker it means much the same as 'gentleman' means in English, and attached to a name it implies the same distinction as 'esquire' might. To the British in India, a *babu* was simply a native clerk who wrote English (it still carries the bureaucrat connotation in present-day Calcutta) and when they found the word applied to the likes of Ramdulal Dey and his contemporaries, they relished the 'jumped-up' image of a clerk masquerading as a gentleman. Manish and his colleagues were using *babu* in the honorific sense, Violet Smith would use it in the disparaging sense.

The palaces were conceived as status symbols, ostentatious displays of taste with a specific desire to impress the Europeans. The architectural style was often European (classical, baroque or Italianate) but the layout was always that of an Indian palace, influenced by the Mughal court: separate living quarters for the men and women, offices, drawing-rooms, servants' quarters and stables, with the central area being the *thakur dalan*, which had evolved from a conventional temple into a courtyard for lavish hospitality. Images of the gods were arranged on a platform that traditionally took up the northern side of the quadrangle.

CRUTA has listed over a thousand *thakur dalans* in North Calcutta, in various states of decay. In some cases, they are all that remain of the palaces.

Often there would be a secondary, more intimate space for entertaining – the *natch ghar*, which translates literally as 'the dance house' but was really a saloon or drawing-room. *Mahfils*, private recitals, were held in these rooms.

In their palaces the *babus* led improbable feudal existences that borrowed freely from both Mughal and European culture. Some of these new grandees indulged in ludicrous extravagance – Tanu Babu, for example, who prospered at the beginning of the nineteenth century, had his entire palace washed daily with rosewater whilst Pradyumna Mallik rode in a brougham drawn by zebras and Bhubanmohan Niyogi distributed a thousand Banarasi saris to the prostitutes of Sonagachi – but the majority were far less decadent, using their wealth for philanthropic purposes, encouraging scholarship and founding schools and colleges.

Their extinction as a powerful élite was probably due to the uncertainty placed in their minds by their education; their cultural identity, their role as a new species of Indian, their reluctant dependence on British trade, all these raised so many questions that they became more occupied with these worries than the cut-throat realities of business.

The *babus* flourished until the middle of the nineteenth century; after that they were represented in popular art and literature as foppish figures, maintaining an absurd façade in the face of encroaching poverty. Wherever, nowadays, their milieu survives it exudes an atmosphere redolent to me of Southern Gothic or Russian literature.

When we got back to the CRUTA office, a remarkable coincidence happened. In walked Mr Rathin Deb, a senior member of the family whose illustrious ancestor Nabakrishna Deb could almost be considered the original 'urban raja'.

Nabakrishna Deb (whom the British called Nubber Kissen) was initially Warren Hastings' *munshi*. Always quick to spot an opportunity, he persuaded the local *zamindars* that their prospects were better with the East India Company than with Shiraj-ud-daula. Soon he had acquired a fortune and, when his village of Gobindapur was levelled to build Fort William and the Maidan, he set himself up in a great residence on the land he was granted in Sutanuti.

'Oh ho, *Baby's Day Out*, is it?' The present Mr Deb was fiftyish, sour-faced, not unlike Albert Lyon to look at. He wore a little Tyrolean hat and a banded sweater that gathered at the back. On his left hand he wore a gold ring with a large pearl on it, similar to one my mother used to wear. Subsequently I discovered that pearl rings are worn to assist digestive problems. He asked how old Llewelyn was, then reproached us. 'Eleven months and he still doesn't walk. All my children were able to walk at ten months. You must stop carrying him.'

Mr Deb asked if we had visited the Shobhabazar Rajbati. In no time at all, we were squeezed into a taxi, three, including the driver, in the front and four and the baby in the back, heading north up Central Avenue, toward the earliest of the Sutanuti palaces, said to have been built in just three months in 1757, with a battalion of labourers working in shifts around the clock.

When it was completed a special Durga Puja ceremony was held to celebrate Clive's victory at Plassey. Clive himself was the guest of honour. The celebration set the fashion for extravagant Durga Pujas to which European guests were often invited; indeed the whole Calcuttan tradition of Durga Puja parties stems from this one glittering occasion.

I had no idea what state the Shobhabazar Rajbati would be in. I imagined it might be preserved as an historic monument though I had never come across it in any of the guidebooks. But as we drove uptown Mr Deb pointed to a small red temple standing on an island in the middle of the traffic. 'That was once part of our estate,' he told me and I realised that what we were going to see were just parts of the whole, scattered about a built-up area. Perhaps I had been naïve to expect otherwise.

We got out of the taxi. We noticed the respect paid to Mr Deb by the local people, some of whom pressed their palms together in salutation as he passed.

He led us towards a muddy open space where several cars were parked. A series of broken pillars stood around its edges. Beyond that stood a small classical *natch ghar*, all that now remains of a second palace Nabakrishna built on his estate for his adopted son. In this *natch ghar*, 100 years ago in 1897, Mr Deb told us, a welcome reception was held for Swami Vivekananda, the great spiritual leader and disciple of Ramakrishna, after his triumphant tours of England and America.

The interior was now almost ruined. Mr Deb pointed out that the columns had been whitewashed so many times over the years that much of their fine detail was buried. Around the upper level ran a screened gallery from where the women of the household could watch the proceedings.

Although restoration was taking place, it looked an over-whelming project, almost more archaeology than architecture.

Mr Deb then led us along the street to the remains of the main palace. This building, in equal disrepair, was less European and more Islamic in appearance. We were shown the *thakur dalan* with its fine chandeliers, mirrors and cast-iron torch-brackets.

Despite its crumbling appearance, part of the structure was lived in; there were figures sleeping under blankets in the courtyard, around the remains of a cooking fire. One of the men woke and sat up, glaring at us for disturbing his rest. 'Who are they?' I asked Mr Deb quietly.

He looked at me forlornly and raised his eyebrows. Then, to avoid further discussion of the embarrassing intruders, he told me that his great-great-grandfather had presented Queen Victoria with a mosquito net made entirely of gold thread.

We learnt that the legendary singer and dancer Nicki had given her début performance in this courtyard. Nicki, or Nikibai, became the most celebrated nautch girl in early nineteenth-century Calcutta, popular with both the *babus* and the British, who called her 'the Catalani of Hindustan'. In her heyday Nicki could charge 1000 rupees for a single performance.

Mr Deb took us into the library that had housed a huge collection of Persian and Sanskrit texts, including some ancient palm-leaf manuscripts.

Radhakanta Deb had worked here on the *Shabdakalpad-ruma*, the famous Sanskrit encyclopaedia, as well as in 1823 a list of the *Respected and Opulent Natives of the Presidency of Bengal* that, along with Loknath Ghosh's volume *The Native Aristocracy and Gentry of India*, became as sacred to snobbish Indians as *Burke's Peerage* is to their British counterparts.

Most of the library is now with the Asiatic Society and the building was dilapidated. A family had moved into one end of it; their angry little dog barked at us as we looked around.

The *natch ghar* formed one end of the courtyard, smaller than the one in the other palace and, again, Islamic in design. A few years ago, its central beam had collapsed with the weight of the chandeliers suspended from it. Only the supporting columns now remained.

It all seemed a bit hopeless but Mr Deb remained philosophical. The objective, as far as I could understand, was to preserve what was left of this magnificent building. Of course, that in itself would be a costly enough endeavour.

Manish told us that the *babus* built their mansions in the middle of bazaars. Often they owned the bazaars. Some Europeans he had taken up to north Calcutta had assumed that the neighbourhoods had deteriorated around the palaces but they were wrong; there was never a distinction between a smart or a shabby district – land was land. Also, there was the question of decay. Monsoon rains accelerate ruin, and termites thrive in unchecked conditions. The moment a house is left unoccupied, it starts to fall apart.

And there was another factor as well: Indians have always tolerated shabbiness and disrepair in their surroundings. It is an aesthetic trait, not a mark of indolence. Eighteenth-century Britons noticed this in royal courts. Dilapidation need not imply that the inhabitants have fallen on hard times. 'But I love the decay,' I said.

'You just love squalor,' Emma teased me. She told Manish that I was a terror for slums.

I laughed. 'Baroque slums, maybe.'

'Actually, don't worry. I am the same,' said Manish.

CHAPTER THIRTEEN

Manish was aghast that we had not been to the Marble Palace. 'We must go forthwith.'

But first we went to Kumartoli, beside the river, a quarter given over to the production of divine images, the Hindu deities. These range from the figurines in household shrines to the lifesize representations that are paraded through the streets on religious holidays. The craftsmen are called *kumbhakars*. Manish said that the next major festival was Saraswati Puja.

Kumartoli was a peculiar place, row upon row of ateliers, straw and cobbles and mounds of grey mud, small children playing in the streets, piles of clay limbs everywhere. On the large models, some *kumbhakars* make the arms, others do the heads and so on. Every now and then we passed the headless naked body of a woman with slender tapering legs, a rounded belly and scooped up breasts.

The models are made of mud around a bamboo arma-ture. The mud itself, collected from the river bank, had sacred properties, coming from a branch of the Ganges. The images are painted and given real hair, dressed in clothes, then decorated with garlands and headdresses cut from the pith of the *sola* reed (the material used for *sola topi* pith helmets).

I remarked how realistic the models looked, like waxworks, whereas a lot of temple images are highly stylised.

Manish said that before the Europeans arrived Bengalis would venerate a decorated pot or a picture as a divine image. Then an eighteenth-century maharaja had ordered images in a European naturalistic style. The *kumbhakars* rose to the challenge and the results were impressive. The rich *babus* commissioned similar images for their *thakur dalans*.

Sometimes they asked the *kumbhakars* to make characters from Shakespeare and the Bible to amuse their European friends. Sometimes they commissioned portraits of themselves. Manish said he had seen one of these effigies once, a ghostly thing, over 100 years old, standing beside a bed.

The common people were enthralled by the new realistic models. They all chipped in and bought deities for their communities. As a result of these expensive images, the puja tradition changed from private to public, from a family affair to a communal celebration, the *baroari* puja, in a public park or any other open space.

'Where are the models kept from year to year?' asked Emma.

'They are not, they go in the river when the festival is finished, they submerge. That is the point.'

'So every year new ones are made,' I said and Manish said the style changes a little each year with women's fashion in hairstyles and cosmetics. 'These days they are getting very Bollywood!'

We found some smaller deities on sale, and secular ornaments as well. The ones that I liked most (and would have bought except that Emma loathed them) were almost like parodies of Staffordshire figures, of turbanned Sikhs, their wives and children all sitting on motor-scooters. I would have liked a pair for a mantelpiece.

There were reproductions of the Venus de Milo, Charlie Chaplin and everywhere Father Christmas. 'These are popular with Anglo-Indians,' said Manish condescendingly and clicked his heels.

Manish insisted on carrying Llewelyn, having realised that a cute red-haired baby attracts feminine attention. Whenever he was surrounded by teenage girls Manish was highly excitable, cracking terrible jokes and laughing louder and longer than anyone else.

As we walked away from Kumartoli, we were approached by a boy, painted blue all over with some kind of woad, wearing a gold paper crown, who asked us for money.

'Is he in fancy dress?'

'Yes. In a way. You see, he is a *bahurupi*. A beggar who dresses up as Krishna. Other gods also, and tigers . . .'

'I've seen monkey people before,' I said, remembering some vaguely sinister Hanuman devotees scampering around with black faces and wire tails.

'Those also were *bahurupis*,' said Manish.

A little further on, we encountered another decorated person, a stout elderly man, stark naked, his body caked with grey mud, tottering along on the cobbles. The mud had cracked in the sun so he resembled a type of pachyderm. His genitals, small and fragile-looking, were the only part of his body left exposed. The man wore dreadlocks, which made me suppose he was a sadhu.

Manish said the man probably was a sadhu, but he might be mentally ill. 'It is often hard to tell. Here we have so many showbusiness sadhus, flamboyant charlatans, and crazy people all mixed in amongst them.'

In the taxi, we talked about British artists in eighteenth-century India: Zoffany (Manish said we had to see 'The Last

Supper' at St John's Church – all the disciples are portraits of Company officials and Jesus was modelled on a Greek priest, which is said to have enraged the Anglican congregation) and the Daniells whose popular pictures, Manish insisted, were the chief inspiration for the Brighton Pavilion.

We discussed my favourite Solvyns and Manish said that his lack of success was nothing unusual at the time. Painters, he said, came to India on the scent of money. The problem, in Manish's opinion, was that the majority of Britons in India at the time cared little for art. Fashionable clients could be found if the artist appeared fashionable himself (that was why Zoffany claimed to have been knighted). To set oneself up as a painter took capital and good connections, both of which most lacked. In Calcutta there were too many painters for the small amount of work being commissioned. Painters were forced to undercut one another's prices or sell their works in lotteries.

'Presumably some made a good living . . .'

'Really, it was only one or two,' said Manish.

Then he told us about a painter called John Alefounder who ran up such debts in Calcutta that he tried to commit suicide and, failing in the attempt, recovered to find that another artist had auctioned all his belongings, including his materials and equipment, to cover the debts. Alefounder placed pathetic advertisements in the papers begging for the return of his equipment, most of which was unobtainable in India, so that he could continue his livelihood. When none of his pencils or brushes were returned, Alefounder turned again to suicide, this time successfully.

Manish said that Chinnery, who is mainly known for his paintings of China, left a wife and family behind in Calcutta and fled to China when his debts got out of hand.

The dashboard of the taxi that took us to the Marble Palace was decorated with hibiscus flowers, sacred to the goddess Kali. Manish explained that the driver would have had the flowers blessed at a temple earlier in the day.

Many Hindu drivers embellished their dashboards with divine images: small framed chromographs and plastic figures of popular gods and smouldering incense-sticks. Others simply scrawled orange swastikas.

Once, unable to find Abdul, we had engaged a taxi that resembled a small mobile shrine. The driver had turned out to be a most alarming man. He was fired with a fierce brand of Hindu nationalism and spoke of an India revitalised by the study of the *Mahabharata* and the *Ramayana*. India, he declared, must find its true heroic nature and the might to stand as a world power.

Foolishly, I asked about Muslims, Sikhs, Christians – all the non-Hindu religions in India. 'The name of this country is Hindustan! We must expel foreign religions!'

The driver had insisted that Hinduism was not a passive religion, it was about the will of God. As his language became more militaristic (advocating weapons of mass destruction) we began to wonder if he was a madman.

Manish said some supporters of the BJP came out with such statements. I told him British taxi-drivers often spout bigotry as well. The conversation turned to political graffiti, which we had seen everywhere, some of it finely executed with portraits and blazing flags. All over India, graffiti is primarily a political expression. The western tradition of 'signing' one's name or trademark as often, as largely and as publicly as possible does not mean much to the Indian graffiti writer whose aims are more classical.

Abdul had told us, 'All these people votes, vote Communist, only these people votes,' which sounded undemocratic. Manish

said that the Communists were not interfering – they had a *laissez-faire* approach to Capitalism – they maintained order and economic stability and everybody voted for them in a non-political but pragmatic way. The Smiths, on the other hand, feared it as a demonic force, even though they had survived unmolested through decades of Communist rule. They identified its hand in all closed shops and failed businesses, in the dryness of the grass on the Maidan and the noisiness of amplified music. They heard the snarl of Communism in all Jamal's wisecracks.

The taxi dropped us on the corner of Chittaranjan Avenue and Muktaram Babu Lane. Manish told us that this area was once called Chor Bagan, 'the thieves' garden', notorious for its pick-pockets, but it looked no more sinister than any other part of North Calcutta.

We walked west along the crowded, narrow thoroughfare. There were carpet shops and shops selling expensive saris. Manish said, 'It is a pity you are married. Nearby here are the *babus*' bordellos. Very old, Sonagachi. It means the Silver Tree. The oldest have kept their original fittings, some say the mattresses and all.'

Soon, on our left, we came across a set of high ornate railings. Behind them we could see an enormous bone-grey Palladian mansion, with Corinthian columns, and architraves that resembled tiaras, all in good shape compared to the Shobhabazar Rajbati, surrounded by palm trees (some covered with ivy so they resembled furled maypoles), set in an eccentric but formal garden, whose centrepiece was a baroque fountain brimming with naiads and caryatids and all kinds of classical sea-creatures. Dotted all around were dozens of statues that seemed to have been chosen at random, unrelated to one another; their only common characteristics that they were all made of marble and roughly the same size; Roman emperors shared the garden with Mohican braves and unmatched lions; the effect was that of a Fellini film.

We had some difficulty getting in; the gatekeeper was armed with a fearsome lance. But Manish was an expert at getting into houses, the lance was withdrawn and we walked towards the Marble Palace.

There was a rococo *thakur dalan*, its floor decorated with lozenges of marble, all different colours. Manish said that over 90 varieties of marble were used in the house. There were more assorted statues and bird-cages everywhere, for the house is also an aviary. Some of the birds were loose, chattering with crows and starlings that had flown in from outside to share the birdseed.

The house was built in 1835, so it was considerably later than the Sobhabazar Rajbati and there was a raffish exuberance to it all. We walked through the long public rooms, on two storeys around the courtyard, rooms festooned with Belgian chandeliers, swathes of dusty velvet; on every wall hundreds of dark pictures: Reynolds, Titian and Rubens all muddled in with Victorian junk, Spanish dancers and soft porn. On the ground floor was a life-size statue of Queen Victoria, carved from solid oak, as sprightly as a May Queen.

'What do you think?' asked Manish.

Emma said it was marvellous, faintly decadent like the Garden District houses in New Orleans.

Manish said, 'A friend of mine calls it Rock Star Taste. You know, these *babus* were sybaritic. You know, they used to load hookahs with opium and *charas*, Scotch whisky in the bowl instead of water, and place bets on who would pass out first . . .'

'What, here in this palace?' asked Emma.

Manish started and looked about. 'No, no, no. I am not saying here they did so. *Babus* in general, I am saying. Please, we must speak softly. The Mullick family even lives here now.'

'I know what I wanted to ask you,' said Emma to Manish. 'What is the Bengali for Grandmother? I wanted to put it in a letter to my mother.'

'*Didima*,' Manish told her, 'and your father is Llewelyn's *Dadamoshay*.'

There were names for every family relationship. Manish told us that, for instance, he would call his older brother's wife *Baudidi* while his mother would call her *Baraobau* and if he were married (which he was not) his mother would call his wife *Chotobau*. His father's younger brother was his *Khura* and this uncle's wife was *Kakima*.

'That is why children address all grown-ups as Auntie and Uncle. English is refreshingly vague on the subject . . .'

CHAPTER FOURTEEN

Then we went off in search of the Armenian Church, most difficult to find. Manish himself had never been there. We wandered around and around the swarming alleyways of Barabazar, receiving complicated directions.

Barabazar was a noisy crowded district of godowns and tiny box-like huts called *gaddis* where suppliers sat on cushions cutting deals on mobile phones. Enormous Tata lorries squeezed through the narrow cobbled lanes; barefoot coolies scurried past bearing every conceivable commodity in sacks and boxes, from betel nuts to toner cartridges.

'So much activity, so much of it illicit, most of this has grown without planning.' Manish showed us several tall modern buildings, built without authorisation, operating without electricity or running water. 'Everything illicit,' he said, 'built with black money and bribes. It is like a separate economy.'

A water-carrier, *bhisti*, from ancient India, ran past us on tiptoe, holding a staff that quivered like a bow from which he had suspended empty oilcans, not clay pitchers or deerskins.

We nipped into a snack bar called Haldiram Bhujiawala, not a Bengali place at all but a Rajasthani import. Manish ordered three helpings of *chaat* that Emma and I agreed was cloying and sickly, like warm Bombay mix served with a sweet yoghurt dressing. Llewelyn enjoyed it. We all sat at a table, beside an old man who promptly took his food away and sat on the floor, facing the wall.

'Have we upset him?' asked Emma.

Manish spoke a few words with the old man. 'Please, it is not personal. He has a delicate stomach and must digest his food calmly.'

During the monsoon, Manish informed us, when the rest of Calcutta floods, Barabazar remains dry, for it is built on higher ground than the surrounding metropolis. Barabazar is actually older than the city, having grown out of the old Sutanuti *hat* (weekly market) that supplied cotton yarn (*suta*) to the weavers of coastal Bengal. It was this ridge of land that attracted Job Charnock in 1690.

The name Barabazar means the 'great bazaar' but many Bengalis claim the name derives from *Buro*, an affectionate name for Shiva, and that *Bara* and its anglicism *Burra* were, initially anyway, mistaken.

It certainly grew into a great bazaar almost as soon as Calcutta was established. Traders came from near and far: Khatris from the Punjab, Marwaris from the Rajput kingdoms, Chinese, Jews, Greeks, Portuguese and Armenians. Solvyns had illustrated the cosmopolitan make-up of the city in a print entitled *Of the Nations Most Known in Hindoostan*.

A town of mud and thatch grew up within a short walk of the classical grandeur of the East India Company's offices, the Writers Building and Government House, and so much of the enterprise was secretive, untaxable, designed for profit. It is the unofficial history of the city, still unfolding.

Manish told us the majority of traders are now Marwaris. They quietly ousted the native Bengalis in the nineteenth century, driving them into the professions. The foreign communities in Barabazar dwindled, assimilated or moved away.

We had been told by Violet there were fewer than 200 Armenians left in Calcutta; when she was a girl, there were ten times as many and even that number was less than in the nineteenth century.

I asked her when the Armenians had arrived in Calcutta.

'Darling, we were here before the British. The Armenians pulled strings for the East India Company, got them trading rights, they negotiated the sale of the land this city's built on. The British couldn't have done that alone, nobody trusted them. But the Armenians were respected by the Emperor in Delhi, you see, and by the Nawab up in Murshidabad. They had to vouch for the East India Company. Nothing would have happened without them. All the history books tell you about Job Charnock but he wouldn't have got anywhere without Khojah Sarhad, his Armenian friend. The Emperor would have booted him out, *ek dum*.'

The first Armenians probably settled in India in the fourteenth century, escaping persecution in their homeland from the Egyptians. There were subsequent exoduses as the Tartars, Persians and Turks invaded Armenia. Certainly there were Armenians at Agra in the sixteenth century. The Emperor Akbar took an Armenian wife, the Begum Mariam Zamani, and allowed her compatriots to build a church in his royal city in 1562.

By the time Calcutta was founded, Armenians were long established in all the important trading centres of the subcontinent, dealing in spices, gems, muslin and indigo. Before long they had set themselves up in the new city as well, in betel and jute. They built homes and businesses and a wharf to receive and dispatch goods that is still called Armenian Ghat. In 1707 they built a wooden chapel on Old China Bazar Street. This chapel was replaced in 1724 by the current church, the oldest surviving church in the city. The money for the church was raised by public subscription, through the efforts of an elder called Agha Nazar, which might be why it was called the Holy Church of Nazareth.

Eventually we found the church gate, along a passageway dedicated to the sale of firecrackers. There are three entrances to the church, which accounted for the confusion. It was striking to walk from the clamour of Barabazar into a churchyard so peaceful that people were sleeping on the paved floor. Most of the paving stones were in fact tombstones.

We immediately sought out the tomb of Rezabeebeh, dated 1630, sixty years before Charnock. This tomb has struck countless visitors as a tantalising mystery. Manish pooh-poohed our speculations. 'It is a memorial, that's all. Why not 100, 200 years later her family puts it there . . .'

The church is odd-looking, making allusions to several architectural styles at the same time; Norman, Baroque, Mughal. There is a toytown steeple with three clocks around it. The architect was apparently Persian.

The interior was spick and span; bourgeois and opulent in an eighteenth-century way, marble floors and polished mahogany, commemorative tablets (mainly in English) and oil paintings around the altar. Everything spoke of prosperity and dignity. I could picture the congregation, stout hoteliers in blue suits and their sallow wives in hats. For some reason, I was reminded of a grand synagogue. I noticed that the descendants of the merchants became lawyers, doctors, administrators; that their names and their memorials grew ever more Anglicised until gradually, at some time around the turn of this century, they had completely assimilated into the British community. But by then it was already too late. What became of them after 1947?

'Most of us went home,' said Violet, 'to England.'

CHAPTER FIFTEEN

Albert Lyon had invited us to an informal gathering, or as he put it an *adda*, at his flat. For Albert to proclaim his party an *adda* was both correct and hyperbolic. The *adda* is what makes Calcutta a soulful city, it is the essence of its culture. *Adda* means a long rambling conversation between a group of friends, their minds all tuned in, the topics ranging freely from politics to aesthetics, from sport to music, everything alighting where it will. The beauty of an *adda* is comparable to the beauty of a kite, its swoops and pirouettes. Marvellous facts are snatched up as it glides on. An *adda* is not an organised thing. On every street corner there is an *adda*, in every sweetshop, on the ledges of private houses. Most public *addas* are exclusively male; women participate only in private situations. The men seem to gather in age groups, but I have seen old men hold younger men spellbound, and a twelve-year-old boy address the elders. It is not idle gossip, although it claims no gainful purpose. It is conversation raised to its highest level, the exchange of ideas. The origins of the *adda* lie in the village gathering at day's end, the *chandimandap*, the discussion in the moonlight in the days before television. It does not have to take place at night, it can happen anywhere and that is its attraction for the stroller with time on his hands. In its urban form, it gives one a voice, an identity. It is often the refuge of thwarted souls, for an *adda* can recompense the disappointments of life. It offers wings to the earthbound.

The British introduced the club to India. What goes on in a Bengali club? *Adda*. Unlike the comparably freewheeling conversations in the pubs of Dublin, the participants tend to be sober; but, of course, there are drunken *addas* as well.

Emma was not at all keen on going. She thought Llewelyn should be kept in the peaceful room. I thought it would be churlish not to go. What was more, Albert had told me there would be a Baul enthusiast there. So, after bathing Llewelyn and making sure he was asleep, I went alone, leaving Emma to her Pat Barker novel.

Downstairs, I told Violet how impressed we had been with North Calcutta. When I compared what we had seen to Italy, she interrupted me. 'Italy? We've been there. A dirty, dirty place. Rome? Quite revolting. Venice, like a sewer. Very dirty people, the Italians. Nearly poisoned us two or three times. We shall never go back there.'

Abdul drove me to Albert's flat. The address was difficult to find, even though I had written it down, and that was because the house was behind another. It was a large Victorian mansion off Park Street and Albert occupied an apartment on its ground floor.

I found him standing alone in the dark on a stretch of gravel between the two houses. I could see that he was wearing a loose shirt over drawstring pyjamas; on his feet were comical Ali Baba slippers, that he called *jootis*, with red bobbles on the toes.

'Am I the first to arrive?' I asked.

'No, most of them are here. I just wanted a moment to think quietly.'

'Shall I go on in?'

'Oh, I'd better introduce you, hadn't I?'

Albert led me into a large, sparsely furnished room with tall shuttered windows and piles of books everywhere. Without putting obvious effort into it, Albert had made himself a stylish nest; his whitewashed, high-ceilinged rooms with their furniture of metal and dark wood could have been in Sicily or Mexico. They were strikingly the rooms of a poet. I was reminded of the picture on the Leonard Cohen record, *Songs From A Room*. There was even a monkey's skull on one of the bookshelves.

And, almost appropriately, there was some Bob Dylan album I didn't recognise playing in the background. I had imagined Albert listening to Indian classical music exclusively. Then it struck me that Albert looked just like Bob Dylan; perhaps there was some identification.

I took my shoes off and placed them on a mat besides those of the other guests: two pairs of *chappals*, a pair of trainers and a pair of pink slingbacks.

Three of the other guests sat on cane chairs around a coffee table, with drinks and *nimkis*: an old man with a thick black moustache, a younger man, looking nervous, and a short-haired weather-beaten Englishwoman in a blue tracksuit, looking like a games mistress.

A fourth guest was in a corner of the room using Albert's telephone; she was, I guessed, the wearer of slingbacks. She was in her thirties, good-looking, dark skin, wide mouth, loose untidy hair, dressed in a black cotton sari with a bright folk-art *kantha* embroidery border. Whoever she was speaking to was making her laugh. I couldn't help noticing Albert shudder when she laughed.

I was introduced to the moustached man. His name was Professor Shastri. The younger man said, 'Happy Christmas, I am also a poet, in both English and Bengali . . .' Both Professor Shastri and the poet wore white *kurta* pyjamas. The poet's hair gleamed with oil.

The games mistress was called Trish Crystal. She had a firm handshake. She had been living in Calcutta for six months (although she had been to India several times before) financed by a grant to study and exchange ideas with Indian dancers. I was a little surprised: she looked too old and chunky to be a dancer.

Albert (who, I noticed, kept his *jootis* on in the house) told her we were staying at the Fairlawn and she snorted derisively about people paying high prices to pretend India was still a British colony. 'It strikes me that if you come all this way, you'd want to stay somewhere more Indian . . .'

She seemed to imply that we were softies, cushioned from the 'real India' that she, no doubt, inhabited. I had come across the oddly competitive attitude that the cheaper and dingier the accommodation the more intrinsically Indian it must be. It hardly seemed worth arguing. I told her that I liked the Fairlawn for its eccentric atmosphere, and it was clean. Llewelyn could crawl on the floor of our room. We did not care how Indian it was, we liked it for what it was. It was, in my experience of India, unique.

'Okay, but it's hideously post-colonial, you must admit,' said Trish.

If I had been in a harsher mood, I would have said that so much in India, especially Calcutta, is post-colonial. It is unavoidable but there are (and always were) other factors at play.

'Actually,' I said, 'we're only staying there over Christmas. We've found a room at Lake Gardens . . .'

'With how many servants to look after you?' asked Trish Crystal.

[123]

I replied, 'Our landlady employs a doorman and his wife works as the ayah. They bring us hot water for our baths, and they bring us meals, that's all.'

Albert, who was offering drinks (beer, or *chai* from a street stall kept warm in a thermos, or Limca or water filtered by Aquagard, all served in stainless steel beakers), told us that, when he had taken on this flat, he had been inundated with people wishing to serve him. He had adamantly refused to employ anyone.

The other woman put the receiver down and joined us. 'Is Trishie being horrid to you? She gets like that. I have to tell her. Always being horrid to Britishers. It's because she won't allow herself to be horrid to Indians.'

'But you should, sometimes,' opined the young poet.

Admonished, Trish Crystal picked up a book about the Khasis of Meghalaya. She struck me as an odd character, maybe a little mad, perhaps driven mad by Calcutta.

The other woman went on: 'I know, I know she should, it's so unhealthy. She keeps all this spite bottled up inside her. My name's Lalitha . . .'

'Which means 'voluptuous beauty' in Sanskrit,' said Albert.

Lalitha waved aside the compliment. 'It's just a name. I expect Albert means something, doesn't it?'

'Yes, of course, it means "shining with nobility" . . .'

'Well, there you are . . .'

It was evident that Albert was mesmerised by Lalitha. Whenever he looked at her, his eyes assumed a faraway mystical look and his jaw went loose and swung forward. It was a peculiar face to pull but one, I was certain, he had practised in front of the mirror.

'Do you know Sanskrit?' I asked him.

'Sanskrit, Pali, Brij, Bhojpuri, Hindustani, Urdu and, of course, Bengali . . .'

Professor Shastri, who had been concentrating on the *nimkis*, looked up and, wiping a rheumy eye with the sleeve of his *kurta*, said, 'This is a remarkable achievement you have made. It begs the question, in a past life were you living here in India?'

'Actually,' said Albert, 'my great-grandfather was Indian. From Delhi, I understand. He changed his name from Singh to Lyon. Went into the linen business.'

I laughed, 'And there I was, thinking you were Jewish.'

'In fact, I am Jewish. He married a Miss Abrahams from Dublin, and converted. That was when he changed his name.'

I turned to Professor Shastri and said, 'The problem with reincarnation is that the population of the planet keeps increasing. Do some of us share past lives?'

The Professor cracked a piece of hard *gram* with his hind teeth, then paused before answering a completely different question, like an evasive politician on *Newsnight*. 'There was something, before the universe is existing. Who knows if this was more, or less? Who knows if the universe was created thus, or these are the broken pieces scattered? Or dust even? Only God can know, and maybe God does not know.'

'It says as much in the *Rig Veda* also,' said the poet.

'So God isn't all-knowing?' I asked. It did not matter that he hadn't answered my reincarnation question, this was interesting stuff.

'Knowing, not knowing. These are human ideas, from human heads. Even the birds are having some questions for God. You must understand, what we are calling God is formless, most immense, very unimaginable. Beyond the imagination of all mankind. And everything is God. You. Me. This chair. Hugli river. All are God. Ask Hugli river how does the universe begin? Humanity must strive to answer the questions it sets, itself. This is why scientists are religious men.'

The poet said, 'Nobody can describe the attributes of God, nor his qualities. There is a phrase in the Vedas: *Neti, neti*. It means 'unknowable': it is not this, it is not that . . .'

'I certainly don't believe in God,' mumbled Trish Crystal. 'In fact, everything you say sounds to me like a rationale for atheism.'

'Ah, that's what you think,' chuckled Albert, 'I've decided it's possible to be a Hindu atheist . . .'

'Or a Hindu Muslim, or a Hindu Christian,' said Lalitha, and Albert gave her a slack-jawed smile for backing him up.

Professor Shastri looked as if he had some misgivings about all this and took another handful of *nimki*. Then the conversation turned to more general topics, and it transpired that Lalitha and Trish Crystal were working together, choreographing a piece to be performed in Calcutta, Delhi and Bombay. Trish Crystal was guarded when I asked about the project, and dismissive of any interest I professed in Indian dance.

'Where's Derek?' asked Lalitha.

'Yes, where's the Contemplative Buddha?' asked Trish Crystal.

'I gave him good directions,' said Albert, 'he wrote them down in a notebook.'

Ten minutes later, in walked an Australian dressed in a safari outfit. A dark, burly sergeant-majorish man. He took about five minutes to remove his high, lace-up jungle boots. Derek Platanias hailed from Sydney; he was an authority on the history of Buddhism, on his way to Nalanda in Bihar, and just in Calcutta for ten days, meeting some archaeologists. Derek was staying at the Tollygunge Club. I asked what that was like. 'Right up your street,' sneered Trish Crystal.

Albert had been there once and loathed the whole atmosphere. But wasn't the Fairlawn just as bad?

'No, the people are different. The Fairlawn is eccentric. The atmosphere at the Tolly is corporate. You could be in Singapore or Kuala Lumpur . . .'

'Ah, you're being a little hard on the place,' said Derek.

'Bob is a sweet potato,' said Lalitha in a put-on American accent, rubbing Trish Crystal's shoulders in a manner that upset Albert. He curled up in his chair, sticking his bobbled *jootis* out like a pouting lip.

'Yeah,' agreed Derek, 'he's a great bloke . . .'

Derek and Lalitha were referring to Bob Wright, the secretary of the Tollygunge Club, a figurehead of post-colonial, ex-pat culture, who has become a minor celebrity in television documentaries.

Professor Shastri joined in. 'Such a character we used to find in the hill stations. That he can achieve such importance in Calcutta is remarkable but there is, I would say, something of the hill station about Calcutta.'

'It is because we love anything British,' said Lalitha. 'All Bengalis are Anglophile at heart. Much more so than in Delhi or Bombay.'

'I'm sick of all this affinity-with-London business,' announced Trish Crystal. 'To me this is Kali's city. It grew from her dance.'

I asked her to explain this, but the young poet answered for her. 'This area was called *Kali-kshreta*. Before it was Calcutta, it was the land of Kali. I think about it, it must have been quite marshy, and subject to Hugli river, like Sunderbans. Jungly, also. Tigers and harmful insects, fevers. Fever, this is Kali also . . .'

'That's right,' agreed Trish Crystal.

Lalitha said, 'We have been thinking about female energy in times of deadlock. You see, the gods and the *asuras*, the demons, had locked horns. Only Kali, the most terrible, could save the gods.'

'Shakti, female energy,' said Trish Crystal, 'this is the age of Kali, the Kali Yuga.'

'I thought you didn't believe in God.'

'I don't, as such. I believe in *dharma*. I'm talking about *dharma*.'

'*Dharma* means righteous living, according to holy laws, doesn't it?'

The young poet raised his finger, 'Actually, *dharma* is more than religion. It does not mean just righteousness . . .'

'What does it mean?'

'The whole picture. The deeds of the gods as well as the deeds of man in relation to the gods,' said the poet.

Derek Platanias interjected that Buddhists define *dharma* simply as the truth.

Trish Crystal repeated, as if I hadn't been listening to her, 'This is the age of Kali, the Kali Yuga . . .'

'And when do we eat?' asked Professor Shastri bluntly. He had looked tetchy when the others were talking about Kali. In fact, he had winced once or twice.

Albert was rather embarrassed. 'I hadn't really planned much in the way of food.'

Professor Shastri said, 'In that case, I shall leave now, if you don't mind . . .'

Albert explained that he was travelling that night to Shantiniketan, in a friend's car, and because he intended to sleep on the back seat he preferred to keep an empty stomach. The Professor said goodbye politely and wished each one of us, in turn, all the best for 1997. When he had gone, Albert took me aside and said huffily, 'I ought to point out that a meal is by no means an essential part of an *adda* . . .'

I reassured Albert that I was not expecting to be fed. 'By the way, who is the Baul fan? Not Professor Shastri, I hope.'

'Trish has worked with them . . .'

When Albert told her we were going to Poush Mela the next day, she said that, as far as she was concerned, the event was now ruined by ignorant tourists. That was as far as she could be drawn on the subject.

Derek and Lalitha were discussing the Prince and Princess of Wales. Derek had met Prince Charles and (unusually, for an Australian) admired him. Lalitha confessed to romantic daydreams about Diana. The poet, eager to join in but without much grasp of the subject, asked, 'Is it true this Camelia woman has a husband already?'

Albert, who regarded such discussion as horribly lowbrow, groaned his displeasure. It was becoming less and less his idea of an *adda*.

I left at around nine o'clock, thanking Albert and saying that we hoped to see him the next day at Shantiniketan, and bought myself a *kathi* roll from a stand on Park Street. Suddenly it started to rain heavily, for the first time, I was told, since September. Again, Park Street looked just like London. I didn't want to get soaked so I took a taxi back to Sudder Street.

It wasn't such a good idea. The taxi had bald tyres and inadequate brakes. As we turned from Chowringhee into Sudder Street we ran straight into the back of a parked car. The bonnet of the taxi was badly dented and the boot of the parked car was crumpled. If I had been sitting in front I would have been hurt but I just suffered a jolt. The driver leapt out and started a loud argument with the car's owner. I tried to pay him but he was so caught up in the row that I could not get his attention so I walked along to the Fairlawn in the rain. I decided not to tell Emma about the collision as she was far from happy about the lack of seatbelts in taxis and Llewelyn bouncing around on our laps.

Apparently Violet had asked where I was and when Emma had told her I was with Albert Lyon, she had voiced her disapproval, warning us about mixing with the wrong set. Emma, as fascinated as I was by Violet's disapproval of Albert, had tried to find out its cause but all Violet would say was that everyone knew everyone else's business in Calcutta.

In bed, I read about an eighteenth-century chaplain at Fort William called Blunt who once got so roaringly drunk that he stripped naked and sang obscene songs to the soldiers. When he sobered up, he was so remorseful that he refused to leave his room. Colonel Wellesley assured the chaplain that one cursory debauch was nothing to be ashamed of, but Blunt was so ashamed that he fretted himself to death within ten days.

CHAPTER SIXTEEN

The next morning we were up at five to catch the early train from Howrah to Bolpur, having been unable to get tickets on the Shantiniketan Express that leaves at the more convenient time of 9.55.

Howrah Station is something between a fortress and a cathedral, a hybrid of Romanesque and Arts and Crafts styles, with eight towers, built at the beginning of this century to a design by an English architect with a wonderful name, Halsey Ricardo. Although the architecture is European in style, the end result looks strangely Islamic; it could have been commissioned by a Mughal emperor had there been one to do this in 1900. It was mosque-like too in that the great dimly lit halls were surprisingly quiet and reverential. The crowds were there but sitting around or lying down and everyone was speaking in hushed voices, as if at prayer.

We boarded our train, in a compartment with the other passengers huddled in shawls and trying to catch up on their sleep.

On the platform, next to our barred window, a teenage beggar sat on a trolley scratching his testicles with one hand up the leg of his shorts. The train started with an asthmatic grumble. It was cold and eerie, and as we moved northwards through the grey squalor of the outskirts, the sun came up, turning the sky a dirty yellow colour.

But as we moved further from the metropolis, rural Bengal came into view, paddies and fishponds, a flat, languid, liquid place that grew cleaner as the train moved on. Sometimes there were moving figures covered with leaves, like Birnam Wood on its way to Dunsinane; these turned out to be fodder-gatherers on their way to feed the cows. The other passengers shed their shawls and unwrapped bundles of food. Each time we stopped at a station, more people got on, everyone going to Shantiniketan.

Vendors came along selling *puri sabzi* (fried bread with vegetable curry) and *jhal moori* (a salad of puffed rice with shallots, chillies, beansprouts and mustard dressing, shaken up in a tin can, then served in a bag made from newspaper). Some of the passengers bought garlands of *mogra* to wear around their necks.

We had been sitting on our own since Howrah, with an empty bench facing us. The bench was now occupied by an old woman, her daughter and son-in-law. All three of them had studied at Shantiniketan: the married couple had met there in the 1970s, the mother-in-law had been there in Tagore's time. One of the advantages of travelling as a family in India is that women, who would not speak to a lone man on a train, will start a conversation. The mother-in-law, whose name was Mrs Majumdar, was bright and garrulous and looked like an Indian Shelly Winters. She told us she had visited England in the 1930s when she was a teenager and she remembered the names of all the matinée idols she had seen. Before long, she was bouncing Llewelyn in her lap and pointing out birds and trees. The sun rose higher and the countryside sparkled with aquatic reflections, verdure and fertility. It was the landscape of *Pather Panchali*. All this seemed apt for Poush Mela.

The son-in-law, Swarup, who had not spoken much because he was reading a John Grisham novel, asked if either of us had read much of Tagore's work. Emma replied she had not and that I had only read a little.

Swarup said that he had written his own translations of Tagore and some had been published in American magazines. Swarup had been a graduate student at Berkeley. 'What were you reading?' I asked.

Swarup mistook the question. 'Oh, Ferlinghetti. Patchen. Mainly I was writing . . .'

His wife, whose name was Took-Took, said, 'He was a wild poet for many years. Now he is in cement.'

'Cement business supports the writing only. I am in contact with an agent in London, actually. Indian novels are the new big thing.'

'Oh, yes indeed.'

'Mine is a thriller, set in the world of international high finance, but magic-realist also with many Hindu gods involved, and satirical too . . .' Swarup smiled with pride, then went back to his reading.

'There are lots of Tagores, aren't there?' Emma said we were confused by all the names ending in '-anath'.

'It is a dynasty in fact,' said Took-Took, 'only Tagore was not really their name to begin with, it was Kushari and they came from Jessore, which is now in Bangladesh.'

Mrs Majumdar told us that the Kusharis were Brahmins but some contact with Muslims (perhaps a forced conversion in an earlier generation) had caused their fellow Brahmins to regard them as *pirali*, impure. About the time Calcutta was founded, two Kushari brothers, Panchanan and Shukdeb, arrived in the city to set up a stevedoring business. Their workers, acknowledging their priestly caste, would call them *Thakurmashai* or 'holy sir'.

Took-Took said, 'The Britishers mistook this for their actual surname, that was shortened to Thakur, which they pronounced Tagore.' She smiled at us, 'I can't see what was so difficult about Thakur. It is a question of a *k* or a *g*, that is all.'

By the end of the eighteenth century the Tagore family had switched from stevedoring to finance and in 1784 they bought land on the Chitpur Road, where the family home, Jorasanko, was built.

Dwarkanath, the poet's grandfather, was the first of the Tagores to enter public life on a grand scale. He invested in industry, gave legal advice to many Bengali businessmen and ran the thriving salt trade. He was director of the Calcutta Steam Tug Association, owned newspapers, indigo factories and real estate. He founded the Union Bank and moved into shipping with Carr, Tagore & Company. When he travelled to England, he went in his own ship. Typically for his time and milieu, Dwarkanath had an extravagant streak – his clothes were laundered in Paris and he threw lavish banquets for his business associates. His manner was so regal that people referred to him as Prince. Besides his involvement with Rammohan Roy and the Brahmo Sabha, Dwarkanath established the Hindu College and the Calcutta Medical College, campaigned for more opportunities for Indians in government service, introduced the jury system to civil courts and brought about reforms in the police force. He was one of the first Indian members of the Asiatic Society.

Mrs Majumdar told us that Dwarkanath's son, Debendranath, continued his father's business interests but his career followed a more spiritual path. Hugely influenced by Rammohan Roy, he studied the *Upanishads*, made pilgrimages around India's holy places, and came to believe in a universal, formless God. For some time he was the editor of the Brahmo journal, the *Tattwabodhini Patrika*; eventually he became the spiritual leader of the resuscitated Brahmo Samaj movement. The Poush Mela celebration commemorates Debendranath's initiation into the movement.

'When you mention Tagore to anyone outside India, they only know about Rabindranath,' I said.

Took-Took said that this was actually the case outside Bengal.

'Don't forget,' said Mrs Majumdar, 'Debendranath had fourteen children, the youngest was Rabindranath. It is tempting to overlook the others. The oldest one, Dwijendranath, not only a mathematician, philosopher, poet and flautist, not only so but invented Bengali shorthand . . .'

'Hemendranath, an educational pioneer . . .'

'Satyendranath and Ganendranath, among the first intake of students at Calcutta University and Satyendranath, first Indian member of the Indian Civil Service . . .'

'And what does '-anath' mean?'

'It means Lord only.'

I had already gathered that Bengalis regard Rabindranath Tagore as their greatest genius. He was born in 1861 and educated mainly at home in Jorasanko. In his late teens he was taken to London where he attended lectures in English literature at the University. He wrote and published prose, poetry and plays from an early age and edited various literary journals. He wrote many songs and some were set to music of his own composition. These, known collectively as *Rabindra Sangeet*, are considered a major Bengali contribution to Indian classical music. *Rabindra Sangeet* was a new genre, influenced by

European song traditions. In 1912 a selection of poetry, *Gitanjali*, translated into English by the author, was published in London. In English the poetry, even in Rabindranath's own translation, comes across poorly. My Bengali friends tell me that the intensity of the original is lost. Nonetheless the book was praised by both W. B. Yeats and Ezra Pound. In London Tagore was lionised and he cut a dramatic, almost Messianic figure with his flowing beard and cassock-like robes.

Tagore received the Nobel Prize for Literature in 1913 and in 1915 a knighthood, subsequently returned as a protest against the Amritsar massacre. Politically, Tagore was an early champion of Indian independence. He composed a song for the nationalist Calcutta Congress of 1911, *Jana Gana Mana Adhinayaka*, that would become India's national anthem after 1947, and he wrote articles and made speeches arguing the nationalist cause.

A few years before his death in 1941, Tagore started to paint in a style that was influenced by both Japanese art and European expressionism. There was nothing amateurish about his efforts, which are now regarded as some of the most important works in modern Indian art.

A little item of trivia I discovered about Tagore: he changed the way Bengalis write, introducing a cursive 'joined-up' handwriting that nobody had used before.

Shantiniketan, 'the abode of peace', is some 85 miles north-west of Calcutta. It is a curious mixture of a garden city and a spiritual retreat that was established by Rabindranath Tagore around the site of his father's ashram.

The whole place, especially Vishwa Bharati, the liberal arts college founded in 1921, was intended to promote Bengali culture. Tagore designed the core of the faculty himself. It was

not a narrowly nationalistic project; there is a fine collection of Chinese manuscripts in the China Bhavan. Nor was it backward-looking; the Kala Bhavan houses many important works of twentieth-century Indian art, including some by Tagore himself as well as his nephews, Abanendranath and Gaganendranath Tagore. Tagore's objective was to revive traditional ways of teaching, with lessons held in the open air under the spreading *sonajahuri* and mango trees. No examinations would trouble the students. Each season would be celebrated with a festival.

Mrs Majumdar remembered the atmosphere as calm and serene. In the rainy season Tagore would rise at dawn and sit on the verandah of his little house on the campus, watching the movement of the clouds. With his white clothes, long grey ringlets, and white beard with two dark streaks on either side, he looked every inch the patriarch, and the students – who addressed him as *Gurudev* – came to discuss poetry, Keats and Shelley as well as Kalidas and Ramprasad.

At Bolpur station we separated from our travelling companions and took a cycle rickshaw the mile or so to Shantiniketan. The road was thronged with people on their way to the Mela; entire bourgeois families, local peasants, vendors bristling with painted flutes or weighed down with painted toys. Many wealthy Calcuttans have second homes at Shantiniketan. We passed bungalows decorated with plants in terracotta pots, their verandahs milling with visitors.

The campus appeared run down, most of its buildings ugly and dated in their rebuilt 1950s way, but the original spirit was intact, with its lanes shadowed by pipal trees and groups of earnest youngsters, seated on the ground, discussing philosophy. I was not surprised to learn the young Indira Gandhi had studied at Shantiniketan.

We walked around for a while and found that the Kala Bhavan museum was closed for the festivities. A long-haired, angular curator in white *kurta* and *dhoti*, who (except that he was clean-shaven) looked remarkably like Rabindranath Tagore, had just bolted the doors. He said, 'I'm sorry . . . any other day . . . come back . . . must dash', and headed in the direction of a hall, surrounded by *sal* trees, from which emanated the reedy plaintive tones of a *shehnai*, the Indian oboe.

Coming out of the hall we saw Albert Lyon, wearing brindled orange *khadi* pyjamas, a garland of yellow carnations and carrying a huge jute satchel. Albert pushed his glasses up and said, 'Listen to that, the *Raga Bhimpalasi*. Perfect. I hear that and I am filled with enormous love.' So we all stood still and listened to the Oboe of Enormous Love.

Albert asked if we had been along to the fairground yet. Emma said we had seen where it was, but nothing had been going on. 'I believe it's starting soon,' he said referring to a timetable, printed in Bengali, incomprehensible to us. The Mela was held on a large dusty maidan; part of it was a dangerous-looking funfair, the rest was given over to craft exhibitions, a village of tents from different parts of northern India, and some crafts-men had laid their wares out on sheets on the ground. Many of the stalls sold textiles, rugs and bedspreads as well as saris and shawls. We saw a lot of *Dhokra* work (exquisite cast brass objects, animals and gods, made using a 'lost-wax' process, covered in minute detail like strands of filigree) and all kinds of terracotta, as well as primitive hand-painted plaster deities (especially Krishna and Kali) that resembled the fairings of nineteenth-century England. Best of all, but expensive, were the kansa vessels, made of heavy bronze or bell-metal, dishes and beakers.

There were lots of food stalls and places selling Kwality's ice cream. In the middle of it all was a large *shamiana*, a marquee without sides, underneath it a stage on which various dignitaries sat listening to a speech given by an old man I took to be the regent of the university. A small crowd sat on the ground in front of the stage. Albert Lyon was plainly well known at Shantiniketan, people would come up and pat him on the back; occasionally he would say, 'Let me introduce my friends, this is Emma and this is Joe . . .' The speeches continued.

I noticed, at the side of the maidan, an area of sack tents, like a tinkers' camp, around which several figures in bright orange and patchwork clothes were milling. They were the Bauls, some of whom would be performing in the *shamiana* later. Some of the Baul women were cooking and there was a strong whiff of ganja. They reminded me of Rastafarians, with their air of aloof detachment and bloodshot eyes. Their costumes were a kind of motley: long patchwork cloaks, belted around the waist with bright, almost fluorescent orange sashes. Some wore loosely tied turbans, again in the brightest possible colours. Both sexes had long hair, untied and shining with oil.

Many of them wore *ghungurs* (ankle bracelets) of small bells shaped like rosebuds as well as *nupurs*, thin brass or silver tubes fitted around the arch of the foot, filled with small beads to produce a musical jangle with every movement.

The Bauls are a phenomenon unique to Bengal, a mystic sect who preach their religious message through their highly distinctive folk music and, to a lesser extent, through dance. Tagore loved the Bauls in much the same way that Augustus John loved the gypsies. He was not the only poet to be inspired by the Bauls. Many years later, Allen Ginsberg took a deep interest in them. Ginsberg introduced Bob Dylan to Purna Das Baul, who toured the West in the 1960s. Purna Das Baul is the dark man standing to the right of Dylan on the cover of *John Wesley Harding*, the one most people assume to be some unknown Mexican hippy.

There is speculation as to the origin of their name. Some say it comes from the Sanskrit word *vayu* (wind), others propose *byakul* (anxious) or *vatul* (frenzied). The image these words suggest is of drifting madmen, blown from village to village, and certainly the Bauls refer to themselves as *khepa* which means 'madcap'. However the Bauls who live in predominantly Muslim areas are called *Auls*. *Aul* might derive from *Auliya*, the Arabic word for a saint (Nizamuddin Auliya, for example, is a Sufi mystic venerated by *qawwali* musicians). In any case, the Bauls cultivate the image of holy fools.

Although the Bauls have been around for several centuries,

not much is known of their origins. Often they are illiterate and because the concept of *trikala-yoga* (harmony between past, present and future, or existing outside of time) is central to their beliefs, they are opposed to written records. They simply do not believe in history, just as they do not believe in the past.

The Bauls generally come from poor rural families, both Hindu and Muslim, but once they are initiated into the sect, all religious and caste distinctions are shed.

The Bauls are similar to other Indian musicians in that their craft and traditions are passed from generation to generation by gurus. In their songs they often refer to their gurus as *sunya*, meaning 'nothing' or 'emptiness'. That is typically misleading – it does not imply the absence of a guru so much as his presence all around them.

They live in small communes called *akharas*, that are to be found all over rural Bengal, particularly around Burdwan and Bolpur. Several *akharas* also exist in Bangladesh. Their beliefs stem from a variety of religious traditions including Vaishnavism, Buddhism, Tantra and Sufism. Teaching might vary from *akhara* to *akhara* but the ideal is to be *sahaj* (simple, natural) and free of worldly constraints.

Unlike sadhus, the Bauls are by no means ascetics; they have no particular dietary restrictions and consider sexual intercourse to be the highest possible form of meditation. They regard marriage as a bogus institution, at odds with their rootless existence, and this means that both male and female Bauls are free to choose lovers at will.

I am told that, after years of practice, a Baul man can, at the point of orgasm, draw the semen back through his penis and make it flow upwards through his body until he spits it out of his mouth. This is probably a practical measure as Baul women are forbidden to bear children.

The human body is regarded as the seat of the Almighty,

[141]

the mind being its guiding force. Some Baul songs describe the body as a magical tree bearing fruits and flowers full of honey, others compare it to a hall of mirrors.

After a lengthy introduction from the speakers, a party of Bauls walked over to the *shamiana* to perform.

Albert told me he knew the singer, a strikingly bardic figure in the full gear. 'He's a legend, has been for about thirty years now.' As he told me the name, I had to attend to Llewelyn who was wriggling to get down and crawl. I did not hear it.

The legend stood at the front of the stage and the other musicians sat down in a half-circle behind him: among them were two drummers, a man playing a three-stringed lute called a *sarinda*, another on a single-stringed fiddle called an *ektara*; the remainder kept time with a variety of cymbals (*kartal*, *khanjani*, *mandira*) each with a different sound.

Slung from the singer's left shoulder and resting on his left thigh was a small conical drum called a *duggi*, that he would beat occasionally with the palm of his hand. He also held a *gopiyantra*, a small single-stringed bass that he played with one hand to produce a pleasant, droning sound.

The music was rhythmic and stringy, the one-string fiddles keening above the beat and the singer with a nasal 'high lonesome' voice. The sound to me was jiggy and Irish.

At the end of each verse the singer would lift the *gopiyantra* above his head and perform a stylised pirouette with odd old-fashioned sashays as if he were dancing a schottische. The formal movements were rendered staccato by the singer's age, so that it was like watching an old Calypsonian playing his guitar with stiff but unfaltering fingers.

Although I found the music perfectly accessible, whenever Albert translated the lyrics for me I found the imagery impenetrable. But perhaps I was trying too hard. There are, after all, many similarities between the Bauls and the *qawwali* singers of the Sufi tradition. With its powerful rhythms, the music of *qawwali* has a religious function, to arouse mystical love, even divine ecstasy in the listener (the same could be said of American gospel music) and even if one does not understand the words, one can understand the driving force of the music.

The Baul singer yearns to be at one with the *maner manush* (man of the heart), the Divine Spirit at the heart of existence. Sometimes it is given other names: *adhar manush* (the uncatchable man), *ajana manush* (the unknown man), *sonar manush* (the golden man) and *manush ratan* (the jewel man).

Albert Lyon told me that one particular song was the best known of all Baul songs. He translated for me:

> Unless you learn to worship love,
> How will you be intoxicated?
> Love is as pure as a virgin,
> Sensuality is her lawful husband.
> Oh mind, oh lust, come together now,
> Come into my yearning heart.
> My prayers can only be besotted when
> Both of you fire my hymns . . .

The Baul ensemble departed, to be replaced on the stage by a troop of Santals, the local tribesmen, who wore white tassels on their heads and performed a conga to rousing percussion. We noticed Mrs Majumdar, sitting on the floor, clapping along to the rhythm. She saw us too and waved, rolling her shoulders and arms like one of those Polynesian women who dance sitting down. Took-Took sat attentively beside her, looking slightly less enthusiastic. Swarup was still engrossed in *The Pelican Brief*; he might have been anywhere. We left Albert talking to a group of professors and looked for somewhere to eat.

As we sat, eating aubergine and potato curry with slices of bread and a garnish of *mulo* (white radish), a sadhu, naked except for an orange hankie around his genitals, his skinny body covered with ash and his dreadlocks tied in a great knot, performed weird contortions in front of us. Llewelyn was most entranced. When the sadhu had finished his performance, he approached us for *baksheesh*. I was about to hand him a few rupees but the stall's proprietor shooed him away with a dish-cloth. 'Bloody vermin bugger-fellow!' he shouted. The sadhu retreated like a dog.

We walked around the craft stalls and bought a blue and white rug, for the floor of our room. It was our Christmas present to ourselves. The salesman wrapped it up in brown paper for us. The parcel was big enough to sit on, so we went back to the *shamiana* to watch the next performer.

This was a weird androgynous figure, a long-haired old man in a white silk sarong, with a *chamara*, a yak-tail fly-whisk (similar to the wildebeest tail that Jomo Kenyatta carried) attached to one wrist. Making elaborate hand movements, the old man preached in a quavering high-pitched voice. Every now and then he broke into song. The crowd was mesmerised. Some of them brought their children to the edge of the stage and the old man waved the *chamara* over the heads as a bene-diction. I looked around for Albert Lyon to tell us who this charismatic figure was but he was nowhere to be seen.

On the train back to Calcutta, an itinerant *paan*-wallah plied his wares through the carriages. He sold cigarettes, *bidis* and *zarda* as well as a selection of catechu and betel nuts, peels, pastes and preserves. The customers would ask for specific combinations of the ingredients, and the *paan*-wallah would wrap them neatly into betel leaf parcels, to be chewed as a digestive or simply to pass the time.

One of our fellow passengers, who'd already asked if we had sterling or dollars to change, suggested we try some *bhang*. It turned out that the *paan*-wallah sold little cakes of the stuff for two rupees each. I decided to buy one for Christmas evening. My plan was to take it to a backstreet café and ask them to whip it into a *lassi* for me.

Emma said, 'You'll give yourself food poisoning, very festive I must say. What if it's too strong?'

I said it was unlikely to be strong if it cost two rupees on a train.

The *bhang* came wrapped up in a leaf; it was the size of a walnut, loose and sticky to the touch, not at all like hashish, in fact suspiciously like silage. But other passengers were ordering *bhang* among their *paan* ingredients so I took it to be genuine.

Many westerners assume *bhang* is just another word for hashish, but it is a cannabis preparation in its own right. Whereas hashish and leaf cannabis are outlawed in most parts of India (the levels of enforcement vary) *bhang* is legal and available from many *paan* stalls. It is looser in texture and not as strong as hashish nor is it smoked but mixed into *paans* and sweets and milky drinks to be consumed on religious holidays and on pilgrimages. In Calcutta (where it is also called *siddi*) a glass of *bhang lassi* is often served as an aperitif. I am not sure exactly how *bhang* is prepared and certainly its texture varies from region to region: the *bhang* in Varanasi looks like jellied mud and the stuff in Puri is mixed with sugar.

Back at the Fairlawn, tired and refreshed by our day in the country, we tried some more of the phone numbers we had been given. We had a list from a woman who had spent some time in Calcutta in the late 1960s and early 1970s; many of the numbers were defunct, and I was sure a ouija board would have been a more effective means of communication.

One of the numbers was for a Mr Agrawal whose personal assistant answered the phone. He told us Mr Agrawal was resting and that he would call us back. Later that evening he did so. I mentioned our mutual friend Mrs Walker whom he remembered fondly and he invited us to tea the following afternoon. He would send his car for us at four.

CHAPTER SEVENTEEN

On Christmas Eve we found the hotel decorated with swags of paper chains and golden lanterns; the effect more oriental than one might have expected, the decorations having come from Chinese paper shops on Free School Street. There were crimson dragons made of pleated crêpe paper. There was also bunting: the flags of many nations, with the Union Jack prominent amongst them. It must have all been put up over night.

A marching band, of the kind that traditionally accompanies the groom's party to an Indian wedding, all dressed up in epauletted Sergeant Pepper uniforms, went from door to door on Sudder Street playing celebratory tunes like *For He's A Jolly Good Fellow* and *Happy Birthday To You*, idiosyncratic renditions with the trumpet fading away halfway through a line and random drumbeats added for jollity. Mr Bose would not allow them into the Fairlawn courtyard so they stood blaring at the gates like the trumpeters at Jericho.

All around New Market it was busier than ever. A flock of small, confused-looking turkeys huddled on Lindsay Street like babes in the wood, overseen by a pantomime villain with curling moustaches and an eyepatch. Hawkers approached us with packets of Christmas cards, tubes of wrapping paper and tinsel rosettes. We were after a dozen roses for Mrs Smith. They turned out to be so cheap that we bought her two dozen instead. Then we walked along to Nahoum's for some fruit cake but the queues were so long that we abandoned the idea. We noticed a tall, professorial man (I thought I recognised him as the curator from Shantiniketan, but he wasn't) serving behind the counter, evidently drafted in for the rush and looking most flustered.

Outside the market and on Chowringhee, we came across Nepalese families, sturdy hill people with oriental features and rosy cheeks, selling machine-knitted sweaters, unattractive patterned acrylic garments. We were told that their presence in the city marked the coming of winter, much as hot chestnut vendors do in London.

Violet was touched by the roses. 'Darlings, you shouldn't have . . .'

Later, there was a knock on our door. Jamal, grinning, handed us a square white box, 'Present from Memsahib.' Inside was a chocolate Christmas cake from Flury's.

Andy Devane crept along to wish us a happy Christmas. He was leaving that afternoon for the Andaman Islands, where he was to join his son's yacht. 'We'll probably do a little scuba-diving . . .' He managed to make it sound as customary a Christmas activity as singing carols or listening to the Queen's speech.

The hotel was filling up with guests. There was a middle-aged couple – the man, tall and Hemingway-like, the woman, also tall and athletic, very glamorous – so wrapped up in one another that Emma and I called them 'the second honeymooners'. He turned out to be the Asia correspondent for *Der Spiegel*. Ted told us he was a superstitious man who consulted astrologers and fortune-tellers.

A woman from Yeovil, travelling with her ten-year-old daughter, told us how brave we were to bring a baby to India, so of course we told her the horror story, at which her mouth formed a querulous O shape. She barely spoke a word to us after that.

A sturdy Canadian family, father, mother with two adolescent sons, both beefy and flaxen-haired, and two Indian children they had adopted two years earlier, a brother and a sister, twelve and ten, the little girl blind in one eye. All six of them wore safari outfits, bushjackets and trousers that unzipped above the knee to make shorts. Emma discovered that the Indian children had grown up on the streets in Calcutta. She wondered if it was traumatic for them to return.

We never really spoke to them, there were enough of them to fill their own table in the dining-room. They said grace in loud voices and we noticed their peculiar Canadian pronunciation: 'For what we are *aboat* to receive . . .'

I overheard Ted asking the Canadian father, just as he had asked me once, if he had been cautious. I had thought it odd then but had assumed it was a question about insurance.

The Canadian's reply was that his family was used to crowded cities. 'Nobody's gonna cut our throats here . . .' To which Ted responded, 'Good, good. Well, I thought so, of course . . .'

Then there was Brenda, a schoolmistress from Taptapani, a tribal area of Orissa, an Anglo-Indian spinster, frumpy and religious, who reminded us of Barbie Batchelor the tragic missionary in the Paul Scott books. She was standoffish to most of the other guests – and once tutted loudly at Llewelyn's dining-room behaviour – but gushed uncontrollably around the Smiths, who treated her with patience and polite condescension. Apparently she had spent every Christmas at the Fairlawn for the past twenty years.

[149]

Harry Dent knew all about Brenda. 'The problem is where to begin,' he told us but, tantalisingly, with the same code of gentlemanly reluctance as Ted, left it at that. Harry and Rosemary were spending Christmas Day with their relatives.

Harry felt the celebrations would be sufficiently jubilant without their presence. 'One year they engaged a projectionist and showed cartoons. Oh ho, I remember that Chilly Willy. He was a penguin, killingly funny. Oh yes, and Woody Woodpecker, of course. Mustn't forget him. Great fun . . .' He chuckled hollowly.

There was a frantic yapping and Fifi came hurtling down the passage from the servants' courtyard. She had escaped from her weekly bath and stood, trembling and drenched, at Ted's feet. Her white curls were matted into stiff peaks and she looked like some small flesh-coloured prehistoric reptile, covered all over in spiky protuberances.

Ted looked down at Fifi proudly, and said, 'Plenty of fight left in you, old girl.' He patted her wet flank. Then he turned to me and said, 'Used to see dogs when I was a boy, coats looked like that all the time. Terriers of some description. Could have been Lakeland Terriers. Very good ratters . . .'

CHAPTER EIGHTEEN

Mr Bose, who had sent for us to say a car was waiting at the gates, was in an excited state and whispered, 'Mr Agrawal, very important VIP,' as a chauffeur in a grey safari outfit held open the doors of the cleanest black Ambassador we had ever seen. The glass in the windows was tinted. In a state of luxurious invisibility, we cruised south towards Russell Street.

We knew little about Mr Agrawal, except that he was an aged bachelor, extremely rich and a member of Calcutta's Marwari community. The term Marwari literally refers to someone from Marwar, the erstwhile kingdom of Jodhpur in Rajasthan, but in colloquial usage, away from Rajasthan, it refers to the business clans of Rajasthani origin who have flourished in all the big Indian cities. In Calcutta the most famous Marwari family are the Birlas. Wherever there is really big international business in India, there is almost always Marwari involvement.

To call the Marwaris successful is an understatement; many are as rich as the richest people anywhere in the world. In fact, many of them would be listed in the *Fortune 500* if it wasn't for their reluctance to declare their wealth. The Marwaris have a reputation for tax evasion.

Historically they were the *seths*, hereditary money-lenders and bankers to the Rajput nobility. They controlled the supplies that were essential to the armies the Rajputs supported. The rulers of the different states would vie with one another to attract the *seths*, offering them tax-free land, armed protection for their trade caravans, even a hand in political matters, for they all knew that a concentration of prosperous *seths* meant a rich and powerful state.

By the beginning of the nineteenth century, feudalism was in decline. Constant infighting had weakened the power of the Rajputs. The East India Company was waiting to move in and take control. The British presence in Bombay, Calcutta and Madras was affecting the caravan routes the *seths* used to move their goods from place to place.

When the impoverished rulers took to plundering the caravans, the *seths* needed little persuasion to relocate in the British garrison towns, where not only were they protected but a whole new area of trade was opened up to them. After 1857, with the progress in transportation and communication, the *seths* expanded their operations beyond Rajasthan. The age of the Marwari plutocrat dawned. British companies looking to sell finished goods in India needed agents, the Marwaris were given the job, and the rewards for such brokerage were high. As British traders developed an interest in opium, tea and jute, so the Marwaris took over those commodities, becoming the mainstay of foreign firms.

In the business world of Calcutta, by the end of the nineteenth century, the Marwaris were overtaking the Bengalis, whose fervour for education and reform had led them to question British rule; a cultural renaissance had given the Bengalis an uncomfortable sense of national pride, they found themselves hovering between dependence and defiance. Without such dilemmas to bother them, the Marwaris used the British simply to get rich. Within a short time, they became property magnates.

The First World War allowed the Marwaris to speculate. They held important contracts. After the war, faced with growing nationalism in India, the government made tax concessions to retain Marwari support. Already making vast profits from the market for imported cotton goods, they were gradually taking over the international jute market.

When the Marwaris, notably G.D. Birla, saw that the nationalist movement was unstoppable, they made their overtures. They persuaded the nationalists that they held the means to strike at the base of British rule in India, economic power. The authorities might see fit to lock up radical politicians but it would be hard to imprison businessmen who were after all playing by the rules the British had introduced; and so, when Independence was granted, the Marwaris continued to flourish, replacing British investment with their own capital and diversifying into a range of industries, from cement to aviation.

We were aware of a definite anti-Marwari prejudice among Bengalis. Having lived beside one another for a century and a half, the differences have widened rather than narrowed. Bengalis tend to think and dream while Marwaris tend to acquire and amass. For generations the most advanced and educated of all Indians, Bengalis shudder to see their great city bought up by outsiders they regard as grasping and unprincipled.

Of course, these are generalisations; the anti-Marwari prejudice is as silly as any other snobbery. Generally it has remained no more than snobbery; occasionally it has flared up into greater hostility. In 1918, after supplies of ghee bought from the Marwari merchants of Barabazar were found to be adulterated, armed guards from Rajasthan were recruited to protect the Marwaris' homes and warehouses from angry mobs.

The Marwaris, especially the Birlas, have given a great

[153]

deal to the city: concert halls, galleries, a planetarium and, most recently a vast, opulent marble temple in the Ballygunge district. I asked a Bengali friend which deity was venerated in the new temple. 'Mammon,' was his flippant reply.

The car turned into the courtyard of a Victorian mansion block. Several khaki-clad security men stood around the porch. The front door was opened by a gigantic *durwan* wearing black pyjamas, who led us to an old-fashioned lift that he entered with us. We rose five floors.

Another muscleman in black pyjamas was waiting for us; he led us to the door of the apartment, which was opened by a man wearing a light grey suit with all three of the jacket buttons done up, a white shirt and a silk tie with a pattern of woven elephants.

'Mr Agrawal?' I asked, ready to shake his hand.

'I am Desai, Mr Agrawal's assistant,' he said, 'please come.'

Noticing his stockinged feet, we started to remove our shoes.

'Please, it is not necessary,' said Mr Desai.

We followed him along a panelled corridor spread with a line of magnificent Persian carpets. I spotted an alcove containing an image of Mahadevi and two Sanskrit mantras in red ink, underneath which incense-sticks smouldered.

Mr Desai showed us into a little drawing-room that seemed to be scented with violet air-freshener, where beside each plush pink armchair stood a spindly table, each one covered with Royal Worcester figurines of English children from the 1920s. These filled me with trepidation as they looked enticingly toy-like. I begged Emma to hold Llewelyn tightly.

In the corner of the room was a vast ivory Ganesh in a glass case.

'Mr Agrawal will be with you presently,' said Mr Desai and left us.

Through the window we could see the shabby rooftops of central Calcutta and the looming, decrepit skyscraper, the Chatterjee Centre, with its burnt-out upper storeys, a peculiar contrast to the neat, fussy little room we sat in.

'Hello, hello, welcome.'

Mr Agrawal stood at the door, a short, elderly man with a bald head and bulging froggy eyes, dressed in exactly the same way as Mr Desai, all the buttons done up on an identical light grey suit, the same elephant tie. One difference was his watch, a gold Piaget with a bracelet strap, and whereas Mr Desai wore socks, Mr Agrawal wore no shoes or socks at all. But they were similar enough to remind us of Gilbert and George, the same look of anonymity heightened into weirdness.

A telephone rang in another room. Mr Agrawal called back down the corridor, 'Desai, that will be the Israelis. Please tell them our position.'

He smiled at Llewelyn and told him, 'When you are older you will look like . . .' he paused for a second to find the figurine he was thinking of, making funny eeny-meeny gestures with his finger, 'this one!' A little ginger boy carrying a ball. I asked if he had found the figurines in England. They were presents, he told us, from an old friend. 'Dead now, I'm afraid.'

Although Mr Agrawal was polite, we had the impression he was in the middle of important negotiations. He told us that he had some business to finalise before leaving for Varanasi, where he was spending a week's holiday, as the guest of some business associates. There would be lectures and discourses from religious scholars, including the greatest living authority on the *Ramayana*.

The two pyjama-clad musclemen came in with a tea trolley. There were all sorts of cakes – eclairs, slices of strawberry gateau, chocolate meringues, all rich and creamy – as well as fried Indian savouries, wadas, samosas and a little bowl of *gulab jamun*. 'Please, tuck in,' urged Mr Agrawal. He sipped a cup of Darjeeling tea but took no food at all, which made us uncomfortable.

We talked about Indian politics. Mr Agrawal's opinion was that Left and Right were irrelevant, the most desirable Prime Minister was the one who least hindered international trade. He talked about the newly appointed British Deputy High Commissioner, who seemed to him just the man to strengthen the links between Calcutta and London. Mr Agrawal was surprised we had not yet met him. There was no mention of disco dancing.

Mr Desai came in again, urging Mr Agrawal to talk to the Israelis himself. 'You will excuse me, please,' he said and padded out of the room. Llewelyn was messy with chocolate and cream, so Emma decided to wash him in the bathroom.

At the drawing-room door stood one of the musclemen. He seemed to be on guard duty, preventing us from wandering about the flat when his employer's back was turned.

She tried to explain that she wanted the bathroom but he continued to block her path. Eventually we were obliged to ask for Mr Desai to come and release her from the drawing-room. 'I'm sorry, they don't speak English,' he muttered, evidently embarrassed.

*

Mr Agrawal returned. More polite, inconsequential conversation, but strained; he kept glancing at his big gold watch and I noticed he was drumming his heel on the floor.

Emma said we should get back and put Llewelyn to bed, a handy excuse.

We thanked him for having us, we all shook hands. He gave me his card and said to let him know if we needed any help in Calcutta and to come again.

The driver dropped us back at the Fairlawn. It had all been somewhat awkward.

Ted asked how we had got on.

'I think we were disturbing him,' said Emma.

Ted raised his eyebrows and coughed. 'Doesn't surprise me at all.'

CHAPTER NINETEEN

We went to Midnight Mass at St Paul's Cathedral. Llewelyn was fast asleep when Abdul drove us there and remained asleep throughout the service. The cathedral was absolutely packed; standing room only at the back, so a crowd had gathered under the magnificent west window (designed by Burne-Jones). The ushers were getting short-tempered, trying to keep order.

All over India there are nineteenth-century Gothic churches. At first glance they look much the same as churches of the same period in England. A closer inspection reveals the numerous adaptations made to suit the climate, such as *punkahs* and extended lancet windows to improve ventilation.

St Paul's was the grandest example of Indo-Gothic ecclesiastical architecture I had seen. It was designed by the military architect William Forbes in 1839. The wide roof is spanned with iron trusses. There is no proper nave nor are there side aisles; the structure was kept simple for fear it might sink in the weak Bengali subsoil. It has had a few wobbles since its consecration in 1847. In 1897 the steeple crashed down in an earthquake. It was rebuilt but fell again, in another earthquake, in 1934. After that it was rebuilt on the pattern of Bell Harry Tower at Canterbury.

There are a lot of Christians in Calcutta, probably even more Catholics than Protestants, but the congregation was by no means restricted to Christians; a party of turbanned Sikhs occupied a pew just ahead of us. We had the impression that Indians of all religions will worship in a church, a temple, a *gurdwara* or a mosque if the occasion is momentous enough.

There were other Europeans there as well – some of the women dressed in saris, which invariably look all wrong on white women – and several Anglo-Indians in outdated western clothes. The only person we recognised was Brenda, the schoolmistress from Orissa, sitting at the end of a pew and scowling at everyone.

The service was quite High Church, a most harmonious choir singing all the responses and the whole cathedral illuminated with candles.

When it came to Holy Communion, there was some confusion. I heard an usher saying that only Christians were allowed to take Communion, another explaining that, no, the bishop was not distributing Christmas presents.

We overheard a heated argument between an usher and a young American who insisted that a Roman Catholic was entitled to take Communion in a Protestant church. The usher asked him why he had not gone to a Catholic church. 'I don't have to put up with this,' snapped the American and pushed past him to join the queue of communicants.

When the service was over, we walked outside and found Abdul sleeping in his taxi. He drove us back to Sudder Street and Emma handed him a Christmas card with a 100 rupee note inside. Abdul, once our friendship was established, was oddly bashful about taking money. Having guessed there was a note in the envelope, he stuffed the whole thing in his pocket without looking at it.

CHAPTER TWENTY

Laxmi, first thing on Christmas morning, showed no such restraint. She burst into our room with cries of jubilation, shaking our hands and shouting 'Happy Christmas! Happy Christmas!' as if Emma had given birth to the Christ Child herself. Of course, we had a card and a tip for her as well, and moments later Osman arrived, smiling shyly, to receive his.

Violet appeared after breakfast, in a gold lamé jacket, looking most festive.

All morning she received floral tributes, dozens of them, enormous bouquets, often worked into complicated arrangements, that put our skimpy twenty-four roses to shame. The bouquets were sent by former employees, old people who wanted Violet to remember them, and sometimes they were delivered by the grandchildren or great-grandchildren of the employee.

'Every year they come, more each time. One year you won't find me, I'll be buried under flowers. Eh, Patrash.'

Patrash started laughing, I felt a little exaggeratedly but maybe the idea was funnier in Bengali than in English, then threw one arm over his head as if to shield off blows. He continued to laugh but the pitch of his voice had risen and the sounds began to resemble stifled cries, then a shrill tom-cat's wail.

Something was wrong. Patrash was crouching on the floor.

Violet called out to Jamal, '*Patrasher fit hochchey*! *Taratari*! *Laxmi jaaney ki kortey hobey. Taratari, Jamal.* Poor chap has these fits. Laxmi knows what to do. He can't help it. I wouldn't dream of firing him. He's been here twenty-three years. The thing is he's completely honest.'

It was clear that Violet cared for Patrash, but in an oddly masculine, military way, as an officer cares for his batman.

'Should we call a doctor?' asked Emma.

'I don't think so. Laxmi knows the drill. He'll be all right after a rest.'

We asked Abdul to drive us to the Kali temple at Kalighat. He was reluctant to take us there, warning us that it was a bad place, not safe for tourists, but we insisted and he drove us south along Chowringhee, dropping us off at the junction of Kalighat Temple Road.

On the way Emma told Abdul about Patrash's fit. There was a misunderstanding. Abdul thought Violet ('Esmiss Eshmit', like 'Esmiss Esmoor' in *A Passage To India*) had had the fit. When she clarified that it was actually Patrash, Abdul smiled, 'Patrash, *yaar*? Many times have fit. Meow, meow, like pussy cat? Nice for Wahlen . . .' His lack of concern surprised us a little.

To the Hindus of Bengal, Devi, the Mother Goddess, the most important deity, takes many forms: Sati (the virtuous, faithful wife), Uma (the bright, shining one), Parvati (the mountain-goddess), Annapurna (the giver of food), Ambika (the moon-mother), Durga (the unassailable). But it is as Kali, the Goddess

at her most terrible, that she is worshipped in Calcutta: a black-skinned woman with blazing eyes and a protruding tongue dripping blood. Around her neck is a garland of human skulls and around her waist is a skirt, like a tutu, of hacked-off arms; she holds a knife and a severed head in two of her four hands while her other two beckon and reassure.

To western eyes, she looks demonic. She is usually portrayed on the rampage; the only power that can prevent her crossing the line between good and evil comes from Shiva, who lies in her path. Some explain her stuck-out tongue as the common gesture for shame (that Bengalis still use) at touching her husband with her feet.

On a daily basis Kali must be appeased with gifts of food and money, even animal sacrifices, to prevent disaster. This sounded to me like a protection racket, until a Hindu friend explained that the whole point of Kali is that she is on our side; with all her ferocity she scares away the demons on our behalf. She is the protective mother, ready to fight like a tigress.

The cult is strongest among the urban poor who live close to horror and disease. A prayer to Kali implores the Goddess, 'Let all your smell be far away from my face, I entreat you. Lead from here the other smelling ones, lead away the other putrid ones.'

The Kalighat Temple Road was like a ragged crusade, pilgrims from near and far, including some impressive trident-wielding sadhus. Beggars swarmed around us immediately, some asking for 'Christmas *baksheesh*'.

We passed shack-like kiosks, selling sweets to be offered as *prasad* to the Goddess. *Prasad* is consecrated food: once presented to the deity who blesses it, eating *prasad* is like taking communion. We saw garlands of jasmine and hibiscus, plaster and brass images of Kali (and Mother Teresa, the Buddha, Jesus and Charlie Chaplin), *prasad* plates made of pale stone, and little *sandesh* moulds, like cookie cutters, in the shape of fish and elephants. Hymns and film music blasted from tinny speakers.

For centuries, Kalighat has been known for its festive carnival atmosphere. Its most typical souvenirs were the Kalighat *pats*, folk-art paintings, produced by *patuas* (scroll painters). In rural Bengal *patuas* used to go from village to village, unwinding their scrolls like scenes from a film, relating the events depicted in a sensational, melodramatic way. It was a popular form of entertainment, a bit like the cinema or the comic strip.

The *patuas* who migrated to Kalighat found that the pilgrims on their way to the temple did not stand still long enough to appreciate the scroll shows, so they switched to making religious paintings, icons and painted toys to sell instead. These items, especially the paintings, went extremely well. Just as Bengali life became more secular throughout the nineteenth century, so the *patuas* diversified their subject matter to take in pretty girls in the latest fashions, scenes of murders (especially crimes of passion) and satirical depictions of babus and their pretensions.

Gradually, to meet the demand for their pictures, the *patuas* turned away from cloth and tempera and started to use factory-made paper and water-colour instead, foreign introductions that dried quicker than the old materials.

The factory-made paper came in a standard size, eleven by eighteen inches. The *pats* were always composed with the shorter edge at the top. This enabled the *patuas* to display more finished *pats* at the small booths in which they worked but it also reflected the scroll origins of the *pats*. The *patuas* were not much concerned with perspective; backgrounds and foregrounds were minimal. When it came to rendering volume, the *patuas* came up with a simple but effective technique: after first drawing the figure in outline with a pencil, they painted over the line with a well-loaded brush, then applied a lighter (tonally gradated) line to the inner edges of the form. This makes Kalighat painting look remarkably similar to the much later work of the French painter Léger. In general, Kalighat *pats* strike me as peculiarly modern, similar in line and composition to the work of the Fauves and Post-Impressionists, even the early Picasso. It would be interesting to find out if the *pats* made any impact in Europe at the time, in the way that Japanese woodcuts did.

At home, Kalighat painting was largely ignored by educated Bengalis who preferred more academic westernised painting. Consequently Kalighat *pats* rarely found their way into the collections of connoisseurs. It was not until 1926, by which time the tradition had all but died out, that the art critic Ajit Ghose wrote seriously about the paintings and trained Bengali painters like Jamini Roy, fired by modernism in Europe, turned to Kalighat painting for inspiration.

The *pats*, and the stylistically related *Bat-tala* woodcut prints, were eventually replaced by the mass-produced chromolithographs we now regard as the definitive temple souvenirs.

Much of the atmosphere of old Kalighat lives on. The red-light district survives a few streets away; along with Sonagachi in the north, it is one of the city's oldest. There was such a lack of solemnity, it was easy to forget that we were walking on sacred ground.

According to the myth, Daksha, Shiva's father-in-law, berated Shiva in front of his daughter, Sati, upsetting her so much that she burst into flames. Shiva was so distraught by his wife's self-sacrifice that he took her burning body in his arms and performed a frenzied, stamping dance to quench the flames. The dance caused the world to tremble. Vishnu was asked by the other gods to stop Shiva's manic tarantella, so he threw a knife-edged discus at the corpse, chopping it into fifty-one bits. The spot where each bit fell became a *pitha*, or pilgrimage-site. The little toe of the goddess fell on what is now Calcutta; the temple at Kalighat marks the spot.

For some time the precise location was unknown, until the hermit Chourangi Giri (for whom Chowringhee Road is named) found an image of Kali's face on a *shalagram* that told him where to find the toe and build the temple.

Both the *shalagram* and the toe still exist, swathed in cloth and preserved in an iron chest in the *garbagriha*, the inner sanctum of the temple; at certain auspicious dates they are bathed in the temple tank, a ceremony called the *Snanjatra*. The relics must not be seen; they are not unwrapped and the ceremony is conducted by a senior priest who is himself blind-folded.

Nobody can say when Chourangi Giri lived, so it is hard to establish just how old the temple is. The land on which the temple stood belonged to the Sabarna Roy Chowdhury family, who sold it to the East India Company in 1698. In those days the temple was in the middle of thick jungle, pilgrims had to travel by boat and the pujas took place at night, but these conditions did not deter the devotees.

In many ways, the growth of the Kali cult, certainly the fame of the Kali temple, is tied in with the growth of the city: the site became more accessible as it was incorporated into the metropolis. To Bengalis, Kali was so closely associated with the city, she became known as Kali Kalkattawali.

There is still something jungly about the place; the palm trees swaying wildly through the pollution, and the muddy smell of Tolly's Nullah, a canal dug by William Tolly in 1774 to bring the Hugli, the *Adi Ganga*, to the temporarily landlocked temple.

The East India Company respected the awe the temple inspired. In 1765, after the Company had obtained official financial control of Bengal, it sponsored a massive ceremonial puja at Kalighat, no doubt to appease its Hindu subjects. The cost of the ceremony is reckoned to have been 30,000 rupees.

The current building, with its squashy dome, was erected in 1809 with money given by a merchant called Kaliprasad Datta. After that, it became fashionable to endow the temple, especially as the city grew and the temple became more central to life in Calcutta. All through the nineteenth century, Calcuttans and visitors to Calcutta trooped to the temple, which grew rich from the constant stream of offerings.

Today there are regular pujas on Tuesdays, Saturdays and on the nights of full and new moons; special pujas for widows and housewives, litigants and businessmen; all bringing in a steady income. The temple also functions as the Gretna Green of Bengal; elopers can get married there and have the union blessed by Kali.

People were queuing to get inside. The beggars became more desperate. We spotted a huddle of white-clad *pandas*, temple officials who assist the pilgrims with their supplications. Seeing us, they all rushed forward, plainly regarding tourists as rich pickings.

One stocky *panda* caught us. He spoke good English and, apart from continually asking us for money, was helpful and well-informed. He gave Llewelyn his finger to hold. 'Do you know the English film, *Baby's Day Out*?' he asked us.

Emma and I glanced at one another. We were still amazed at the impact this obscure film had made on Calcutta. 'Is it an English film?' We were under the impression it was American.

'English language,' said the *panda*. 'Starring Joe Mantegna . . .'

We removed our shoes and socks ('Please open your shoes,' commanded the panda) and stepped into a courtyard, where the headless carcass of a goat was being dragged away. The flagstones were smeared with its blood and women were dipping their fingers into the blood and marking their foreheads. The *panda* told us the sacrificed goat was cooked in the temple kitchen and fed to the poor.

Such a crowd swarmed around the central shrine that we could not see in. Many were holding offerings of sweets and hibiscus flowers. It was not a beautiful building, bits and pieces in a variety of styles were thrown together.

The panda was keen for us to make puja. I said we hadn't brought any *prasad*. He waved this technicality away, 'You can put money there . . .'

We joined the crowd at the sanctum sanctorum. All around us people were muttering prayers or *japam*, the repetition of mantras. *Japam* seems to me a particularly Indian form of prayer; Indian Sufis use the same technique, the ceaseless repetition of God's name, which they call *zikr*.

The image, as far as I could make out, was primitive, no more than a head with four arms, the body only suggested by the red garment and garlands. It was impossible to ascertain whether the image had feet at all. Then I wondered if the image was really a rock transformed into a sacred image, as is sometimes the case in older Hindu temples.

To Emma's annoyance, I gave 100 rupees, adding an extra rupee for courtesy – the standard etiquette for cash offerings, like buying a racehorse with guineas.

Emma was looking green and said the smell of blood was making her feel sick. We sat beneath a tree, sacred to the goddess Manasha, Queen of the Snakes, with little ragged bundles tied to its branches. People made these offerings to ward off snakebite. I asked our *panda* what was in the bundles. 'Small stones, usually,' he replied, 'but you can put money . . .'

We walked over to the Kalikunda, the temple tank, and another *panda* joined us, his mouth and teeth crimson with betel, which gave him a vampiric appearance.

Without asking, he started blessing us, then produced a book of previous donations given by foreign visitors.

It was clear that he had doctored the figures, turning 100 rupees into 1,000 and even 11,000 rupees. I asked where the money went and he said to feed the poor. I gave him fifty rupees, the same amount to our guide, then we retrieved our shoes and left, feeling confused and alienated.

Walking back towards Chowringhee, we passed an old mangy dog that had survived a road accident, leaving its spine in a mangled state. It was hopping along in agony and people were shooing it away.

'This place is horrible,' said Emma, 'I don't know why we came.'

'I don't think it's horrible. I think we need to come with someone who knows the place well, so we won't be bothered by *pandas*. I mean, it is a bit extreme, with decapitated goats and everything, but it's really important. The city is named after this place.'

'This is supposed to be Christmas. All we're seeing is blood and guts and beggars and suffering animals.'

CHAPTER TWENTY-ONE

There were faxes waiting for us at the hotel that, even after such a short time in India, seemed like news from another planet.

Patrash was back at the reception desk, as if nothing had happened.

Emma asked if he was better and he replied, 'Yes, madam. Don't mention . . .'

We ate a light lunch at Khalsa, a Punjabi *dhaba* on Madge Lane, then went back to our room for some chocolate cake and a rest. Emma wrote some letters that she faxed to her parents and sisters.

While she was sending these, I walked along Sudder Street in search of a café to make my *bhang lassi*. I found a suitably clandestine place called Annapurna, up a narrow alley near the corner of Free School Street.

The other patrons, eating lunch at five o'clock on Christmas afternoon, included the German Hare Krishna fugitive, two Buddhist monks and an aged Italian hippy reading Brunton's *A Search in Secret India*; an odd crowd, made even odder, no doubt, by my arrival and request.

The proprietor of the Annapurna café, a young man dressed in a brown bush-shirt and a *dhoti*, was quite agreeable, taking my little cake of *bhang* and returning a few minutes later with two glasses of khaki-coloured yoghurt. I said I only wanted to drink one glass, so he drank the other one.

It tasted like grass to me, actual grass from a lawn. I asked the proprietor if it really was *bhang*. Yes, he assured me, it was *pukka*.

'I hope it won't knock me out,' I said.

'Don't worry. This is very light. We drink this at weddings, even.'

Sudder Street was crowded that afternoon. There were lots of Europeans around but also more Bengalis than usual. Perhaps people had converged on Sudder Street expecting wild celebrations. A family of entertainers had gathered a huddle of spectators. I watched them for a while. The troop consisted of a man who banged a drum and blew a whistle, a woman performing a folk dance and two small children who took it in turns to walk a tight-rope that was actually a length of bamboo stalk suspended between two posts. When the children shimmied along the bamboo, the man chanted '*Shabash*! *Shabash*! *Shabash*!' They were small children, no more than four years old.

The Christmas celebrations at the Fairlawn took place in the evening and had, in previous years, attracted such a crowd that it was necessary to purchase tickets in advance. The gates were locked to prevent intruders; children from Sudder Street had crept in to watch.

There were to be carols, accompanied by the Salvation Army choir, a conjuror and, of course, a special dinner. The tables in the dining-room were joined together into one long

দত্ত প্রেস

[173]

row and all the places were laid with festive hats and crackers.

We bathed Llewelyn and came downstairs as the carols were ending. There were people everywhere, in the lounge and in the garden, laughing and drinking. Phil Spector's *Christmas Album* was playing above the noise of talk and laughter, which gave the scene a Disney atmosphere.

The *bhang* was taking effect and I felt expansive and light-headed. I told Emma it would be most suitable for weddings, much cheaper than champagne. It did have one devastating effect, though. I found myself craving a cigarette.

'Darlings, you've missed the singsong,' said Violet. She was still dressed in gold lamé, enthroned in a loom chair with a glass of pink gin in her jewelled fist. Beside her sat a younger woman, looking chic in a red velvet dress, about forty years old with auburn hair and a long humorous face.

Llewelyn immediately picked up a balloon. 'Don't bite it, darling,' said Violet; turning to her companion, she explained, 'Brand new teeth, cut them the other night . . .'

Violet introduced us to Catherine Berge, who had come from Paris to direct a documentary film about the veteran actor, Soumitra Chatterjee, the star of *Charulata* and many other films by Satyajit Ray. The film was being produced by Merchant Ivory.

I begged a cigarette from her. Emma frowned at me. It was my first since Llewelyn was born and it tasted rich and mellow, more intoxicating than the *bhang*. But the *bhang* intensified the swirl of the nicotine and for a moment or two I felt pleasantly giddy.

Catherine told us she was in a state of hysteria, having just arrived from the airport; she'd stayed awake throughout the flight and now she had found a second wind. It was her second visit to Calcutta: the previous time had been during the monsoon, when she had waded through knee-deep water from meeting to meeting. 'I was so scared I would fall in a hole!'

'I don't think the holes are all that deep.'

'Some are. Straight down to the mud. The road caves in,' said Ted, who had sidled over and was standing next to Violet's chair. He was wearing a grey tropical worsted suit and carrying Fifi under his arm; there were white hairs all over the back of his jacket. 'Due to the damn underground railway, if you ask me. Probably cause the whole place to collapse . . .'

'Ted has strong views, you know . . .'

'Know a thing or two about cut and cover, anyway.'

'The monsoon must be terrible here,' I remarked, thinking of the nightmare of sloshing through filthy water to get anywhere.

Ted said that, over the years, he had come to feel about the monsoon much the same as Indians felt about it, that it was the time of renewal and cleansing. I asked if the hotel was ever flooded. 'Not once,' said Ted, 'in all my time here. We're on raised ground. There's a slope, you see, from here down to the gates . . .' The courtyard looked level to me. Catherine confirmed his statement. When Sudder Street had been a pool, the Fairlawn had been an island. Ted continued on the subject. 'All these plants get a proper drink. You should see them. Green as jade. And the air feels wonderful, moist and alive after the heat. You probably can't imagine how hot it gets before the rains. I've seen grown men buckle under. Prickly heat, inflamed sweat-glands, that's no joke . . .'

Jamal was turning up the music, urging everyone to dance, but he received a sharp word from the Burra Bearer who was busy collecting empty glasses. Laxmi scooped Llewelyn up and danced with him at the foot of the stairs.

Brenda walked past. Ignoring Catherine and ourselves, she curtseyed to the Smiths. 'Look at you two, the King and

Queen of Old Ireland.' It was a peculiar compliment but well intended.

Ted said, 'Liked your singing, my dear. Very good at it. Beltin' out those carols loud and clear . . .'

'The way you do,' remarked Violet.

Violet said, 'We had Clifford Anstey here.'

Ted said, 'You mean Clive Andrews, darling. Yes, filming with the BBC. Not so long ago . . .'

'Clive Ellington,' said Violet.

'Not Ellington, darling. Anstruther . . .'

'Clive Anderson,' said Emma.

'That was the fellow's name, by God.'

'Clive James,' said Violet, throwing everything back into confusion.

'Was it Clive James?'

'No, it was Clive Anderson,' said Emma. She had seen the programme.

A loud explosion. Llewelyn had bitten his balloon. Laxmi brought him over to Emma. The explosion had shocked him initially into silence, followed by a keening wail. Brenda said we should not have given him a balloon to play with.

Fifi, unused to howling infants, gave a worried bark. Ted offered a few words of comfort. 'Don't worry, old thing. Balloons go off like that all the time. Don't trust 'em myself . . .' I couldn't tell if he was talking to Llewelyn or Fifi but both calmed down.

'I love this place,' announced Catherine, yawning. 'The only person missing is Albert Lyon . . .' She pronounced the name, wittily, in French.

'He's at Shantiniketan,' I said.

'Catherine is being facetious,' said Violet. 'Do you know,

[176]

that fellow wants our monarchy abolished? He told me himself . . .'

I was sitting, with Llewelyn on my lap, waiting for the magic. A table of props had been set up under the columns and a small, anxious-looking conjuror in *kurta* pyjamas was standing with his palms pressed together, trying to get everyone's attention.

When the tricks started, they were old ones: he poured water into a paper cone where it transmogrified into sand; he turned one handkerchief into a string of handkerchiefs; he turned eight separate metal rings into a chain that resembled the Olympic symbol.

The audience groaned affectionately at his patter and clapped their encouragement. The conjuror, selecting a member of the audience to assist him with a trick that involved playing cards, chose the blind girl standing with her Canadian family. Jamal, who was wrapped up in the performance, loudly pointed out that the girl was blind and the conjuror, flustered, looked for someone else. I don't think Jamal was being unkind, he was more concerned that the conjuror might cheat.

Unwisely, perhaps, the conjuror chose Brenda. No, she kept insisting, that was not the card she had chosen. The conjuror said that it had to be. Brenda was adamant that she had chosen the four of hearts. The conjuror said that was impossible, he knew she had chosen the six of diamonds.

Catherine burst out laughing. Everything wound down and before long the gong sounded for dinner.

We sat at one end of the long table with Ted and Violet and Catherine. Emma held Llewelyn on her lap. Violet told her to give him to Laxmi but Emma said she wanted him to eat something.

'Plenty of tucker round here,' said Ted.

To my left sat a Japanese social scientist, all bundled up in a hooded tracksuit that looked less athletic than protective. Opposite him sat a suave Argentine, with a deep tan and bulging facial muscles, wearing a crested blazer; he looked a bit like Ralph Lauren. It was clear that Ted regarded both of them as potential agitators.

Violet insisted we all wear our paper hats. The social scientist put his, a golden crown, on top of his hood, a curiously Plantagenet effect like Richard the Lionheart.

'Don't cry for me, Argentina,' Violet sang. 'Have you seen the film *Evita* yet?'

The Argentine had not – nor had any of us. Violet had seen the stage production in London. She told us she had great respect for Madonna. 'You must understand she is an artiste, one hundred per cent. You can't judge her like anyone else . . .'

'Staunch RC, so I'm told,' said Ted.

'It's not had good reviews, that film,' I said.

'That doesn't matter,' said Violet, then snorted, 'the critics are pygmies.'

'Look at how they treated Mrs Thatcher,' said Ted, suddenly looking bewildered.

'There you are. Pygmies, the lot of them.'

Violet turned to the hooded scientist. 'What about the hostages in Peru?' He just blinked at her, so she repeated the question. 'What about the hostages?'

'P-prostitutes?' he stammered in a loud voice.

'Good Lord!' exclaimed Ted. Fifi yapped in outrage.

'And what can you tell us, sir? You're South American, aren't you?'

The Argentine smiled as Violet pointed her spoon at him. 'I'm sorry, I don't have an opinion . . .'

Emma asked him if he played polo.

'As a matter of fact, yes . . .'

'Barbara Cartland!' shouted Violet. 'She's another. One hundred per cent artiste.'

'Marvellous woman,' said Ted, 'she came here once . . .'

'Here,' said Violet.

'How fabulous,' laughed Catherine.

'Ninety-six years old . . .'

'Doesn't look it. Marvellous woman.'

'I'm 96,' announced Violet.

'Darling, you're in a muddle . . .'

By the time the pudding came, everyone at our end of the table, including the social scientist, was in a muddle. My *bhang* high was feeling more like sedation, but enjoyable enough. I felt removed from everything, like a contented ghost. I finally asked the social scientist why he kept his hood up.

'It is too noisy and I have running ears,' he shouted.

Violet kept blowing a whistle at him, insisting we all show some spirit.

Halfway along the table sat a party of Indian Christians whose conversation turned on religious themes, and beyond that sat the Canadians and Brenda, apparently at loggerheads. And there seemed to be any number of couples, Indian and European, who would rather have dined on their own and found themselves embarrassed at the communal celebration.

'Come on, you lot, misbehave!' shouted Violet.

A young Indian couple got up to leave and thanked Ted and Violet as they passed. The girl was pretty, with a hint of Burmese ancestry around the eyes and cheekbones and a serene smile. After she'd left, I commented on her looks to Violet. 'Very beautiful, oh yes,' she hissed, 'they can be lovely, but treacherous, treacherous . . .'

The crackers turned out to be empty, which sent Catherine into fits of laughter, and few of their explosive strips seemed to work. The Japanese social scientist, perhaps misunderstanding the nature of a cracker, set his alight with a candle.

'I say, steady on.' Ted (who had been waiting for something like this to happen) clicked his fingers and immediately the Burra Bearer carried the burning cracker off into the kitchen. Ted shook his head sadly. 'Extraordinary thing to do . . .'

Violet announced that she was bored. 'God, what fun we used to have. People nowadays, ugh. We used to play games after dinner. We need dancing, love affairs . . .'

'Proper games,' said Ted, 'like 'Are you there, Moriarty?''

I suddenly had a glimpse of the fierce and disciplined pursuit of pleasure that must have driven Violet in her night-club days. The trappings of age fell away from her and I could see her as a small dynamic figure, worldlier than the English girls, ready to take charge. How she must have appealed to Ted, who probably needed a bit of chivvying.

I was enjoying this revelation when Ted, like the person from Porlock, disturbed it by shouting, 'Irawaddy!'

'Darling, what are you talking about?'

'The longest river. That conjuror asked the name of the world's longest river. Whatever he said, he was wrong. It's the Irawaddy.'

'I don't remember this question,' said Catherine.

'That's because he didn't ask it,' snapped Violet.

'Actually, I believe he did,' said the Argentine.

Just after that, I slipped out to Sudder Street to buy a

packet of cigarettes. When I came back, the Smiths had gone upstairs and the party was evidently over. Jamal was busy clearing the tables, jamming away to *Sleigh Ride* by the Ronettes.

CHAPTER TWENTY-TWO

On Boxing Day afternoon we loaded our belongings into Abdul's taxi, settled the bill with Patrash and moved to Mrs Lahiri's house.

The gate to Mrs Lahiri's house could only be unlocked by Sushil the doorman. We were never given a key to the gate. To enter or to leave, we had to summon him with a buzzer. He was a small slender man in his thirties, and like many doormen in Calcutta he was of Nepalese descent. His parents had left Nepal when he was a small child and we learnt that he had come to Calcutta from Cooch Behar.

Sushil had a wife, Malina, a robust Bengali woman who worked as Mrs Lahiri's ayah. Twice a day she swept the entire house with a short broom (called a *jhadu*) and wiped the floors with a moist grey rag. To begin with, Malina had an air of not suffering fools gladly: as foreigners, we were most certainly fools, or at least I was, especially when I attempted to speak Bengali.

I think, in her taciturn way, Malina liked Emma and, as a mother herself, she took an interest in Llewelyn. Sometimes when Emma was bathing Llewelyn she would slip into the room (as she always did, without knocking) and offer to dry him. To do this, she sat on the floor and, holding him on her lap, thoroughly massaged his little body, working baby oil into his skin and dusting him with powder. She spoke a soft repetitive baby language to him, as if she were saying 'Abracadabra cadabra cadabra' over and over again like a mantra.

Llewelyn relished this treatment and would scramble towards her, beaming. Malina would smile down at him and then we would see that she had a sweet gentle smile, but as soon as she looked up at us the smile would vanish. We didn't take this personally, it was just some notion Malina had about deference.

Sushil and Malina had two children, a son of ten called Manu and a daughter of eight called Mina. Manu played fast, ramshackle cricket with his friends in the street. The ball slammed against walls and rebounded. I was always expecting to hear breaking glass. At other times he flew a small kite of his own construction from the roof of the house next door (where Malina also did some cleaning) and challenged other boys to aerial combat. The object was to break the rival kite's string. The winner would shout, '*Bhon kattya!*'

Mina regarded Llewelyn as a marvellous doll; she would sit and play with him for hours on end and when we got to know her well and trust her, we would let her take him off on her own, to carry him up and down the street, to the envy of all the other little girls in the neighbourhood.

Sushil's family lived in a small annexe at the back of the house. The rest of the ground floor was unoccupied although we noticed there were two rooms that could feasibly be rented out.

There were seldom any other guests staying and when there were, we were hardly aware of them. Once I passed an albino man on the stairs. With his blond hair and grey suit, I took him at first for another foreigner. The red eyes identified him. He was visiting from Bhubaneshwar, being interviewed for a teaching position.

On the first floor there was an office that ran courses in computer science. Mrs Lahiri's son took some interest in this enterprise but he was, in fact, employed as a travel agent.

Mrs Lahiri, being a widow, took withdrawal seriously; she cultivated a roof garden (rose bushes, bougainvilleas, lemon trees, all in containers) and sat for long hours in prayer. At certain times of day she sang hymns, *gayatrams*, in a trained soprano voice, accompanying herself on a portable harmonium, and her clear, measured syllables poured down through our windows. It was ironic that, to our western minds, Mrs Lahiri's conformity, her adherence to the strictest conventions of Bengali widowhood, made her stand out as someone otherworldly and exotic, whereas her intention was to fade gently into the background.

We rarely saw her. When we did meet, it would be on the stairs. She would stand one flight above us. This was oddly appropriate for talking to her was like talking to someone sitting on a cloud. We would have long conversations over the banister. Her speech (at least in English) sounded like a string of quiet sighs, every sentence trailing downwards at the end, as if sent down from above.

She was, we reckoned, in her mid-sixties; a small compact figure, not hunched at all. In fact, Mrs Lahiri was as supple as a girl, the result of a lifetime's yoga. Sometimes, when she spoke to us, she sat in the lotus position at the door of her apartment and a mystical aroma of sandalwood incense wafted down the stairs, like the rose odour that is supposed to accompany visions of the Virgin Mary.

In her prime, Mrs Lahiri must have been quite alluring.

Now she wore her long grey hair untied and her face was composed of little puffy muscles, half-moons under her eyes and at the sides of her mouth. Sometimes she oiled her hair, which seemed out of keeping with the rest of her austerities (she told Emma that the best hair oil was called *Jabakusum*).

She smiled constantly but it was a serene, distant smile transfused with gentle mockery. I told Mrs Lahiri how much we liked her singing. She had, she told us, studied music in Varanasi. Before her marriage, she had given recitals of devotional songs. 'Always my parents chose the songs. It was their decision.'

Mrs Lahiri never collected our rent. All financial transactions were handled by her son, whom she talked about as Mr Biswajit, just as she called me Mr Joe. Actually, Bengalis pronounce the consonants *z* and *j* the same way, which is basically *zh*, and when confronted with an English word beginning with *j*, some get flustered. At first Mrs Lahiri had difficulty with my name, the *j* as well as the *e* at the end which she could not accept as silent. For a while I was Mr Zöe. Emma was always referred to in the third person, as Llewi-ma.

Mrs Lahiri only left the house in the company of Mr Biswajit. He visited her once or twice each week and then he would hover at the door of our room, making strained conversation.

In marked contrast to his serene mother, Mr Biswajit was a jumpy, agitated man, and her English was far superior to his. Mr Biswajit could only relax when talking about the Internet. 'For my different interests, you see.'

'What are your interests?'

'Actually, information technology, er, different aspects about information technology . . .'

Mr Biswajit told me he regarded the Internet as a global *adda*. Who needs a global *adda*, I asked, when one can just walk to the sweetshop? He pointed out the world needs an *adda* as a forum for discussion. Unfortunately cyberspace is full of people like Mr Biswajit, who are not much use at the *adda* to begin with, nattering away like virtual crickets.

CHAPTER TWENTY-THREE

The nameless street in Lake Gardens, although generally quieter than Sudder Street, seemed to us, at first, as noisy as a jungle. Every morning we would hear the cries of itinerant tradesmen, in some cases not cries at all but a type of *musique concrète*: the jazzy rattle of the key-cutter and knife-grinder, and the jew's-harp twang of the cotton-fluffer, reviver of cushions and mattresses, whose curious instrument is known as a *ping-jam*. If we looked over the balcony we might see a *bhel puri* vendor with a tray of puffed breads, piled like profiteroles, on his head; we heard him shout '*Be-hel poori-ya! Be-hel poori-ya!*'

The deep squawk of a cycle-rickshaw's horn, ayahs singing as they carried baskets of bed linen to the *dhobi*, the incessant conversation of crows and *shaliks* and the chanting of schoolchildren learning to march for Republic Day, '*Ek do, ek do, ek do, ek.*' A series of loud 'flups' meant that Malina was washing her own saris, beating them on the concrete of the passage, then wringing them into long colourful ropes before hanging them out to dry.

Whereas Sudder Street would drop by night into an almost rural silence, all our first nights at Lake Gardens were disturbed by the barks and howls of pariah dogs. I would lie awake and the weary rotation of the ceiling fan would defract the sounds from outside until it was like listening to a radio drama through poor reception. Whenever a dog from another street wandered into ours, the place erupted. Occasionally a fight ensued; usually savage threats from the dominant male would cause the interloper to retreat. The dominant male was a sturdy bruiser whose brown and white coat was, for some reason, dyed with magenta splotches (possibly medicinal, applied by some human well-wisher to counteract mange). The effect, given the size and belligerence of the dog, was that of war paint, which became our name for him.

Then one might suppose the disturbance to be over, but the excitement generated by the intrusion lasted for a long time. Junior pariah dogs pretended that more enemies were approaching and sent out ferocious warnings. Many of the bitches sang, or howled, praises for the mighty War Paint, and dogs from neighbouring streets responded, until the whole of Lake Gardens rang with canine hymns and curses. None of the human occupants did anything to stop the pariah dogs' noise. Perhaps nothing could be done.

One night in that first week I was woken, not by pariah dogs, but by a scratching, tapping noise and the shuffle of feet. Blind Pew finding his way home, I thought, and sure enough down on the street was a man with a long cane like a fishing-rod touching all the walls and doors and windows as he stumbled along. I presumed he was blind until, under the glow of the streetlight, he drew the cane back to inspect its tip. Whatever he found proved insignificant because he promptly continued his slow progress, tapping and running his cane along all the walls, as well as the sides and roofs of cars.

On one morning each week (but never on the same day two weeks running, so it was always a surprise) we were woken at 5.30 by Malina knocking on our door (which we locked at night) to say that the sweeper had come to clean our bathroom. This would mean pulling clothes on and letting a silent angry man into our bedroom. He carried a bucket of hot water, some scouring powder and a stiff spiky brush and he worked for half an hour, scrubbing the floors and walls, the sink and the lavatory. Sometimes I made a cup of tea and sat vigilantly on the edge of the bed, watching him while Emma and Llewelyn slept on. The sweeper was an Untouchable, who performed duties that caste Hindus considered polluting and yet, with his jet-black skin and fiery red eyes, his thin face like a drawing by Daumier, his long sculptural arms and long tapering hands, he had a defiant, dignified grace. I offered him tea once, which he refused without looking at me, but he did accept a tip of a few rupees.

Later I discovered that tipping the sweeper was a faux-pas; Malina paid him with money she received from Mrs Lahiri. From what I could understand, my tip was more than the sweeper was paid.

I also learnt that the Bengali word for sweeper is *mehtar*, which was actually a courtly rank in Mughal Murshidabad. It was initially a sarcastic joke, to give an Untouchable such an aristocratic designation. Over the centuries the irony has evaporated. Nevertheless, until quite recently, sweepers greeted one another as 'Maharaj'.

CHAPTER TWENTY-FOUR

We shopped locally for items like bottled water, bananas and tea. Most days we shopped in the early evening, the time when our neighbourhood was busiest. We started to recognise faces and to be recognised. People asked after the baby. Many of the women gave Emma advice about teething and its attendant problems; one presented Emma with a green tube of antiseptic cream called Boroline.

We always tried to buy our oranges or bananas from a man who crouched on the pavement next to a small general store that displayed notices of what it did not stock, 'no medicine', 'no Coca-Cola', anti-advertisements to prevent customer disappointment. The fruitseller, who resembled Charles Hawtrey, was limited in the range of fruits he sold. Usually it was just oranges, sometimes bananas as well, and then only a few of them displayed in a shallow bowl. It was a shoestring operation, a few steps from begging. I bought cigarettes from the general store sometimes.

The most crowded business was the local travel agent. There was a constant demand for tickets to all parts of India and, occasionally, overseas. Lake Gardens being a middle-class neighbourhood, its inhabitants had outposts of their families all over the world. We were often told by people in the street of trips to Toronto and Los Angeles and sometimes unexpected British destinations like Dewsbury or Frinton-on-Sea.

The men stood around the *paan* stalls, smoking cigarettes they would buy individually and exhaling the smoke through their noses, like schoolboys on a bus-trip, while discussing the chances of Mohan Bagan the football team. Sometimes there was a strange effect of glowing embers floating around the men at the *paan* stalls; it took me some time to ascertain that these were fireflies.

Near our house, at a crossroads where taxis and autorickshaws waited for customers, there was a *chai* stall. It was a little cement hut where various snacks, *wadas* and *bhajis*, were fried in buckets of oil over butane. We never tasted the food but I regularly drank the tea, strong and sweet and with the kick of a double espresso. The tea was made by a boy, eight or nine years old. He mixed the ingredients – tea dust, grey sugar, milk and water – into a kettle that, with the force of the butane jet, boiled in seconds. Then I would stand there, waiting for the tea in its tiny clay pot to grow cool enough to drink.

At the *chai* stall, I met a man with an excited fox terrier. When the man passed me, he laughed and said that the terrier had also just arrived from England. I stroked the dog. Everything smelt wonderful to him, richer and more pungent than anything in Britain. 'How will he cope with the heat?' I asked.

'He is only here in the winter. Then he is moving with my father to Darjeeling.'

'What's his name?'

'Jack Russell.'

'But he's not really a Jack Russell, is he?'

'Actually, he is named for the English cricketer. This is the second dog my father has called Jack Russell. The last one was a cocker spaniel, killed by buffalos.'

I was just reflecting on this ghastly story when the dog-walker asked how I liked the tea. I replied that it was more like drinking coffee.

'No, no. Coffee is heating. Tea refreshes. Even when it is hot, June month July month, the tea will refresh you . . .'

'Do you ever drink iced tea?' I asked him, stroking the terrier's head.

'For full absorption of tea's properties, it is better consumed hot.'

When we had first seen the room at Lake Gardens, it had looked, compared to the clutter and chintz of the Fairlawn, attractively simple; but once we had moved in we found the spartan furnishings a little too austere. We bought the items we needed – bedside lights, a kettle, beakers, a teapot and strainer, plates, a broom, dustpan and brush – from the various emporia on Southern Avenue.

To get to Southern Avenue we had to walk back across Dhakuria Lake, past a cricket ground on one side of the road and on the other a small maidan that, in that last week of the year, was given over to a craft fair whose elaborate entrance featured Santa Claus and reindeers and a snow-capped mountain range all made out of painted tarpaulins.

Craft fairs are ubiquitous across India. Visit any town when a religious festival is in swing and, without a doubt, there will be a craft fair. The phenomenon is, I think, more to do with retail methods than enthusiasm for traditional cottage industries; I have found nylon bedspreads and mass-produced kitchen appliances on sale in some of the tents.

Lake Market was a pocket of South India in Calcutta, its pavements vibrating with Tamil and Malayali conversation, and the cafés selling *idlis* and *masala dosa*. Inside the market we found twisting snake gourds and banana flowers and brown cakes of date palm sugar, and even though I knew that these were Bengali ingredients, their presence, after the more familiar produce of New Market, made me feel we were entering a different world, that we had left the Anglo-Indian ambiance of Madge Lane and Sudder Street for somewhere altogether more foreign, that we might as well have been in South India. I could look at a stall of produce and realise that I had no idea how any of it would be cooked. I felt that we had moved to a world we understood less, because the language was no longer English. We had to respond to people and situations with instinct and intuition, and what understanding there was came through our senses: sounds, smell, taste. In Lake Market we were actually walking over food, the floor was covered with cabbage leaves and husks.

There was a pottery stall where Emma bought a cylindrical terracotta pot. Fresh flowers were so cheap and plentiful there that she would buy a massive selection every time we went. If there were any left when the pot was filled, Emma gave them to Mrs Lahiri.

Emma was deliberating between some tuberoses and some variegated lilies when a voice called my name. It was Lalitha, whom I had met at Albert Lyon's *adda*. I was relieved to see that the poisonous Trish Crystal was nowhere in sight. Lalitha, who was wearing a heavy blue silk sari, was accompanied instead by a tall Indian man in early middle age.

The man was flamboyantly dressed in traditional clothes: a cherry-pink *kurta* over loose white pyjamas and a little biscuit-coloured embroidered waistcoat, buttoned at the throat and extending no further down his body than the end of his ribcage. On his feet the man wore *jootis*, like Albert's but without the bobbles.

As the majority of men on Rashbehari Avenue were decked out in western-style polyester (in fact, Rashbehari Avenue contained dozens of shops selling polyester shirts) Lalitha's friend looked magnificent, like a Nawab from Murshidabad strolling through the bazaar in the company of his most beautiful courtesan.

I introduced Emma and Llewelyn to Lalitha. Her friend's name was Jayabrato Chatterjee. 'Please, call me Jay,' he insisted, pronouncing his name *Joy* in the Bengali manner.

Lalitha said, 'Jay stays in Southern Avenue, back that way. He is practically your neighbour. Not only so but the most brilliant novelist and, you know, I don't hand out such praise to all my literary friends. Albert's poetry, for instance, leaves me cold . . .'

'Oh God, Albert,' groaned Jay, throwing one shoulder forward in a witty gesture as if the name were the last straw, 'that moaning minnie, I call him Eeyore . . .'

'Did you enjoy the *adda*?' Emma asked Lalitha.

'*Adda*? Oh, Albert's! There are *addas* and *addas* . . .'

'And cocktails and blackties . . .' Jay pronounced both these words with the emphasis on the unexpected syllable: cock*tails* and *black*tie to rhyme with blackfly. I could tell he was mentioning what he perceived as more sophisticated (Bombay-style) gatherings so that we didn't think Calcutta provincial. 'We've never read any of Albert's poetry,' said Emma.

'Then you must count your blessings,' said Lalitha.

'The poetry is one thing,' Jay said, 'the real torture is when he sings . . .'

'Albert sings?' I was genuinely surprised. 'What does he sing?'

Jay said, 'All kinds. *Rabindra Sangeet*, Baul songs. Irish folk songs. Some by Le-o-nard Cohen, even. He has a whining voice.'

Lalitha said, 'He plays a Spanish guitar . . .'

'I didn't notice one in his flat.'

'That is because you did not go into his bedroom. It is there beside his bed always. He sings himself to sleep, apparently.'

'When he first arrived in Calcutta, he gave recitals. At first we all went,' said Jay. 'Then not so many went. I believe he only sings now to his close friends . . .'

'He didn't sing the other night.'

'That was because Trishie was there,' Lalitha explained. 'She's very blunt . . .'

'So I gathered . . .'

'Now he gives more formal readings, from the great work in progress.'

'Enough of Albert,' Lalitha moved her hand horizontally to close the subject. 'You must read Jay's novel. It is a Penguin. *Last Train to Innocence*.'

'What's it about?' asked Emma.

'Growing up,' said Lalitha, 'in a particular time and milieu . . .'

The conversation turned to flowers and Lalitha decided to buy some as well and then with both her and Emma bearing enormous bouquets, we crossed the road to a café called Prema Villas where, she told us, they served proper South Indian coffee. It was a bare room, like a works canteen, where grey-overalled waiters stood wiping trays. There were a few other customers in there, eating *idlis* and *sambar*. We all sat down and the waiter brought us typewritten menus.

We took Llewelyn out of the Dream Rider and he started squealing to be fed. In the drab surroundings Emma resembled some allegorical *tableau vivant*, suckling her infant in an arbour of tropical flowers.

Close to, we noticed that Lalitha was wearing a wonderful perfume. Emma asked her what it was and she said that it was not really a perfume at all but an oil extracted from the *champa* blossom. She believed it was a kind of frangipani. She told us that musicians will sometimes wear a scrap of muslin, scented with *champa* oil, behind their ear to inspire them while they play.

Jay said he longed for a *paper dosa*. 'The trouble is my teeth are in agony . . .' He was, I thought, handsome in a weary, slightly decadent way, his plump face full of wit and mischief. Dark bags around his eyes looked like make-up.

Lalitha frowned at him. 'Darling, it is quite simple to have them straightened.'

'Oh God, I wish it were. I don't think there is a dentist in this bloody town up to the job.'

'Maybe you've left it too late . . .'

'Lalitha! Don't tell me what I know already. It's my own fault for refusing to wear a brace when I was a teenager. Now I must suffer for how devastatingly good-looking I was then . . .'

'How are you finding your flat at Lake Gardens?' Lalitha asked us.

'It's only a room,' said Emma, 'and we've just moved in.'

Jay broke into song: 'All I want is a room somewhere, far away from the cold night air . . .' His attempt at a Cockney accent made us all laugh; he sounded like Dick Van Dyke. 'Where in Lake Gardens is this room?'

Emma told him the address, which meant nothing to him until I added that it was on the same street as the Adhunika Housing Colony. 'Ah, then it's not so difficult. I shall send my driver Sukumar to fetch you. You must have a telephone number?'

'Mrs Lahiri will take messages for us.'

'I shall invite you to dinner, to meet my wife and daughter.'

We were both a little surprised. 'How old is your daughter?' asked Emma.

'Shahana? A grown woman!' Jay replied, raising his eyebrows.

The waiter brought four foaming glasses of sweet milky coffee. It would have been churlish to say so but it was not at all strong. Its chief distinguishing feature was foam, which I could have done without.

'How ancient we have become,' sighed Lalitha.

'How do you two know one another ?'

'We go back all the way to childhood,' said Jay.

'Jay is like a brother to me . . .'

Jay called a waiter over and ordered a *paper dosa*. 'We can all share, it's very light . . .' He took a few sips of his coffee, then asked how we were coping with Calcutta.

I said it was full of surprises. There was so much to interest a visitor. 'It ought to become one of those cities, like Prague or Saint Petersburg, that people go to because they like cities . . .'

'I love cities,' said Lalitha.

'Most westerners have such bullshit ideas about Calcutta,' declared Jay. 'They come here expecting a disaster zone and they're not really contented until they've seen the worst of it . . .'

'They don't even want to see what else there is . . .'

[197]

'If you ask me,' said Jay, 'it's Mother Teresa's fault. She is our most famous citizen. All these foreigners think she looks after the entire city. They think we all sleep on the pavement . . .'

I told them I sensed a certain resentment towards Mother Teresa from other Bengalis.

'But she must do *some* good,' said Emma.

'Of course, of course. But it is all tied up with moral superiority. There are tourist buses passing through the *bustis*, the poorest areas of the city, and these outsiders are made to think that only a foreigner, a representative of a European religion, can help these benighted creatures . . .'

'Tell them what Subhra was saying . . .'

'My wife Subhra does voluntary work for the cerebral palsy children. Money had been raised to build a day centre and there were enough facilities for spastic children from Mother Teresa's orphanages to come along. Subhra approached the Missionaries of Charity. She said 'We can do something for these children' but the nuns told her God's love was enough for them.'

Jay's *paper dosa* took a long time to arrive. It was a thin, crisp pancake rolled into a tube about two feet long, stuffed with mashed potato flavoured with mint and coriander.

When we left Prema Villas, Jay gave us his card. We wrote our address and telephone number down for him and he promised to get in touch.

CHAPTER TWENTY-FIVE

Each night we took our dinner in a large room across the landing, empty except for a table and chairs. There Sushil spread the bakelite serving bowls of food that had been prepared by Mrs Lahiri, brought down in stages by tray.

The first few nights Mrs Lahiri sent down bland fare: boiled potatoes and slices of scarlet carrot. She evidently believed we would find Bengali food too spicy. Tactfully, we managed to dissuade her of this notion; we told her we had no problem with spices and that we wanted to taste Bengali food. After that the food improved, although we often had no idea what we were eating because to Sushil all fish was *maacch*, all vegetables *sabzi*, even though we were served a broad variety of both.

We bought a book on Bengali cookery to try to identify the offerings, and now and then we managed to prise the name of a dish from Mrs Lahiri. This was difficult as she seemed loth to discuss cookery. She was a widow and had sworn to forego certain foods, including fish, as a mark of respect for her departed husband. It was poignant to think of her spending hours preparing elaborate meals that she was forbidden to taste. On the eleventh day of each fortnight Mrs Lahiri fasted completely, a custom called *ekadasi* that only the most devout widows observe.

We did learn that a Bengali meal is taken in separate courses, instead of mixing everything together on the plate. Condiments were usually arranged around the upper edge of the plate – sea salt, a wedge of lime, a couple of fresh green chillies – as well as small appetisers, such as roasted jackfruit seeds, aubergine fritters, or *dal bories* that are little fried dumplings made of lentil batter.

When people think of Indian food, they usually think of cumin and garlic and chillies. I am most reminded of Bengali food when I cook and eat an aubergine. I never salt it to remove the bitter juice for it is that bitterness, erupting on the palate along with the sweet taste of the flesh, that makes an aubergine delicious to me. Bengali food uses a palate of bitter and sweet that reminds me of that taste; it is there in the preparations of squashes and the greens as well. Chillies play a relatively minor role in this cuisine but there are many sour tastes. The regional salt tasted harsh at first, too mineral and with a bleachy taste.

As the meal was to be eaten with the right hand, a glass of water was placed on the left of the *thala*. The food was served in bowls that were arranged, in order of courses, from right to left, starting with the *dal* (lentil soup). In the centre of the plate went a mound of plain boiled rice (*bhat*) that could be replenished throughout the meal. The appetisers were taken first, then the *dal* was taken with rice, then *ghonto* or perhaps *shukto*, both complex vegetable preparations – the *ghonto* would usually contain large chunks of root vegetables while the *shukto*, more bitter-tasting, would contain greens – also taken with rice. Then came the *maachher jhol* or fish stew, again with rice. A meal without the fish course would be considered incomplete and some of the other courses, such as

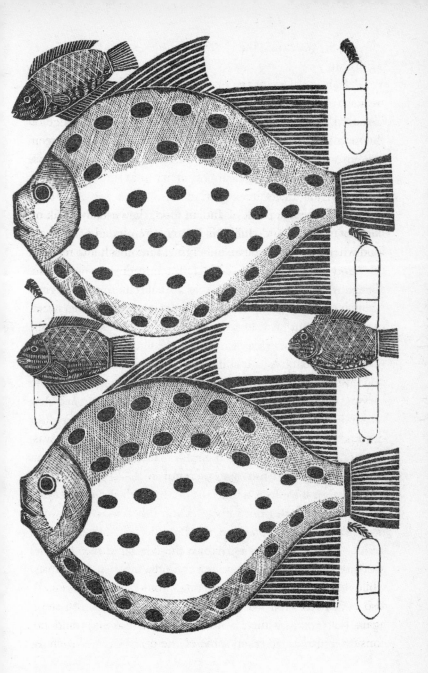

the *dal*, the *ghonto* and the *shukto* might be seasoned in some way with fish.

Fish is the mainstay of Bengali cuisine, especially fresh-water fish, whose flavour is best appreciated cooked with mustard oil. That, to me, is the flavour of Bengali food. It seems a peculiarly Northern European notion, like herrings in mustard, and it works sublimely; the mustard oil brings out the delicacy of the fish, the cleanness of it.

Bengalis make an important distinction between fresh-water and saltwater fish, *mishti jhol* (literally, 'sweet water') and *nun jhol* ('salt water'). *Mishti jhol* fish, from rivers and ponds are considered the more desirable. The distinction between *mishti jhol* and *nun jhol* is, however, full of inconsistencies. Most Bengalis regard *mishti jhol* fish as cleaner than *nun jhol* even though certain pond-bred fish, such as the carp and the catfish, are omnivorous scavengers. The most prized fish of all, the hilsa, is actually a sea fish that swims upriver to spawn – however, in that it is caught in a river, it is regarded as *mishti jhol*.

Bengal is also the only region in India where Brahmin priests, elsewhere strictly vegetarian, eat fish, even though they observe other dietary restrictions such as the avoidance, for instance, of onions and garlic which are supposed to inflame passion. Perhaps the Bengali Brahmins do not regard fish as flesh at all; indeed fish is so plentiful in the region that it is often referred as 'fruit of the rivers'. In medieval times, faced with disapproval from other Brahmins across India, the Bengali Brahmins consulted the Puranas and other Sanskrit texts to justify their eating habits; they declared that fish was permissible, except eels (because they resemble snakes) or any fish without scales.

All parts of a fish are eaten. The head is considered a great delicacy, as is the roe. Even the tails, skin and bones are used in a dish called *kanta-chachchari*, rendered down with herbs and red pumpkin. Qualities that many westerners might find disagreeable in fish – smelliness and boniness – were not considered negative at all. Hilsa is a notoriously bony fish. The ability to eat hilsa gracefully (removing the flesh from the needle-like bones inside one's mouth) using deft movements of the tongue, then placing the clean bones on the side of the plate is regarded as proof of a good upbringing.

On the odd occasion, about once a fortnight, the fish course was followed by a small portion of meat curry such as *mangshor qorma*. These were never up to much. Meat cookery is best in restaurants and prepared by Muslims; the quality of the meat is better. *Halal* butchers are infinitely more skilful than their Hindu counterparts.

The remaining rice was then finished with an almost jam-like sweet chutney and the meal ended with fruit or *mishti doi* (sweet yoghurt) or possibly some sweets, such as *sandesh*. We bought the pudding or fruit ourselves, enough for Sushil and his family as well.

Many Indian housewives make sweet dishes at home and the Bengali housewife is no exception with her *pithas* and *payesh*. Mrs Lahiri, however, did not provide pudding for her lodgers, which was fair enough because it gave us a chance to visit the local sweetshop.

The sweetshops produce a range of confections that are quite unlike the home-made variety, and the sweetshops of Calcutta are quite unlike sweetshops in other Indian cities. In Delhi's Chandni Chowk, for example, there is an old Jain establishment called Ghantewala that once supplied the Mughal court; the sweets, with names like *sohan halwa* and *emarti*, are based either on flour and ghee or on the boiled-down milk preparation called *kheer*. Calcutta's sweets, distinctively, are based on *chhana*, a type of cream cheese, or the solid part of curdled milk, strained through muslin.

The production of *chhana* is definitely European in origin. It might have been learnt from the Portuguese; certainly it was unknown in India before the Europeans arrived and, in fact, to adulterate milk in any way, especially to cut it with citric acid, was regarded by orthodox Hindus as sinful. But once the use of *chhana* was established, around the middle of the nineteenth century, the *moiras* (confectioners) revelled in the creamy, adaptable substance and a new range of sweets was established. The most ubiquitous is *sandesh*, which literally means 'good tidings' (and it is traditional to send sweets with a message); *sandesh* is a small sweetened cake of *chhana*, pressed with a mould into the shape of a fish or a flower or what have you. *Sandesh* tastes like a bland but delicate fudge and often has a curious, almost 'squeaky' texture from being heated until all the moisture has evaporated. The moulds themselves have a striking folk-art quality; a *sandesh* fish looks just like a fish as drawn in a Kalighat *pat*.

The sweetshops came into their own just as the Calcuttans grew comfortable with their own urban identity and the sweetshops catered to the leisured, discerning bourgeoisie in much the same way as did the patisseries of Vienna.

The initial success of any *moira* was based on novelty and they were always inventing new delicacies – such as the *rosogolla* (*chhana* balls floating in warm rosewater syrup) and the *rosomallai* (*chhana* balls floating in thick cardamom-flavoured condensed milk) – to please their enthusiastic patrons. Recipes were closely guarded and passed down from generation to generation, and as every Bengali seems to be a connoisseur of sweets, the quality has been retained over the years; the freshness and purity of the *chhana*, the subtlety of the flavourings are all important and the use of adulterated or synthetic ingredients would be anathema. Some sweets have charming names like *nayantara* ('sparkle in the eye') or *abar khabo* ('I'll have another').

Many of the sweetshops produce *mishti doi*, which is a thick, almost caramelised yoghurt, sold in spiralling terracotta *handis*. Llewelyn was very keen on it. It is a light brown colour and has lumps of clotted cream in it. No one seems to make *mishti doi* at home. It is always bought from the sweetshop. A pot will be brought home by the husband after he has finished work, which gives him the chance to sample a few favourite sweets at the same time.

Many sweetshops, including ours, had tables where customers could sit and eat their purchases on the premises. The customers were usually groups of men, engaged in the *adda*, which was generally conducted in fast, animated Bengali but sometimes an English sentence dropped into the flow so that, as eavesdroppers, we were given cryptic hints as to the topic of discussion.

'Horse power? What is the power of a horse nowadays? Nothing in this day and age . . .'

'I say he is puppet only, his strings are pulled by business-men . . .'

'Sunil Ganguli, Pranabendu Dasgupta, proper poets. Nobody since has come close . . .'

'That would make perpetual motion. What for? Losing money?'

These men were not, as you might imagine, all fatties. Some, of course, were. We came to recognise a distinctive Bengali physique in the men. Many are tall and prone to stooping; they have long necks and large heads with long fine faces; their limbs are long and slender and gangly in their movements. If they do put on weight, they carry it on their stomachs which feminises their appearance, but most remain slim. They have long hands and often wear rings. I started to think that Solvyns was not far off the mark with his elongated figures.

In the afternoons the sweetshops make savoury snacks: *singharas* (samosas), *luchis* (puffed breads, similar to *puris*) that are served with *dal*, as well as a range of savoury mixes, generically known as *nimkis* ('salties'). These are consumed with tea at four o'clock. Bengalis still take afternoon tea.

Our local *moira* was a tall, stout man who usually wore a grubby white vest. The shop was a little flyblown but we were not squeamish. He seemed pleased that we liked his creations and urged us to try different sweets each time we visited. All the customers would turn around and watch us as we sampled a *pantua* or a *ladikeni* (named after Lady Canning, the Vicereine), all anticipating our approval. I don't think many Europeans had been into his shop before.

CHAPTER TWENTY-SIX

It was in a sweetshop, of all places, that I learnt about the Great Bengal Famine of the early 1940s.

I was walking along Chowringhee when I (almost literally) bumped into Professor Shastri outside Ganguram's sweetshop. He recognised me and smiled. 'I was just considering some refreshment. Will you join me?' he asked. He was wearing a beige cashmere shawl like a poncho over white pyjamas and looked, with his luxuriant black moustache, like a Kalighat depiction of a walrus.

'Let me pay,' I said and we went to the counter and ordered. I asked for a pot of *mishti doi*, Professor Shastri for a pot of *mishti doi*, a black *kalojam*, a *ladikeni* and two pieces of *sandesh* shaped like elephants. We stood at another counter to consume our sweets and several nods of recognition greeted the Professor.

'You do not know the value of nourishment until you have seen starvation,' said the Professor tucking into his *mishti doi*. I thought this rather glib and protested that – 'walking around with my eyes open' – I had seen it everywhere in Calcutta.

Professor Shastri put his spoon down and his facial muscles went firm. He looked at me coldly. 'My young friend, what you have seen is hunger only. You have not seen the dying attempt to eat the dead. This I have seen with *my* eyes open. You have not seen a starving man unable to digest a handful of rice, vomiting and dying, and a rush of children trying to scoop up the vomit . . .'

I felt reprimanded. Meekly, I asked if this was during the Bangladesh War of the 1970s. Professor Shastri told me he was referring to the Second World War when he was a young student in Calcutta. 'It was the most terrible famine Bengal has suffered.' He pronounced it *fah-meen* in the French way.

'But surely Calcutta was full of troops then?'

'Precisely. It was the war effort that caused the famine only . . .'

'But I would have thought a famine would have weakened the front. It would have been in their interest to relieve the problem immediately.'

'You may well have such thoughts. Their interest was entirely the war, Bengali people were on the back burner in their minds.'

Professor Shastri explained that, for a long time, Bengal had been importing rice from Burma and Thailand because it could not grow enough to feed its population. The Japanese invasion of Burma in 1942 had made this impossible. As soon as the invasion took place Bengali civil servants had started warning of food shortages. The Governor of Bengal had dismissed the warning.

There were parts of Bengal that were dependent on river trade for food supplies. The government requisitioned all boats in case of invasion.

'The Bengali civilians protested, "This will make them deplete their village supplies. It is most unwise!" My own father was one such civilian.'

Professor Shastri's moustache, despite the flecks of cream

that adhered to it, looked as dark as the anger with which he spoke. It was a tale of dark, disgusting tragedy.

'The bloody fools ignored him. He knew what he was speaking about.'

Calcutta was full of munition factories and, once the government realised there were going to be shortages, they requisitioned all the rice from the countryside and brought it to the city to feed the workers. People in the villages were left to starve. The Governor insisted that Bengal went on exporting rice to other parts of the empire. A cyclone devastated the coastal villages and hunger spread like fire.

'Tens of thousands of starving villagers creeping here to die on the streets. Dead-body corpses defiling their village water supplies, famine *and* disease. Every street, every square park laid out with groaning misery. Eighteen months or more, two, three years even before it had passed, this agony, and then famine has come to the city and everywhere. There was no relief. Linlithgow Viceroy wouldn't come here, even. No Emergency Powers Act.'

'People in Britain must have read about it . . .'

'My dear friend, the government had the power to ban newspaper coverage. And don't forget bloody arrogant Churchill, bloody fat-bottom, saying, "Too many of the snivel-ling, disloyal bastards anyway . . ." '

I had a nasty sensation of being held to blame for the incompetence of my countrymen. All heads in the sweetshop were turned towards me.

'The only ones getting sufficient food,' declaimed the Professor (and everyone in the shop stopped eating), 'were the crows. Those that could do so were eating crows even. Jackals came into the city, drawn by the odour. Once I chased a jackal with a child's arm in its mouth . . .'

There was a gasp from the audience.

'The people of Calcutta directed the dying to the pavements outside Government House, you know this Raj Bhavan today. Corpses were removed to this pavement. Piled up. Let them see what is happening. Why did they do nothing? Every day the railings piled with dead-body corpses. Every day there were more . . .'

A man holding a bowl of *rosomallai* said, 'My father as well he talks of this . . .'

'I saw this even myself,' whispered one old man who pressed his palms together and smiled bashfully at Professor Shastri, 'many many bodies . . .'

The Professor continued. 'Only until Wavell Viceroy to show commonsense decency. Grain was brought in from other parts of country. Export stopped. Soldiers breaking open godowns of profiteers . . .'

'Who were these profiteers?'

'Oh, Britishers and Bengalis too . . .'

'Marwaris,' murmured a voice.

The *rosomallai* man pointed his spoon at me. 'Britishers must be held responsible first and foremost.' He seemed to be goading me for a reaction.

'This is something I was barely aware of until now,' I confessed.

If pressed, I would have denied any personal remorse. All I am responsible for is my own behaviour. I asked Professor Shastri if he despised the British.

'The British I do not despise. No, it is only the folly of your men in my country at that time I despise. As I have despised also my own national politicians in years since. Each day has its own potential, it is the balance we endeavour to maintain.'

With these words, calm was restored and I ceased to represent a regime I had nothing to do with. Professor Shastri chatted about his retirement and his newly discovered enjoyment of Dorothy L. Sayers' fiction. Albert Lyon he considered a philosopher-poet; he praised the vigour of his insight.

Walking south, after leaving the Professor, I realised that I had seen references to the Great Bengal Famine but, in my ignorance, had assumed the famine to have been in the nineteenth century, not just a few years before Independence.

When I next met Harry Dent, I asked if he remembered the famine.

'I can remember the groans from the pavement and passers-by reacting with fear and disgust and I can remember British soldiers weeping at what they saw . . .' He said that the display of corpses on Government House railings was the most powerful and terrible demonstration of civil disobedience in the entire Independence struggle. Harry believed the corpses had polluted Calcutta in the national mind. He felt that Calcutta, Bengal in general, had never received a fair deal from the national government. This was due to Hindu notions of death pollution. At the same time, he told me, the famine had increased the devotion shown to Kali by the common people of the city.

I thought to myself: 'Lead from here the other smelling ones, lead away the other putrid ones . . .'

CHAPTER TWENTY-SEVEN

When we were in the city centre, we had lunch at the Fairlawn.
Partly this was because Llewelyn liked the food so much. He
would eat Indian food but it was hit-or-miss. At the Fairlawn we
knew he would stuff himself with *bekti* fillet and crisps and he
liked what Jamal called 'essepard pie' – really an ordinary
shepherd's pie, made with mutton, rendered exotic by the
addition of cinnamon. As Emma and I are both adventurous
eaters, we were dismayed at our son's preference for more
familiar fare, but we agreed that if his appetite was healthy, it
was a good sign.

Ted approved of Llewelyn's enthusiasm. 'Quite right.
Doesn't want to be eating all that sloppy food. Needs something
more substantial.'

Violet said, 'You see, our food is safe. He knows it. They
can tell, you see. Babies. Intuition. It's the survival instinct . . .'

'It's clean food, every single person in the kitchen wears
gloves,' boasted Ted.

'Anyone found without them, out. No questions asked.'
Violet clicked her fingers to illustrate the speed of the dismissal.

'Problem is the way they wipe their, wipe their, you know.
Let's not put too fine a point . . .' Ted looked down at his
gleaming brogues, as if overcome by this indelicacy.

Andy Devane tiptoed downstairs, tanned from the Andaman Islands which made his hair seem whiter than it had been before Christmas. 'It'll go back,' he said, 'it's the sea that bleaches it . . .'

Rosemary Dent told us all about the wedding, that had taken place the previous day. At the reception Daphne, the groom's first wife, had turned heads with a short red dress and all afternoon she had sparkled and gushed, upstaging the bride Ursula. At one point she had danced in a slithering, lascivious way with Patrick, the bride's father. The song they danced to was *Lady In Red*.

Emma laughed, 'Chris De Burgh. Princess Di's favourite . . .'

'Ah, well,' said Andy Devane, 'the De Burghs are a well-known family in Ireland. I believe his mother was musical as well . . .'

Rosemary told us that the song caused Emerald, the little daughter, to burst into tears. The groom, Barty, had been calm throughout all this until, dismayed at Emerald's anguish, he finally rounded on Findley, his quiz team rival. A bizarre duel had taken place.

'What is the population of Louisville, Kentucky?'

'All right, who wrote the screenplay of *The Maltese Falcon*?'

It had lasted twenty minutes with the wedding guests clapping at each correct answer. Happily for everyone, Barty won. Harry smiled when we laughed at Rosemary's description of the duel. He said, 'Actually, once upon a time, duels of this kind were common. They were called *kabis*, and they were entirely verbal. Not these quiz-questions but hurled insults, in front of a crowd, until one or the other backed down. And, of course, you could hire a *kabi*-wallah to perform on your behalf. All kinds of disputes were settled that way.'

Shortly after the duel, Findley and Daphne left. What

became of Emerald? Rosemary told us she joined her father and Ursula on their honeymoon at Gopalpur-on-Sea.

Among the denizens of Sudder Street, Abdul was regarded as Llewelyn's godfather and whenever we met him, there would be five minutes before we got into the taxi that he spent holding Wahlen Bachcha and telling the other taxi drivers and any passers-by the story of the hospital dash. Abdul had great charm so nobody felt he was blowing his own trumpet. Llewelyn was enthralled by Abdul; he would often spot him before we did and would cry 'Dur-ba! Dur-ba!'

Before he could speak, Llewelyn made up names for things: *bur-la* for music, *bed* for breast-milk and so on; Abdul was one of the few individuals to whom he granted a name in this language. Fittingly, Llewelyn's first true words were in Bengali for Mina taught him to recognise elephants (*hathi*) and tigers (*baag*). We occasionally called Llewelyn by a whimsical Hobson-Jobsonism of Wahlen Bachha: Waylon Butcher. Waylon Butcher, Bible salesman from Waxahachie, Texas.

Abdul would take Wahlen Bachcha from us and seat him on top of his head. He spoke to him constantly in a quiet high-pitched voice. Sometimes, when in a traffic jam, Abdul would reach back and take Llewelyn and place him beside him on the front seat. Emma would always retrieve Llewelyn as soon as the traffic resumed motion; she worried constantly about the absence of seatbelts.

At the corner of Minto Park there was always a beggar in a handcart, a thin teenage boy with polio. Abdul generally spoke to the boy, enquiring after his health (the boy suffered from burning fevers), and gave him a few rupees. Once when

Llewelyn was in the front seat with Abdul, the boy gave him a smile of such Dickensian sweetness that Emma had to wipe her eyes. I gave the boy some money and felt an unusual sense of communion, to be giving to a beggar with tenderness instead of embarrassment. I could not trust my instinct completely: the beggar showed no emotion of any kind in return and I tend to eschew pious self-congratulation.

CHAPTER TWENTY-EIGHT

Some time after that, Abdul drove us to the Nakhoda Mosque. I think he had assumed we were on some kind of religious quest in Calcutta, continually visiting places of worship. 'You go say prayers cathedral church?' he asked us. Then he asked if we prayed at all. I just said, 'Now and then, you know . . .'

Abdul told us he prayed at a mosque at least once a week, generally on Fridays.

'You go *Shaitan khana*?' he asked, startlingly. 'Mishter Eshmit, anyways, he go every week *Shaitan khana*.' *Shaitan* I recognised as the Muslim name for Satan. *Khana* means hall or building. So, Satan's hall? I asked Abdul what he meant.

'*Jadu ghar.*'

This was equally cryptic. I knew it meant 'magic house' in Hindi. I had also read that the Indian Museum used to be called *jadu ghar* by rural people visiting the city. 'Do you mean Mr Smith visits the museum every week?'

'*Nahin*, museum *nahin*,' Abdul clicked his tongue, evidently a little frustrated that I was so slow on the uptake. '*Shaitan khana* . . .' He drove on for a while, then when the taxi came to the junction of Chowringhee and Esplanade, turned around and tried again, '*Aacha*, my sons.'

'I'm sorry, Abdul. I really don't understand . . .'

'My sons. Mishter Eshmit, my sons. Free my sons . . .'

'Oh, Freemasons!' I told Abdul that I was not a Freemason. I wasn't surprised about Ted.

'*Han*, anyways, Free-my-sons we says *Shaitan khana*. Englishmen *jadu*. Indian men come along some, anyways. Mishter Eshmit *burra sahib* at *Shaitan khana*. Big fish, very magic . . .'

I had noticed that the taxi drivers treated Ted with fearful respect whenever he appeared at the gates of the Fairlawn. It was possible they regarded him as a magus.

Chitpur Road is Calcutta's oldest, older than the city itself; it was the original pilgrim's path from the village of Chitpur, past the Chitteshwari temple to the Kalighat temple. Shops and hostelries along the path flourished over the years and became markets; the names for the different stretches of Chitpur Road come from these markets and other landmarks: Murghihata (chicken market), Kasaitola (slaughterhouse), Jorasanko (twin bridges).

A section of Chitpur Road skirts Barabazar and much of the bazaar's frantic atmosphere overlaps on to the street. It is almost impenetrably crowded, and taxis and trucks move slowly through the crush of pedestrians. There are pavements but the shop displays extend right to the curb. Many of the shops seem to be small factories as well. A senior member of the firm generally sits cross-legged in the middle of the display, barking for trade.

Leaving the taxi, we were surrounded by shoeshops. Every imaginable type of shoe was for sale: men's, women's, children's, army boots, trainers, loafers, brogues, Albert's *jootis*, mules, mary-janes, pumps, sandals, *chappals*. Bizarre fantasy footwear: riding boots with leather wings at the heel ('This for jockey, anyways,' explained Abdul) and sandals covered with plastic flowers. Then we entered a stretch of shops selling handbags and wallets.

Further along, a shop sold twisted gold braid for epaulettes and caps; no doubt their customers were the marching bands that performed at weddings. Another sold tinsel and another sold *chamaras* (yak-tail fly-whisks like the one the ancient androgyne had swished about with at Shantiniketan) and horse-hair wigs for *jatra* actors. We saw stalls selling pigments and large phallic pumps for spraying coloured water. Violins, trumpets, cymbals. Various Indian drums, *tablas* and *dholaks*. A stretch dedicated to marble: flat slabs, lozenges, Italianate statues (from some ruined palace in the vicinity), samples of carving, tiles. Huge clouded mirrors with gilt frames. Birdcages. Swords. Hookahs. Plastic buckets. Kettles. Televisions. Ornately carved bedheads and footboards. Brocade waistcoats. White-on-white embroidery, *chikan*, from Lucknow, and crochet prayer-caps. I noticed the Royal Indian Hotel that Manish had recommended.

Before long we became the focus of everyone's attention, a small crowd following us as we passed through the hubbub. If we stopped to look at some copper taps or chromolithographs of heroes, these spectators questioned Abdul on our motives. 'American?' we were asked.

'*Ingresi*,' Abdul answered for us. He also told them an abbreviated version of the hospital story.

We passed a man selling bowls of a dense sticky buttery substance like clotted cream.

'*Rabri*,' said Abdul, 'is like ice cream.' More like custard, I thought, as people were eating it warm.

'*Mallai*,' said one of our audience, meaning 'creamy'.

'UK Prime Minister is come here Calcutta,' another chipped in.

'*Han*, is visit soon Eshmister Major,' said Abdul.

Emma was looking at off-white saris, decorated with a pattern of silvery metallic stripes, that she could turn into curtains.

Around the Nakhoda mosque, the shops and their customers took on a Muslim character. We noticed old men with hennaed beards, which meant they had made the pilgrimage to Mecca. Abdul said it was an old Muslim neighbourhood and later I learnt that in the eighteenth century the Deputy Nawab of Bengal, Reza Khan, built a palace on the road and the area became a haven for Bengal's old Muslim upper class who had started to arrive in Calcutta from Murshidabad. With these courtiers came a coterie of Muslim tradesmen and artisans who are still evident today.

The mosque is not old. It was built in 1942 by Cutchi Memons, merchants from Gujerat, in white marble and red sandstone in a Mughal style, modelled on Akbar's tomb. It is on four levels like a car-park and it can hold, on a Friday evening when it is traditionally full, ten thousand worshippers. They are summoned to prayer from minarets 150 feet high.

It was more or less empty when we looked around. The floors were swept and washed and little piles of prayer-caps lay here and there. Abdul, who insisted on carrying Llewelyn, spoke to a man lying on the floor near the foot of the stairs, then came back to us. 'Is nice, *yaar*, peaceful time . . .'

I wanted to know more about the Cutchi Memons. Abdul implied they were the Muslim counterpart of the Marwaris. I asked if there were many of them.

'Is not so many here now, anyways . . .'

'Do the Cutchi Memons still maintain the mosque?'

'*Han*, these people and all kinds Muslim people . . .'

We wandered around the mosque in an aimless way. I felt that to see it full of worshippers, as I have seen mosques in Istanbul, would be more exciting. As it was, it had the atmosphere of an empty theatre.

We took a different route back to the car and found ourselves in a bazaar full of fresh and dried fruit: apples, guavas, Kashmiri apricots, all kinds of roasted nuts and mounds of crisp vermicelli.

Abdul became very animated. He sensed we had been disappointed by the mosque and was keen to show us something memorable. 'Okay. One hundred-year-old Jewish man. I take you . . .' He led us to a stall selling dates and there, seated beside the proprietor, was a skeletal figure in white pyjamas and a purple v-neck pullover. The old man held a walking-stick in both hands and his left thumb constantly caressed the handle with an involuntary palsied movement. He was certainly very old, the skin stretched tight across his skull reminded me of Richard Avedon's photographs of his dying father. 'One hundred-year-old Jewish man,' announced Abdul again with evident pride.

'I am,' said the old man in a faint voice that sounded like an ancient cylinder recording, 'I was born in 1896 . . .'

'Here in Calcutta?'

'No, not in Calcutta. I was born in Aleppo . . .' His accent, when he spoke English, had a peculiar old-fashioned briskness to it, like a voice in a newsreel.

The proprietor muttered a few words to the centenarian in Bengali. We felt uncomfortable, as if we were gawping. I asked him what his occupation had been.

'Oil business,' he replied.

'Petroleum?'

'Mustard oil, gingelly . . .'

'He was famous sportsman,' announced the proprietor, handing Llewelyn a date.

'That's right,' said the centenarian, 'two years champion, Indian Empire Weight Lifter's Association. Backstroke champion, Wellesley Square Tank . . .'

'That's probably the secret of your longevity,' said Emma.

'*Acha*, diet, exercising,' nodded the old man. 'Let me show you,' and (muttering 'Oh! Oh! Oh, Antonio,' in the way that Cockney geriatrics used to) he rose slowly to his feet. He flexed the bicep of his right arm and invited us to feel the muscle. It felt like a marble egg while the rest of his arm was soft and frail.

He lowered himself back on to the stool. 'Soon I will have lived in three centuries . . .'

'You're sticking around a bit longer then?'

'Oh yes, I have five more years.'

'But how do you know?' asked Emma.

The old man smiled wisely and said nothing. His thumb kept brushing the handle of his stick. The proprietor laughed, shaking his head and wiping his eyes. Abdul shook Llewelyn and grinned. 'One hundred years, *yaar*. Old Jewish man . . .'

'How did he know?' Emma asked Abdul as we headed back to the taxi.

'One hundred years, knowing many things . . .'

CHAPTER TWENTY-NINE

On the stairs at Lake Gardens, Mrs Lahiri dwelt so much on spiritual matters, it was inevitable that religion came into our conversations. She was a follower of Ramakrishna and his disciple, Swami Vivekananda. One day Mrs Lahiri spoke to Emma about maternal duties. It was a matter of some importance to her because her voice took on an uncharacteristic directness.

'The mother should feed the child with faith. That is what so many mothers are forgetting today. You must teach him faith in himself because Godness is there too. I am saying this because the art of living is the art of following Godness. So many have children and what is happening? It's so easy to say everything is going wrong. The mother today also has a great responsibility.'

'I'll do my best,' promised Emma.

Back in our room, we wondered what Godness meant. The Goddess, Emma thought, but to me it suggested godliness or goodness.

One Sunday evening when we passed through the bazaar, we heard raucous chanting and metallic percussion (a number of people banging triangles and cowbells). The chanting came from the first floor of a block of shops, and I saw a man in an orange headscarf standing on the balcony smoking a *chillum*. I asked the Banarasi *paan*-wallah if the noise came from Bauls. He shook his head and told me there was a Hanuman temple up there.

A few days later, on my own and noticing an open door, I crept up the stairs to look at the temple. I found myself in an empty sky-blue room, smelling of incense and body odour: somebody who did not wash often lived there.

At one end of the room was a large Kumartoli-style representation of the monkey-general, as muscular as a super-hero. I was just walking up to inspect the image further when a bare-chested, dribbling priest staggered out from behind it. He was flabby, unshaven and probably drunk. My presence caused him to laugh convulsively, wobbling his oiled breasts. As I retreated, he called after me, 'Very welcome! Very, very welcome!'

CHAPTER THIRTY

On New Year's Eve, Manish had arranged to take us to the Dakshineswar Kali temple in the northern suburbs of the city, where Ramakrishna had preached. This, he had assured us, was quite unlike the temple at Kalighat.

'Good,' said Emma.

I told Manish that I had not disliked it as much as Emma had.

'You have to understand how much Calcuttans love Kali,' said Manish, 'and you have to see her as we see her to love her . . .'

'It's hard for us. We're told about this holy mother and, instead of a gentle madonna, we see a harpie.'

'One aspect only,' stated Manish firmly.

'It's not even that,' said Emma, 'it's the horrible greediness, everyone trying to rip you off. It didn't feel spiritual to me at all. Just a free-for-all, exploiting people's superstition.'

There was a rapt pause. Manish was plainly troubled that she had that impression. 'OK, at Dakshineswar you will see another side.'

We introduced Manish to Mrs Lahiri; his good manners came to the fore, and they spoke for some time in Bengali. Mrs Lahiri's half-smile was evident: she was pleased we were going to the temple, which she regarded as the holiest in

Calcutta, and she plainly regarded Manish as a respectable young man.

Emma suggested that she come with us to Dakshineswar but, of course, that was out of the question without her tiresome son to accompany her. So off we set in a taxi that Manish had engaged for the day. It was a fine, clear morning. 'Your landlady resembles Mona Lisa, don't you think?'

Manish asked, 'And how was Christmas?'

'Like a Mike Leigh play,' said Emma.

'Oh ho, *Abigail's Party*,' laughed Manish. 'Do you know our Bengali director, Ghatak? He is something similar.'

'Do you know of a Bengali writer called Jayabrato Chatterjee?'

'Of course, he often writes for the *Telegraph*. I believe he is the confidant of many beautiful women.'

On the way across town, Manish told us that the temples at Dakshineswar were nowhere near the age of those at Kalighat. They had been built in the last century by a woman called Rani Rasmani, an immensely rich widow who used her wealth to champion the working people of Calcutta. Rani Rasmani was notoriously shrewd. When the revenue department imposed a tax on all fish caught in the Hugli, thus threatening the livelihood of many fishermen, Rani Rasmani came to their aid; for a large sum, she obtained sole fishing rights to a long stretch of the river. The authorities, supposing that she was opening a fishery, rubbed their hands; it would be much easier to collect the taxes from one source than to chase hundreds of reluctant fishermen. But as soon as she owned the fishing rights, Rani Rasmani had chains hung across the river to prevent ships from disturbing the fish. When confronted, she agreed to remove the chains only when the tax was lifted, which it was.

Rani Rasmani was not actually royal at all. She was born into a working-class family of the *sudra* caste. Rani was simply her name, like Queenie. She was, however, beautiful and, as beauties often do, she married a rich man, the philanthropist Rajchandra Marh, who died when she was forty-three. She was very religious, a devotee of Kali, and in 1848 the goddess appeared to her in a dream, asking her to build a new temple. She purchased twenty acres of land at Dakshineswar to the north of the city and set about building a complex of temples there.

There was a snag. It was customary for the patron of a temple to offer cooked food to the deity as *prasad*, that would then be eaten by the resident priests, who were essentially employed by the patron. But no Brahmin priest would eat food given to him by a *sudra* and furthermore no *sudra* was allowed to offer cooked food as *prasad* to a deity. Rani Rasmani sent letters to various pandits who were experts on the *Shastras*, the scriptures that deal with ritual worship. All of them confirmed that her low caste was an insurmountable barrier. Eventually, one pandit called Ramkumar suggested Rani Rasmani make a formal gift of the temple property to a Brahmin who could then oversee the installation of the Kali image and the cooking of the food that was to be offered to her.

Rani Rasmani followed Ramkumar's advice and legally made over the temple to her personal guru, while retaining the right to act as his business manager. The other pandits regarded this as no more than a trick. When the temple buildings were completed, Rani Rasmani found that the priests were unwilling to serve at Dakshineswar. The job of officiating at the main Kali temple went to the helpful Ramkumar.

Ramkumar came from the village of Kamarpukar, about seventy miles north of Calcutta. He had a younger brother called Ramakrishna, who had come to live with him in the big city and who joined him at Dakshineshwar. Ramakrishna was still a teenager when Ramkumar took up his new position. He was a solitary, dreamy boy who spent his time singing hymns to Kali. People began to notice the boy and the joyful intensity with which he sang and the deep, almost deathly stillness that came over him when he meditated before the Goddess. Ramakrishna came to be regarded as the holiest of all the Brahmins at Dakshineshwar and eventually he took over from his brother as the chief priest at the Kali temple.

Ramakrishna's methods of worship were far from orthodox. His mind was so absorbed in prayer that occasionally he would put a flower, offered to Kali, on his own head and sit for hours without moving. He began to have visions of the Divine Mother, and when the visions subsided he would roll on the floor, crying like a child for her to return. This was strong stuff and there were people who regarded him as a madman. Certainly his behaviour could be weird. One day Rani Rasmani, who admired Ramakrishna for his passion and simplicity, came to the temple and asked him to sing for her. While he was singing, Ramakrishna noticed that the widow was not concentrating and he stopped and slapped her across the face. Rani Rasmani's attendants and some of the older Brahmins were horrified at the insolence and called for her to dismiss the crazy priest once and for all. But Rani Rasmani would not hear of it: she admitted that her thoughts had been elsewhere and she was convinced that it was not the priest but Kali herself who had slapped her.

Over the years Ramakrishna's fame spread far and wide, and people flocked to hear him preach. Manish said it was important to remember this was the first time it was possible to become famous, in the modern sense of celebrity, in Calcutta. There were newspapers, there were photographs, and the bush telegraphs of the bazaar and the *adda*. Ramakrishna was talked about everywhere. To the masses who worshipped Kali with devotion, Ramakrishna's acts of rapturous adoration expressed what they wanted to say themselves. Intellectuals also kept their eyes on the charismatic priest. At a time when Hinduism was challenged by Christianity, Ramakrishna's sermons offered a powerful affirmation. He spoke simply and powerfully, using parables. I hadn't realised that the well-known parable of the blind men and the elephant came from Ramakrishna.

Ramakrishna's sermons were written down by a school-master called Mahendranath Gupta, who assembled them into a book called *Sri Sri Ramakrishna Kathamrita* (translated as *The Gospel of Sri Ramakrishna*). The book made an extraordinary impact. Ramakrishna was open minded towards other religions: he had learnt about Islam through a Sufi master, and once he had a vision of Christ that lasted three days. Ramakrishna also studied Tantrism and Vedanta, acknowledging the separate strands of his own religion.

Above all, it seemed from what Manish was telling us, Ramakrishna was a showman. When he worshipped the heroic god Rama, whose divine sidekick was Hanuman the monkey-general, Ramakrishna turned into a monkey, climbing into a tree and eating unpeeled fruit. It was reported that a protrusion, several inches long, grew from the base of his spine. When he came down from the tree Ramakrishna was a priest again, and the rudimentary tail slunk back into his spine.

A sadhu called Jatadhari arrived at Dakshineshwar with a beautiful image of the child Rama. Through adoration of the image, the old sadhu had visions of Rama. When Jatadhari met

Ramakrishna, he felt compelled to leave the image with him. Ramakrishna treated the image as a living infant and called it Ramlala. He played with Ramlala as a child might play with a doll, bathing him, putting him to bed and feeding him, and all the time Ramakrishna, like Jatadhari, saw visions of Rama.

'But weren't these obvious publicity stunts?'

'No, no, no. He was simply tuning into a set of values that devotional Hindus understood.'

Manish explained that there were recognised stages of devotion. The most straightforward is *shanta*, which is the basic approach of the worshipper to the Worshipped. Then there is *dasya*, that resembles the relationship of a child to his parent, a servant to a master. Throughout most of his life Ramakrishna regarded himself as the child of Mother Kali. *Dasya* defines the relationship between Hanuman and Rama: Hanuman, Rama's trusted servant, was privy to his words and deeds, which is what Ramakrishna became.

Sakhya is when the devotee regards himself as a friend or companion of a god; he might, for instance, identify himself with Krishna's playmates, the young shepherds of Brindavan. *Vatsalya* is when the devotee thinks of himself as a god's parent or protector; that was how Ramakrishna worshipped Rama through Ramlala.

The deepest devotion of all is called *Madhura Bhava* that means 'the sweet mood' and that is when the devotee approaches the god as a lover. The chief exemplar of *Madhura Bhava* is Radha, the beloved of Krishna and the state can best be described as one of intense spiritual eroticism. Manish thought that a western example of *Madhura Bhava* was Bernini's sculpture of Saint Teresa.

When Ramakrishna took on the *Madhura Bhava*, he went all the way. He identified so strongly with Radha that he dressed as a woman with a sari and a wig. 'There were, of course, whispers.'

Transvestism was not unknown among ecstatic priests. Ramakrishna's feminine role was so convincing that his women followers could accept him completely as one of their own gender. It might have been because he was naturally hermaphroditic; the photographs we saw of him record a slender man with breasts.

According to Manish, Ramakrishna was heterosexual. Sometimes, in the years before his marriage, Ramakrishna went to brothels, but he tended to see the girls as apparitions of the Goddess, and everyone would end up on the floor in prayer. Later he acquired a comely, intelligent wife, Saradamani, some years his junior, who, after Ramakrishna's death, would take on sainthood in her own right. The marriage produced no children. In photographs Saradamani resembles Yoko Ono in the 1960s, peering out through curtains of hair.

The taxi left the broad main streets and trundled along some narrow and crowded sidestreets and soon we were in a traffic jam. Manish said the approach to Dakshineswar was always problematic. 'You see, in the last century everyone would come on foot only.'

We were in a lane where every shop sold pickles, some in huge gallon jars. The jars were arranged with the visual flair that constantly surprised us in India. Emma commented upon it to Manish. He said it was because there was comparatively little packaging; in the West, goods come in boxes or with labels and we look for brands we recognise, but in Asia most goods are sold loose and vendors must catch the customer's eye in their own way.

'But they're all so good at it,' said Emma. 'Market stalls in England look like, well, market stalls . . .'

'To your eyes, this is exciting. If you presented this driver with, I don't know, a Budweiser bottle, the label would excite him as much as the beer. If he could read English, he would study every single word on it. It depends what you are used to.'

After about ten stationary minutes, the driver and Manish got out to see what was causing the hold-up. A lorry, some hundred yards ahead, had a flat tyre and no spare wheel. A boy had been sent to fetch one. In the meantime, nobody could move forward or backward. As Manish was telling us the state of affairs, a khaki-clad policeman marched past holding a *lathi*, which is a long baton.

'Oh God, now there will be trouble.'

'What's happening?' asked Emma. Llewelyn was pressing his palms against the window, then licking them.

'The policeman is about to punish the driver . . . Ow, yes . . . There he goes . . . Ooh, ow . . . and another, ouch . . .'

'Is that normal?' I asked, shocked, 'I mean, do people let the police do that?'

'Why not?' asked Manish, 'A fine? He would not pay. This is immediate punishment. The end of the story.'

Thank heavens we never drove our own car in India, if a flat tyre meant a mandatory *lathi*-thrashing.

The traffic started moving again and we arrived at the temple. There were several coaches in the car park and as we walked towards the entrance, we joined a crowd of visitors. There were sweetshops and flower-stalls and beggars, of course, but they were less persistent than those at Kalighat. The whole place felt more open and clean. There were other family groups walking around, and a few western visitors, some of whom were actual devotees, for Ramakrishna has a large international following.

In the main courtyard of the temple, the Kali temple was very ornate, like a three-tiered wedding cake all covered in patterned stucco. Its roof was a shallow arch, upon which a smaller version rose, surrounded by spires, and on the roof of that rose another even smaller version. Manish told us this was a traditional Bengali temple design.

The temple stood between two other buildings, a pillared *nat-mandap* that would be used as a stage for religious plays and dances, and a smaller Radhakanta temple devoted to Krishna and Radha. Ramlala, the sacred doll, had resided in the Krishna temple for many years before he was stolen.

Opposite these three structures, and forming one wall of the courtyard, were twelve small Shiva temples, almost identical, each one containing its sacred *lingam*. The other three walls, opening on to colonnades, were made up of rooms, offices, living quarters. At the end of one row was Ramakrishna's bedroom.

There were long queues outside both the main temples, and even the smaller Shiva temples were bustling with devotees. In the middle of the row of small temples was a portico leading to a bathing ghat. We walked through and sat for a while on the steps leading down to the river.

I found it embarrassing to watch the bathers; the women were fully clothed but wet saris cling and I could not help noticing the shapes of buttocks and thighs, parts of women one rarely saw in India. I felt that we were being intrusive, sitting there, watching people washing. Manish was not embarrassed at all; he sat and watched the sodden women with an appreciative smile; not quick, lecherous glances but steady concentration, as if watching a ballet. He even lit a cigarette.

Ramakrishna's bedroom, cool and comfortable, facing the river on one side and the courtyard on another, was a big attraction. There were two high beds, side by side, with bolsters. Emma assumed the second bed was for Saradamani but Manish said that one bed was for sleeping, the other for resting. Around the walls were pictures of his many disciples, including the Irishwoman Margaret Noble who took the name Sister Nivedita.

As we were looking at the room, a large American woman came through the door, accompanied by two Indian women. She gasped and covered her mouth with her hand. I wondered if she had accidentally bitten her tongue. 'Oh! Oh, sweet Lord! I can't believe it. This is his bedroom! I can't believe I'm standing here!' Her Indian companions smiled calmly and one of them gently patted her arm.

When we stepped outside, some Indian tourists asked if they could be photographed holding Llewelyn. This happened often. His likeness must be in photograph albums all over the subcontinent.

Manish kept asking if Llewelyn liked monkeys. Occasionally, he told us, monkeys came into the temple grounds, even inside the temples, where they behaved impeccably out of respect for Ramakrishna.

We sat and watched the American woman join a party of devotees in the courtyard. They were middle-aged women, Indians and Americans and Australians, gathered around a short, cropheaded Indian woman of the same age, dressed in loose orange pyjamas with several garlands draped around her neck. I took her to be a guru of some kind, possibly connected to the Sarada Mission, founded by Ramakrishna's widow. The woman spoke softly, I couldn't make out what she was saying but I noticed her large expressive eyes. She looked soulful and tough, like a woman who had lived a bit, a compassionate version of Trish Crystal. The cropped hair was her renunciation. She seemed to regard her followers with a mixture of derision and love, and she appeared to be bracing them, her body language telling them to straighten their backs and, in spite of her baggy body, demonstrating a posture of fierce strength. I guessed she was talking about Kali and, in doing so, assuming the attitude of the Goddess.

'Who is that woman?' I asked Manish.

'Which one?' He was looking at the followers.

'The guru.'

'Woman? The guru is a man. Actually, I don't think he is a guru.'

'He looks just like a woman . . .'

Emma said, 'No, he doesn't, he's got short hair and he's wearing men's clothes. He's got great big hands. Stubble on his cheeks. There's nothing feminine about him . . .'

'Oh no, quite the reverse,' Manish added, 'this fellow has the women following him. He is not Calcuttan, I think, more like Bombay side.'

When I looked back, I could see that my guru was indeed a man, by no means androgynous, and younger than his followers. It was weird. I would have walked away thinking about the woman guru. When I looked hard I could still see the woman's face (it was rather haunting) in his features but I could not see why I had mistaken him for a woman. I suppose his rotund figure could have been taken for feminine.

'Actually, he has an awkward physique,' said Manish as the group wandered over to the *lingam* shrines. I wondered if it had been an instance of *Madhura Bhava*, but I felt it was more likely a surfeit of tea at the crossroads in Lake Gardens.

I asked how Swami Vivekananda fitted into all this and Manish said that Vivekananda took Ramakrishna's teachings to a worldwide audience. If Ramakrishna became a celebrity in a surprisingly modern sense, so did his disciple. Vivekananda was a precursor of all the Indian gurus who have gained devotees in the West, from Krishnamurthi to Osho, but whereas some of these later preachers have proved fraudulent, Vivekananda was always heroically sincere.

When Vivekananda (then called Naren Datta) first visited Dakshineswar as a young man, it was with a spirit of intellectual curiosity and mild scepticism; Naren was closely associated with the Brahmo Sahmaj and, like many of his congregation, inclined to regard Ramakrishna as a madman who now and then came up with lucidities in his ravings. Imagine his embarrassment when Ramakrishna greeted him like a lost relative returned to the family. Ramakrishna shed tears of joy: 'You have come, at last! You have come!' The priest fed Naren sweets by hand, and showered affection upon him. Ramakrishna started going into Calcutta to seek Naren out, once he even disrupted a Brahmo meeting Naren was attending.

Once Ramakrishna asked Naren to take him to the zoo so that he could look at the lions. They travelled across the city in a horse-drawn cab, accompanied by another member of the Brahmo Samaj. Naren's companion was taken aback by Ramakrishna's behaviour in the cab; the prophet threw his shawl over his face and pressed himself next to Naren, so that people would assume he was the young man's wife. He spent the journey cuddling and fondling his disciple.

Naren became one of a group of disciples, mainly young intellectuals, who engaged the priest in long, philosophical discussions. Much of the *Gospel of Ramakrishna* is drawn from these discussions. For five years, Ramakrishna led them through a series of intense spiritual practices, training them to realize God as fully as he himself had. In 1886, shortly before Ramakrishna fell ill with cancer of the throat, he declared that the disciples had succeeded in their objective; he distributed ochre robes and rosaries. They were to be monks, dedicated to continuing his teachings, and Ramakrishna declared Naren their leader. A few days before his death, he called Naren to his side and mystically transferred all his powers to the younger man.

After Ramakrishna's death, Naren travelled about the country, mixing with all kinds of people, from maharajas to peasants. He saw that India's greatness was fundamentally religious, but religion alone failed to ease her suffering. He saw the need for education and progress but felt these were meaningless unless directed by people alive to the spirit of Indian religion. It would be the mission of the monks to educate the masses and spur them on whilst preserving and strengthening their spirituality. Of course, this would take funds. Naren decided the money should come from the West, which he regarded as weakened by its lack of spirituality, just as India was weakened by poverty. He would present India's spiritual strength to the West and in return he would be granted the resources to make India a place of proper importance in the modern world.

In 1893 there was to be a Parliament of Religions in Chicago, the perfect opportunity for Naren to put his plan into action. The Raja of Ramnad and the Raja of Khetri offered to buy his ticket. Naren had a vision of Ramakrishna that convinced him he was doing the right thing. Around this time, at the Raja of Khetri's suggestion, Naren took the name Vivekananda (it means 'the bliss of spiritual discrimination') and the designation Swami ('honoured religious teacher'). Dressed in orange silk robes and an ochre turban, Swami Vivekananda set sail to America.

Some 7,000 people attended the Parliament of Religions. When it was Vivekananda's turn, he spoke without notes on the subject of universal harmony. By all accounts, he was the most charismatic of all the delegates and, instantly, he was lionised. Photographs appeared everywhere of the handsome Swami, looking princely in his long silk coat and loose turban.

Vivekananda went on the lecture circuit and, like Oscar Wilde, he lectured in major cities and small frontier towns. At times he was no more than a curiosity. At other times he met audiences that were familiar with his discourse: Unitarians, Transcendentalists. Vivekananda stayed in America for three years, travelling back and forth to Britain in that time. Funds poured in for the Ramakrishna Mission.

In 1897 he returned to India a national celebrity and he travelled the country to address the multitudes. Vivekananda spoke of an invigorated India. He did not criticise the British in his speeches. He praised them and told his countrymen to learn from their example. He set about instilling national pride without upsetting the establishment. National pride inevitably leads to nationalist politics and Vivekananda was certainly aware that his teachings would raise political questions, but he regarded himself as a patriot rather than a revolutionary, and his aim was only to disseminate the teachings of Ramakrishna.

The Ramakrishna Mission was established as soon as Vivekananda returned to Calcutta, participating in famine and plague relief and establishing schools and hospitals. In January 1899, Belur Math, the new headquarters of the Mission, was consecrated on land that the brothers had bought, just across the river from Dakshineswar. In June 1899 Vivekananda went back to the West to raise more money and to attend the Congress of the History of Religions in Paris. The voyage exhausted Vivekananda and when he returned to India, the effects of all those long sea-voyages and national tours had visibly taken their toll. Vivekananda died at Belur Math in July, 1902. He was thirty-nine years old. On the spot where his remains were cremated, a magnificent temple now stands.

On our way out of the Dakshineswar temple, we wandered over to a little park near where the taxi was waiting. Manish told us that hundreds of monkeys lived in the trees there. We looked around but saw none at all. 'They must be hiding from us, how peculiar.'

Belur Math was a spacious, tidy place, like a small American liberal arts campus. Manish pointed out that that the gate to the compound was influenced by early Buddhist architecture whereas the mission buildings themselves took in elements of Hindu, Islamic and Christian architecture, and the whole plan of the compound was cruciform. We walked around the various buildings and looked at the mission bookshop. There was a bathing ghat at Belur Math. Manish said, 'Come, let us all sit here for a moment. There is nothing more relaxing than watching bathers.'

CHAPTER THIRTY-ONE

Manish had spoken of us to a friend of his, a musician called Pandit Dey whom he wanted us to meet. Pandit Dey played the *surbahar* which is like a *sitar* but with thicker strings and heavier frets; it produces a deep, dignified sound. He was also a teacher of music. 'I think you will like him. Not only so but, you must see his flat. It is quite extraordinary.' Manish suggested that, on our way back to Lake Gardens, we should stop for lunch at the Elegant Hotel and then walk over to Pandit Dey's flat, which was in the Beadon Street area we had visited before.

The Elegant was not a hotel in the western sense; there was no accommodation, but across India cafés call themselves hotels (and transport cafés are sometimes called Line Hotels). In Calcutta there is another tradition whereby little eating-places call themselves cabins, as if to suggest a rustic atmosphere and 'country goodness' to the food. The cabins tend to be slightly cheaper than the hotels.

The hotel occupied a corner at a junction of Central Avenue. It was quite elegant, as it happened, decorated with sage-green tiles. A large photograph of the original proprietor (pencil-moustached and brilliantined like an Asian Clark Gable) hung on one wall, its frame festooned with garlands of yellow flowers. On another wall was a lithograph of Guru

Gobind Singh, similarly festooned. The current proprietor, tall and stoop-shouldered, sat at a little desk reading a car magazine.

Manish ordered three helpings of the house speciality and we sat and pulled at *naan* bread until it arrived. The speciality, *kabiraj* chicken, was a flat chicken rissole fried in an egg batter. Manish explained that a *kabiraj* is a doctor of ayurvedic medicine. I asked if the dish was considered healthy (minced chicken, after all, has invalid connotations in England) and Manish laughed. 'No, no. Actually, the name is misleading, a bit like your toad in the hole. *Kabiraj* is just an Indian way of saying 'coverage', you know, this coating of batter . . .'

Emma and I found it rather boring. Far too much of the batter, which could have done with more seasoning. What chicken there was seemed as tasteless as cloth. Llewelyn, perversely, thought it very good indeed. The best thing at the Elegant Hotel was the *masala chai*, made with ginger and cardamom. It was so thick; I think it was made with milk and no water at all. A skin formed on the top of each cup that reminded me of hot chocolate when I was a child.

Pandit Dey lived just a short walk from the Elegant Hotel, near the CRUTA offices. Emma asked if he was a descendant of Ramdulal Dey and Manish replied that he probably was but not a direct descendant. 'There are many different Dey families now.'

We arrived at a tall narrow house with all its shutters drawn. The walls of the house were painted geranium red and the door-knocker was an *art nouveau* elephant's head. 'No need to knock,' said Manish, pushing open the door.

We found ourselves in a dusty hall painted the colour of

tea, with black and white tiles on the floor and a heavy marble table bearing a jumble, several inches thick, of unopened letters. A little chandelier, furry with dust, was suspended from the high ceiling. 'Come,' said Manish and we followed him up a creaking mahogany staircase. On one landing there was a large gilt mirror facing another smaller one so that the double reflection formed long repetitive tunnels, an illusion that made the landing seem wobbly and unsafe, as if it might fall through and cast all four of us into the Twilight Zone.

We climbed a few more stairs and Manish led us into a dark room lit only by dusty shafts of daylight where the shutters were pushed together but not bolted. There was a heady floral scent in the air that mixed with the smell of old furniture. Manish pushed the shutters back and we saw that we were standing in a nineteenth-century bourgeois salon. There were two photographic portraits on the wall, both hand-tinted but faded to sepia beneath their glass. The portraits were from the 1890s and the room was so perfectly preserved that the couple could have stepped down from the walls and carried on with their lives. One, in a fine ivory frame, was of a middle-aged man wearing a long paisley shawl. The man was sitting on a chair whose high back was embroidered with flowers. Beneath the photograph stood the actual chair, its flowers faded over a century. The other portrait was of a matronly woman standing with one arm leaning on another embroidered chair. She had covered her head with her sari and wore numerous bracelets on both arms. Her expression was both nervous and proud. I looked, in vain, for her chair in the room.

The rest of the furniture reflected the Europeanised taste so typical of the old Calcutta bourgeoisie. The room looked more French than English. Two chaises-longues and four upright chairs; everything muted and brown with age. The floor was parquet and the walls were papered with a stripy zigzagging material in shades of chocolate and decorated with dusty crystal sconces. In the middle of the room, on a Persian carpet, we noticed a harmonium, similar to the one Mrs Lahiri played.

'Manish, Manish . . .' A young man in white pyjamas entered the room from the other door. He greeted Manish with a hug. Manish said, 'This is my cousin Arun. He learns *tabla* . . .'

'Singing and *tabla*,' said Arun, shaking our hands and wishing us a happy new year.

'I too took instruction from Panditji,' said Manish.

'Do you play the *surbahar*?' I asked.

'No, no. Mainly I learnt singing. That is the basis, you see. All our music is based on the voice . . .'

As if to illustrate Manish's point, a high male voice sang from the other room, '*Sa Re Ma Pa Ni Sa.*' Manish laughed and said the singer was teasing him. We didn't get the joke but, before there could be any embarrassment, in walked the singer, Pandit Dey, pressing his palms together.

He was a small man, about fifty, quite lithe, with a nimbleness of movement. Extraordinary looking, I thought, like Nureyev or Mick Jagger; great thick lips and ruffled 1960s hair, a wrinkled face that could have sprouted goat's horns at any moment. He was wearing blue silk pyjamas, all crumpled as if he had just got up.

The Pandit invited us to sit down and arranged himself gracefully on the floor. 'Please,' he asked, 'do you have an English cigarette?' As he asked, he parted his fringe with both hands, just like Jagger in *Performance*. Arun left the room to call for tea.

'This room is remarkable,' I said. 'It looks as if nothing has been changed for over a century . . .'

'Well, actually, much I have patched up here and there. I

am glad you like it. But I ask why make change for change's sake? This furniture is comfortable and well-made. Why change?'

'Manish says you are interested in raga music,' said the Pandit.

'I like what I hear,' I said, 'I don't know how much I understand.'

'Actually,' said the Pandit, 'unless you are a musician, there is nothing to understand. You need only listen and what you hear is enough. Any knowledge about music is like knowledge about God. Knowledge doesn't help us to understand God . . .'

'No, I mean that Indian listeners recognise each raga's melody in the same way that westerners recognise the standards that jazz musicians play. It doesn't matter how much the musician improvises around that melody, it remains something the listener already knows . . .'

The Pandit nodded and said, 'This familiarity you speak of, it would come with listening only. Our Indian classical music even is not popular with our own masses who know only film music. Maybe it is too demanding.'

'What I would like to know,' asked Emma, 'is how one decides what is a morning raga, afternoon, evening or night-time raga. Why can't you play any raga at any time of day?'

'There is nothing stopping you but all this music is what you would call chamber music and the chamber is important, the musicians play their instruments and the room itself, the ambience. When better to describe night than night-time or morning than in the morning when dawn light fills the room? It would be no good to describe the sun coming up when, actually, it is going down.'

To illustrate this remark he reached over to the harmonium and, pulling it towards him, played a rising scale that, almost miraculously, evoked the first glinting of dawn.

'But, you see,' the Pandit continued, 'it is more specific than morning, afternoon and so on. We divide each day into quarters and also each night. And for all eight sections, there are ragas . . .'

Manish said, 'Six to nine a.m, you could play *Bilawal* raga . . .'

Pandit Dey specified, '*Shuddh Bilawal, Shukla Bilawal* . . .'

'Nine until noon, *Miya-ki-Todi* . . .'

'*Asawari*, perhaps . . .'

'Noon until three, *Bhimpalasi, Dhanashri* . . .'

'Well done,' said the Pandit to his former pupil.

'Three until six p.m, let me see, *Triveni* . . .'

'Yes, yes, yes . . .'

'First quarter of the night, six until nine, you could have *Shuddha Kalyan*. Nine to midnight, *Shankara, Durga. Bageshwari* at midnight. Then midnight till three, why not *Kaunsi Kanada*? Three until six, *Purvi, Marwa* . . .'

'Raga round the clock,' said Emma.

'And not just around the clock but to celebrate each season of the year as well.'

Arun came back carrying five glasses of tea in a frame that reminded me of the frames for milk-bottles one used to see on doorsteps in Britain.

Pandit Dey talked about something called *Srot*. As far as I could understand, *Srot* is a mystical energy that drives music along. This is not to be confused with rhythm; the *tabla* rhythm is merely an expression of *Srot*, as are the other components of the raga.

I wanted to know if *Srot* was universal. Could western music express *Srot*?

The Pandit nodded, chewing his lip. 'Yes, indeed yes. All spiritual music . . .'

Arun was more doubtful, 'Western music goes in many directions. Only some of it is concerned with these matters.'

Then Manish spoke about *Bhakti*, which is the devotional form of Hinduism that has a strong hold on Bengalis. *Bhakti* and *Srot* are interwoven.

I confessed to listening to Indian music as contemplative gospel music or jazz. I heard its yearning and its mystical joy.

'That is not wrong, but labels are unnecessary,' said Pandit Dey.

But I realised that Indian music has a formality that I had been missing, a set of codes and traditions. There is a ritual to it. This idea excited me but daunted me as well; I might never be able to hear it as an Indian aficionado might and trying to would take my concentration off the music itself.

When he learnt that we had just been to the Dakshineshwar temple, Arun mentioned a vision of Kali that Ramakrishna had related to his disciples.

Ramakrishna had watched a beautiful pregnant woman emerge from the Ganges, give birth and nurse the child tenderly. Seconds later, she turned into a terrifying harpie and, devouring the infant, slinked back into the water as she gnashed her blood-drenched fangs.

'That's what I don't understand,' confessed Emma. 'How can that be an image of compassion?'

Arun sighed, 'Kali is the all-creating, all-nourishing, all-devouring . . .'

Pandit Dey smiled at the story. 'There is no need to understand her. She is here anyway. Agni, God of Fire, has seven tongues, meaning seven colours of flame, that spring up when butter is offered. Kali is the name of the black tongue.

[246]

She is Smashanakali, always wakeful at cremation ground, the compassionate black tongue in the flame, incinerates' – Pandit Dey raised his hand palm outwards, flickering his fingers – 'pain, sorrow and anxiety, and bestows' – his right hand made a graceful caressing gesture – 'everlasting peace . . .'

In my imagination, I had a picture of Kali looking like Frida Kahlo, with one eyebrow and a mantilla.

Emma remarked that the room was like a time capsule. She asked Pandit Dey why he had preserved it so carefully. The Pandit just nodded and, touching his chest with one hand, gestured the other towards the photograph of his ancestor. For a moment he seemed to be praying.

'Everything goes brown,' he said eventually. 'You see, this wallpaper was red.'

'There's a lovely smell, like roses.'

The Pandit's face creased into a smile that, with the exaggerating effect of his wrinkles, threatened to cut his face in two. 'Come.'

He sprang to his feet and, still smiling but stifling a yawn like somebody at breakfast in a hotel, led us to a door at the end of the room. He asked to hold Llewelyn. 'First he must see.'

It was a shrine in a cupboard, like an altar entirely covered with red roses, and in the middle stood a stone image of two lovers entwined. Little lamps burned all around it. The lovers were Krishna and Radha. My first reaction was that it was kitsch but, within an instant, I saw that it was altogether deeper than that and the shrine appeared a strange erotic secret, as red as a heart pumping blood into the drained walls of the old apartment, and Pandit Dey stoked this throbbing heart with prayers and roses.

CHAPTER THIRTY-TWO

That evening we went to dinner at the Grand with Catherine Berge.

Since her arrival in Calcutta on Christmas Day, Catherine had worked continually on her documentary. The crew were soon to arrive so all the interviews had to be fixed in a rigid schedule; not a moment could be wasted. There had been countless discussions with Soumitra Chatterjee, meetings with two of his great leading ladies, Aparna Sen and Madhabi Mukherjee, and audiences with Satyajit Ray's widow. Catherine had been visiting locations; the old film studios in Tollygunge and ancient, ramshackle theatres that smelt like lavatories. Catherine had been expecting her producer, Nayeem Hafizka, who is Ismail Merchant's nephew, to join us but on the day he was detained in Bombay.

Catherine was carrying a book she had just bought from the Ritika bookshop called *Crafts of West Bengal*. She told us she was impressed by Kalighat paintings. She liked their stylised simplicity, their wit and she had wondered, as I had, about their impact in Europe.

Dinner was a special event at the Gharana restaurant. The Gharana served the sophisticated Mughlai and Hyderabadi cuisine that Catherine, like many of her compatriots, took great delight in. This type of cooking is probably more exciting to French people than it is to the British; they're not over-familiar with the debased version that most high street curry-houses serve.

The restaurant was an elegant, softly lit room, with a dais for the musicians behind a shallow pool. We were greeted by an usher wearing a long black *achkan* coat done up with twenty-four brass buttons. He looked at our son with some disapproval. I said we had asked if we could bring Llewelyn when we had made the booking and we had been told there was no problem; we had arranged for a high chair and we had even brought a large pillow from our flat that would serve as a mattress should he fall asleep. 'There will be music. People have come to listen.'

'If he's disruptive in any way, at any time during the meal, one of us will take him outside,' said Emma firmly.

As soon as we sat down we were brought beakers of *thandai*, a yoghurt drink flavoured with almonds and rose petals; a pleasanter taste than *bhang lassi*.

For some reason, we talked about Patrash and his fit on Christmas morning. Catherine, like Abdul, found the story amusing. She couldn't stop laughing. 'You see, he is so pompous all the time. If Violet and Ted are not there, he is not helpful. But when they are there, because they are my friends, he smiles and smiles. I'm sorry. It just seems hilarious that he should make a cat's noise.'

'He's very loyal to them, I think . . .'

'Violet gives him far more respect than she gives to the other staff . . .'

'She is kind to Mrs A, don't you think?'

'Yes, but she only confides in Patrash. The funny thing is that she assumes only Patrash understands her. Harry Dent speaks Bengali fluently. I wouldn't be surprised if Andy Devane knew what she was saying.'

'Albert Lyon speaks Bengali,' I said.

'Well, he gets the full force of her invective every time he sets foot in there,' said Emma.

'But this Albert, he has a thick skin,' said Catherine, tapping herself on the skull. It transpired that on her previous visit to Calcutta, Albert had fallen in love with her. I asked if he had made his amorous expression and imitated it. Catherine burst out laughing. 'Yes, this peculiar look in his eyes and this thing he did with his chin. I thought he was trying to hypnotise me or something . . .'

One Sunday afternoon Albert had declared his feelings for Catherine by the famous banyan tree in the Botanical Gardens. He had recited a poem he had written for her, in French ('He speaks and writes French well, of course'), in which he called her *Ganga Ma* ('The strange thing is that Ismail, he calls me by this name. I told them both, this river, it is too much responsibility').

Catherine sighed, 'I suppose it was flattering. But it was also a little awkward because we had to share a taxi back to Park Street. After I had said I wasn't interested, he sulked . . .'

'You're lucky he didn't serenade you,' said Emma.

'I have heard him sing. He brought his guitar to the Fairlawn one evening. He was singing morbid Scottish songs about crows. He had a horrible voice, nasal and high-pitched.'

'Was he well received?'

'You know what it's like, nobody paid him any attention. I think Ted told him to stop it . . .'

Emma asked how Albert had treated her on this visit.

'Well, I've only seen him once and he said nothing . . .'

The food started to arrive. We were served several small courses at once, like a Greek *mezze*. Fish, chicken and cheese kebabs, a creamy chicken soup, a lamb biryani flavoured with sandalwood, prawns in almond gravy, a rich black lentil *dal makhani*, various vegetable preparations and all kinds of wonderful breads.

Some musicians appeared on the dais, bowed, sat down and started to play low thrumming music on a *tabla*, a *tambura* and a harmonium. After a few minutes, they were joined by a soignée young woman who sang *ghazals* in a wavering contralto. As she sang, she fidgeted with a heavy silver bracelet. I guessed she was singing well-known songs because the Indian diners smiled at one another; some of them mouthed the words.

Later the singer was joined on stage by a tall, obese man, evidently a star turn because he was greeted with loud applause. When he sat down and spread his bulk around him, Catherine remarked that he looked like Nusrat Fateh Ali Khan. But his singing was more controlled, reined in, with none of the soaring improvisations associated with the great *qawwal*. For a while the two singers performed duets: I didn't think these were *ghazals* so much as film songs. Some of the guests clapped along.

Then the obese singer sang a few songs on his own and his voice started to quaver and distort the phrasing with rubato. He was warming up. The musicians played faster and louder. The next song was some kind of folk song, like the *bhangra* music of the Punjab, highly rhythmic, with a clapalong chorus.

One of the diners, a short bald patriarch, got up and performed a loose, hilarious dance (like a man caught in a whirlwind) to the song and when it ended he took a handful of notes from his wallet and threw them at the stage.

After that there were more film songs and more guests got up to dance and by the time midnight struck the whole restaurant had erupted into a happy swaying mass. One Junoesque mother bent backwards in a descending version of the twist, as if about to undertake a limbo but never quite summoning the agility. A bouffant-haired man gyrated his pelvis in front of a teenage girl who squealed 'Uncle! Stop it! Everybody is looking . . .' The stage was soon covered with money. Through all of this, Llewelyn slept peacefully on his cushion.

A little after midnight I went to the lavatory and found the place full of teenage boys who had been celebrating at the Pink Elephant discotheque, which is also in the hotel. They were all combing their hair and excitedly discussing the girls they had kissed at midnight. The New Year's Eve kiss was obviously a big deal to them. It was like the 1950s in there.

We eventually left the hotel and walked back along Chowringhee to Sudder Street to see Catherine safely back to the Fairlawn and to find Abdul. We were continually accosted by groups of revellers, always groups of tipsy young men, shouting 'Happy 1997!' Some of them wore conical straw hats.

One of them crooned, 'Happy 1985,' to a lilting melody.

'You've got the wrong year,' I told him.

'No, no. This is a song I am singing. Very popular.' he explained.

Then they lurched forward to kiss the women, and both Emma and Catherine complained that some of them attempted the full-blown French kiss.

When we reached Lake Gardens it took twenty minutes to rouse Sushil. Eventually he shambled along the passage, wrapped in several blankets and wearing a balaclava, coughing and muttering. We had told him we would be returning around one in the morning so we did not feel guilty for disturbing him, but it was obvious that he wanted us to feel very guilty indeed.

CHAPTER THIRTY-THREE

During the second week of the New Year, John Major arrived in Calcutta on a high level trade mission, accompanied by Ian Lang, the Minister for Trade and Industry, and fifty leading British businessmen. Everywhere we noticed railings being painted and scrubby grass verges being spruced up. The presence of the British Prime Minister meant that Calcutta was on show and for days the smell of new paint mingled with the more familiar street smells.

I had always imagined that abroad Major came across as a decent, benign fellow, less charismatic but more affable than his predecessor, so we were shocked by graffiti that proclaimed *Go Home John Mazor* and to read that his effigy had been burnt outside the British High Commission.

I was commenting on this to Mr Biswajit, explaining that, although the Conservatives were unpopular and would certainly lose the next election, Major himself was not the type to inspire effigy-burning.

Mr Biswajit told us that the protestors were unlicensed *puchka*-wallas, hawkers of street food. For some time the civic authorities had wanted to remove the *chai*-stalls and street-kitchens that had sprung up like weeds along the centre of some of Calcutta's busiest streets, from which children were dispatched bearing *singharas* and glasses of tea whenever there was a traffic jam, which was often. Some of the hawkers had operated in this manner for decades. The authorities felt that their presence had transformed roads designed as broad efficient thoroughfares into narrow congested lanes.

Using the state visit as an excuse, the authorities issued final warnings to the hawkers and then, a few days before the British Premier's arrival in the city, in a gesture they called Operation Sunshine, they bulldozed the shacks and lean-tos. I don't think Major knew anything about all this but he was certainly seen in Calcutta as the enemy of the Common Man.

With nowhere else to go, the *puchka*-wallas regrouped in the *paras* and overnight the streets around our little park were transformed into a food fair. We found this fascinating. In the evening we would stroll past the stands, watching people tucking into all the different comestibles on sale. The most basic was *chhatu* which is just raw gram flour for the customer to mix with water into a stiff dough, to be consumed with chili and raw onion. Some sold hot buttered toast and hard-boiled eggs. Some sold *pau bhaji*, which is a bright yellow vegetable curry served with a soft white roll. There was also a type of chow mein. All kinds of fritters and cutlets. None of the food was particularly appetising to us but all the stands seemed to be doing a roaring trade.

Through all this marched, one of those evenings, a parade of sadhus, a dozen of them, all men, of various ages, some very wild-looking and some only remarkable for their orange loincloths; one beating a drum.

'*Makar Sankranti* time,' explained an egg-boiler. 'These fellows, saints. Staying Nimtolla Ghat, passing into Capricorn . . .'

We learnt that thousands of Hindus were converging on an island called Sagardwip, some distance south of the city, in the mouth of the Hugli, where they celebrated the Winter Solstice. It was a gathering especially popular with sadhus.

Emma had read about this festival; apparently, in the past, mothers would sacrifice their first-born babies to the sharks.

'Maybe,' said the egg-boiler, 'maybe, not now.'

'So what goes on?'

'Praying. Actually, too many people. Millions people . . .'

The hawkers stayed in our neighbourhood for about a week, then dispersed.

When we next went to the Fairlawn the news was that Ismail Merchant was staying there. Violet was cool about it. 'Darling, this is where all the film people stay. We're known for it.' Her manner was light comedy, actressy. 'Isn't it fun?'

We caught a glimpse of the famous producer a few minutes later when Catherine and her entourage returned to the hotel. Ismail Merchant arrived separately from the rest of the crew in a white Contessa. In his *kurta* pyjamas and sleeveless *sadri* jacket, he resembled a politician.

Catherine introduced us to him; he was civil but disinterested, like a man with more important things to do. He told us he knew Bath, having filmed *The Remains Of The Day* at Dyrham and Badminton. I imagined that he flew all over the world checking his various productions. Both Emma and I noticed that he had elegant table manners, especially when he ate a tangerine: he removed the peel in one piece that he folded to make a little bowl in his left palm, then he broke the fruit into segments that he picked, one at a time, from the peel bowl. No doubt tangerines were eaten that way by Wajid Ali Shah.

The film crew occupied two tables at the back of the dining-room. Ismail Merchant was very much in charge, checking what had been done and what was to be done, dismissing each possible variation with a sharp clap. They all deferred to him; it was clear that the producer had the final word on everything. Catherine sat through the meal doggedly trying to hold on to what was hers.

Then, having finished his lunch, Andy Devane approached Ismail Merchant with his hands pressed together and held above his head in a gesture of homage. Whatever he said was too soft for me to overhear but it seemed to catch the great producer off guard; after that he was calmer, his manner was more collaborative.

Later on I asked Andy what he had said: it was just how much he'd enjoyed *Shakespeare Wallah* when he had first seen it, decades ago, in Dublin.

CHAPTER THIRTY-FOUR

I had plugged some speakers into my Walkman so that we could all listen to music in our room; we had brought a selection of cassettes with us and I constantly bought new ones, generally of Indian classical music, from Symphony in New Market. Mrs Lahiri was pleased that I took an interest in Indian music. Sometimes she pointed out that the words were a prayer to a certain deity or a verse from a sacred text.

Whenever we played English or American music, Mina and Manu would come into the room to listen and Mina would dance around holding Llewelyn. Once I was playing some Clifton Chenier and both of them said, 'Crunchy music.' Sushil, who was standing at the door, nodded, '*Han*, crunchy music.' Neither Emma nor I understood what they meant.

A day or two later, Sushil came in with a cassette. 'Doctor Cassette.' He waited while I put it on. It was a line dancing compilation; one continuous rhythm track over which inane Nashville pop songs (*Achey Breaky Heart* and so on) came and went, choruses for the dancers to sing along with.

'Crunchy music,' explained Sushil, tapping his foot to the beat. Mina suddenly burst in doing a funny stamping dance that caused us all to laugh.

'Kind permission, Dr Bagchi Sahib,' said Sushil.

Some time after we had returned the cassette, we were

approached in the bazaar by a sleek young man in designer jeans. 'So you like dancing?'

It was Dr Bagchi. Somehow I managed to thank him for the loan. 'The classical music of Europe myself I prefer,' said Dr Bagchi merrily. 'At the moment, I am enjoying Albinoni. Only this line-dance tape I lend to my patients when they are a little overweight. Everyone dances. It is a lot of fun. Off come the kilos.'

As we were carrying two pots of *mishti doi* at the time, we felt this might be a pointed comment. Emma and I were both losing weight without trying (from walking and forgoing second helpings) but we still looked big and pink in Calcutta. Llewelyn seemed to be growing stronger all the time.

Dr Bagchi continued, 'I am always reading of the dancing rave-ups you have in England. Tell me, have you tried the Ecstasy? Come on, come on, you can tell me in confidence, I am a doctor . . .'

CHAPTER THIRTY-FIVE

Sushil came to the door. 'Mr Joe, telephone.' He led me down to the computer office to take the call. It was Jayabrato Chatterjee, inviting us to dinner that evening. He said that an old friend of theirs was in town, a tribal princess who had worked with him at *Society*, a glossy magazine from Delhi. She came from Mizoram, the narrow little state that runs between Bangladesh and Burma, although she had lived for many years in Delhi. She was bringing her new husband, a younger man whom Jay described as her toyboy. Her name was Zothanpari but everyone called her Parte.

'What do you mean, a tribal princess?' I suspected it might just be an expression.

'Well, you see, Mizoram is very tribal.'

'But is she really a princess, I mean?'

'Yes, yes. Of course she is,' said Jay, a little disappointed in me.

'Is the toyboy much younger than her?'

'There is maybe twelve or fifteen years between them. In actual fact, he seems older than she does.'

'Why's that?'

'Oh, I don't know. We met him once and he was rather serious. But he is very rich and very clever . . .'

Jay arrived at Mrs Lahiri's around seven. He looked splendid in a long cream silk *kurta*, frogged across the chest. His driver Sukumar, in white shirt and grey slacks, looked drab beside him.

Emma asked Jay if he always wore Indian clothes and he answered that they were, after all, designed for the climate; western clothes he found restrictive after the lightness and looseness of *kurta* pyjamas. There was also a tiny suggestion of nationalism in his reasoning: 'Why should I pretend to be anything other than Indian?'

We all squeezed into his car for the short journey to his flat. Jay sat in the front and we discussed buttons and fastenings and the Persian origins of Bengali clothing, while he played a cassette of Julie London songs. When *Cry Me A River* came on, he joined in with the line, 'Told me love was too plebeian, told me you were through with me and . . .' He giggled and said the line was worthy of Noël Coward, whom he revered unreservedly.

Then the little white Maruti turned into a large garage beneath a modern apartment building. We followed Jay into the lift and rose several floors.

Subhra Chatterjee was waiting on the landing. She was very composed, with a wide, almost Slavonic face: high cheekbones and liquid eyes. Her sari was made of moiré silk that shone gold and blue like the Mediterranean. She was, we guessed, in her late thirties. 'Come, come in and relax,' she said.

Behind Subhra stood a tiny ayah, no more than four foot nine, wearing an orange sari, who beamed and bowed her head and took Llewelyn from Emma. The ayah's name was Menuka.

We were shown into a small living-room. Three of the walls were covered with framed drawings and watercolours, some Kalighat *pats* and some in the Beardsleyish style that trained Bengali artists went in for around the turn of the century. The fourth wall was mainly taken up by a large window with a broad, uninterrupted view across Southern Avenue to the lakes.

The room was full of ornaments, figures of gods and animals and especially fish in a variety of folk-art representations.

I found fish to be particularly auspicious to Bengalis. They figure prominently in wedding celebrations. Wedding invitations are usually decorated with a fish motif, symbolic of wealth and prosperity. Fish figure in the festive *alpana* patterns traced in rice, chalk or coloured powders that decorate walls, thresholds and seats. As part of the prenuptial puja to Lakshmi, the goddess of fortune, a fish will be drawn on the floor. A couple of days before the wedding, relatives and friends of the bride visit the groom's house bearing gifts that include a large carp decorated with vermilion and flowers. Often the fish is wrapped in a sari. This comical anthropomorphism of fish is carried even further in Bangladesh, where a 'bride fish' will wear lipstick and a 'groom fish' holds a cigarette in his mouth.

Three bedrooms and a bathroom led off this room, and a small kitchen ran alongside the entrance passage. In one of the bedrooms lived Jay's widowed father, a scholarly man who had devoted his old age to reading. Once I glanced into his room and saw shelves stuffed with books and papers. Jay's father was a respected poet who had studied at Shantiniketan, in its early days, under Tagore himself.

In another bedroom Jay and Subhra's daughter Shahana was revising for her A-levels. She emerged to greet us but clearly wished to return to her books as quickly as possible. As frail and as delicate as a leaf, she had that peculiar characteristic, not uncommon in India, of looking unlike her parents; she might have been an actress engaged to play their daughter.

It felt odd to sit talking in one room, flanked by these two cells of concentration; we automatically lowered our voices as if chatting in a library.

Jay poured drinks in the kitchen while Subhra spoke of her work with the Spastic Society. I told her we had heard the story about the Missionaries of Charity and Subhra's eyes welled up as if it still upset her.

At the other end of the room, under the dining table, Menuka played *agdum bagdum* (the Bengali equivalent of 'pat-a-cake').

After twenty minutes the other guests arrived. Princess Zothanpari (who did not look at all as I had imagined, no long heavy ear-rings, no nose jewellery) was about forty, tall and comely, dressed in a relaxed western style: a loose green paisley-patterned shirt, untucked over jeans. She had a Mongolian appearance, and her sallow complexion was accentuated by chocolate-brown lipstick. Parte (as she immediately asked us to call her) was old friends with the Chatterjees and soon she was pumping Jay for gossip. She asked Emma if it was true that Prince Andrew had AIDS.

Her husband was called Neville, which initially led us to suppose he was Anglo-Indian. In fact, at one point in the evening Parte mentioned her Christian upbringing, so I asked Neville if he was a Christian. He replied that religion had played a small part in his life and he didn't feel that he belonged to any one faith. Jay subsequently informed us that Neville is a common name among Sikhs.

Neville was in his twenties (and so slim I reckoned he had a 26-inch waist), smartly dressed in clothes from London: a blue Jermyn Street shirt with folded cuffs and a red parachute-silk tie from Paul Smith, pale trousers and brown suede Patrick Cox loafers. He spoke with an odd shifting accent, sometimes it was glottal-stop Cockney (with Arabic undertones, like the kebab-vendors of Queensway) and sometimes it was pukka and drawling like some Old Etonian maharaja of the 1920s.

Neville had written and published himself a large book about contemporary art in India. Now he was completing a novel about incest; a subject, he told me, that scared most English publishers away. I thought the opposite was true and I listed several popular novels that dealt with the subject. Then I realised I was deflating his self-esteem so we talked about other things.

Subhra told Parte that she had prepared *rui* (a type of carp) in her honour, knowing how she loved traditional Bengali food.

Parte said, 'Neville hardly eats a thing.' She sounded like the mother of a toddler.

'He will take some *rui*, I hope,' said Subhra.

'That I can't promise,' said Parte.

We sat and chatted for a long time before we ate. We moved to the table around half past ten, by which time Llewelyn was asleep on Jay and Subhra's bed.

The food was extremely good. The *rui* tasted fresh and succulent. Parte was not joking, Neville turned out to be the fussiest eater I have ever come across. Emma said later that she felt he was rude to Subhra. He did however confess that he had just recovered from a debilitating illness, cerebral malaria. This alarmed Emma because it combined her two worst fears for Llewelyn, meningitis and malaria.

'It does not happen often,' Neville reassured her. His bout had left him with a condition that was like constantly being on the verge of a migraine. Unfamiliar tastes could bring on a sick headache that lasted for days.

In every other respect the party was a great success.

When Emma asked Parte about her title, Neville cut in dismissively, 'You are too easily impressed, one can be a king with a country the size of a cricket pitch.' The conversation turned to the British treatment of Indian royalty and especially what became of those whose kingdoms were annexed by the East India Company.

Neville told us the poignant story of Duleep Singh, Maharaja of the Punjab, whose kingdom was lost in the Second Sikh War of 1849 when he was just eleven years old. One of the chief spoils of that war was the famous Koh-i-Noor diamond that the boy-king was advised to offer Queen Victoria as a present. Duleep Singh was made the ward of a Scottish doctor who converted him to Christianity and in 1854 he travelled to England, where he was entertained by the Queen at Osborne. He remained in Europe for the rest of his life, with an allowance of £25,000 a year from the India Office. He bought a large country house called Elveden on the border of Norfolk and Suffolk that he decorated in the style of an Indian palace, using white Carrara marble and panels of beaten copper. The effect, in East Anglia, was cold and tomb-like. Nevertheless Duleep Singh threw lavish parties; the Prince of Wales was a frequent visitor to Elveden. It was Duleep Singh's extravagance that led to his downfall; when the money started to dwindle, he asked the India Office for the return of his private estates in the Punjab. This was refused, so he started complaining that he had been cheated of his most valuable possession, the Koh-i-Noor. In 1886 Duleep Singh renounced Christianity, reclaimed the Sikh religion and set off for India where his plan was to raise an army and fight for the return of his lands. He was arrested at Aden. Instead of going back to the Punjab, Duleep Singh ended his days, with neither friends nor money, in Paris. When he died he was buried in the grounds at Elveden. Everyone agreed that it was a sad business.

Jay said, 'You know, this Lord Dalhousie made a hobby of deposing kings. The same fellow deposed Wajid Ali Shah, the King of Oudh . . .'

I said, 'I've heard of him. Wasn't he a composer?'

'He was a very talented man,' said Subhra, 'and, of course, in Calcutta we regard him highly because he lived here for many years.'

'He was exiled in Metiabruz,' explained Jay.

'Where is that?' asked Emma.

'It is where the shipyards are today.'

Jay began his story. 'Lucknow was the capital of the Mughal province of Avadh. You British called it Oudh. It covered most of what is now Uttar Pradesh. As the power of the Mughal empire declined, Lucknow stayed rich from the revenues of the province. It grew more powerful and became an independent kingdom. Its rulers, the Nawabs, planned Lucknow as the last bastion of courtly Islamic culture. They built great palaces, mosques and *imambaras*. Their courts attracted the finest musicians, dancers and Urdu poets. It was like a city from *The Arabian Nights* long after such cities no longer existed. This was the middle of the eighteenth century.'

At the same time the British, in the form of the East India Company, were snaffling up what remained of the Mughal Empire and putting pressure on Avadh. In 1773, the Nawab Shuja-ud-Daula accepted a British Resident and allowed the Company to dictate its foreign policy. Little by little, the Company gained control. By 1801, the Nawabs were no longer allowed their own army but had to pay heavily for one controlled by British officers. Vast tracts of the kingdom were ceded to the Company. The Governor General in Calcutta was able to decide the line of succession and, crucially, he was entitled by treaty to depose any king he regarded as unfit to rule.

In 1848 Wajid Ali Shah succeeded to the throne. His father, Amjad Ali Shah, had been a religious fanatic who paid more heed to considerations of piety than affairs of state; this disinterest had suited his British overlords. Wajid Ali Shah was a very different character: a corpulent dandy, similar in some ways to our Prince Regent, he preferred music to religion, and was most at ease in the company of singers and dancers.

Jay told us that Wajid Ali Shah was responsible for the development of the *thumri*, a new (mainly vocal) type of Indian classical music whose melodies derived from folk tunes. The lyrics were sung in a living language that everyone understood. These lyrics usually concerned love and were immediately popular. Because *thumri* was closely associated with *kathak* dance, it was as if the king had invented pop music.

Jay explained that Wajid Ali Shah was also a poet. There had existed for centuries a type of Urdu poetry known as *masnavi* where the poet would declare his passion for a beautiful woman; the poets, especially those that were Sufis, used the image of the woman as a mystical symbol of their love of God. When Wajid Ali Shah composed *masnavi*, he caused a sensation by ditching the symbolism. He wrote about actual love affairs, often putting blatantly erotic and occasionally obscene imagery into the verses. As heir to the throne, he could take his pick of the female servants and courtesans and he had hundreds of lovers. In his poetry Wajid Ali Shah characterised himself as an insatiable satyr. As soon as he was crowned, he set about building a vast palace called the Qaisar Bagh, larger than the Louvre in Paris. 'Some of the rooms had silver floors,' said Subhra.

'Solid silver?'

'No, covered with beaten silver.'

'And in the *zenana* lived 365 *begums*,' said Parte, 'a different wife for each night of the year . . .'

'I can't believe it,' gasped Emma.

'There are many myths circulating around him,' said Neville.

At the Qaisar Bagh, each spring, the Hindu festival of Holi was celebrated with operas or masques of the young king's own composition, with the king performing the role of Lord Krishna and the most beautiful ladies of his court playing the cowgirls of Brindhavan. The palace gates were thrown open and anyone could attend the celebrations so long as they wore red clothes.

By all accounts, his subjects loved Wajid Ali Shah for his

generosity and flamboyance. Like Elvis Presley, he enjoyed surprising ordinary people with gifts of jewellery, and sometimes he granted people marvellous titles.

The British, of course, were horrified. In 1856, Lord Dalhousie, the Governor General announced that the kingdom of Avadh was to be annexed. Wajid Ali Shah was removed to Calcutta. This unpopular gesture was one of many that led to the Mutiny of 1857.

Jay told us the exiled king was taken to a suburb in the south of the city called Garden Reach, so called because it was directly across the Hugli from the famous Botanical Gardens. Wajid Ali Shah was installed in a place called Metiabruz, which means 'the earthen dome'. There he was given three houses and a generous allowance.

If the authorities thought he would settle down to a quiet life in exile, they were gravely mistaken, for a massive entourage followed him, and if the real Lucknow had been lost to the British, a second Lucknow sprang up in India's most British city. Aristocrats, noblemen, poets and wits, courtesans and dancers; all the merry-makers of the Qaisar Bagh followed their monarch to Calcutta, and so did the craftsmen and tradesmen who had served the court. Metiabruz was nicknamed Mochikhola, 'the earthly paradise'; it became a whole township whose inhabitants observed the same ceremonies and enjoyed the same pastimes as they had in Lucknow. A demesne wall was erected around Metiabruz so that it resembled the Muslim notion of heaven as an enclosed garden. There was a small zoo with a pair of giraffes, flocks of exotic pigeons and a trench filled with snakes.

It was a splendidly defiant gesture, a doomed culture in one last flamboyant display, right on the doorstep of the new industrial, colonial India.

Jay said, 'It turned into a duel for the sympathies of the Bengalis. So many at that time were becoming Anglicised. The *babus* were sending off to London for their furniture. Along comes this ghost from the past and everyone is excited again by Indian taste.' It was because of Wajid Ali Shah that Calcutta became a centre for Indian classical music; his patronage laid the foundation for its appreciation.

Subhra told us how his style was imitated, even the way he ate. Wealthy Calcuttans drank a glass of buttermilk with a gold coin in it each night before retiring.

'What for?' asked Emma. Subhra said it was for medicinal reasons, and to keep them wealthy. It reminded me that credulous European nobles of the eighteenth century bought Goa-stones from Portuguese monks. Goa-stones were polished gallstones removed from Indian cows, supposed to hold the properties of longevity; a tiny flake was consumed in a glass of wine each night.

'But gold is proven, it is old medicine,' said Parte.

'We must go to Metiabruz.'

'You see, Wajid Ali Shah lived to a great age and took on religious duties. When he died the government reclaimed the land to build shipyards. There is nothing left now except some mosques and *imambaras*. Otherwise it is just docks. There are Lucknowi *paan*-sellers still, and many, many tailors.'

'I still want to go.'

'I will take you,' said Jay.

CHAPTER THIRTY-SIX

Llewelyn's first birthday present was a drum I bought from the toyshop at Lake Gardens, decorated with pictures of Indian wildlife (tiger, rhino, peacock, elephant, monkey) and a muscle-bound Tarzan swinging on a vine.

'Mowgli would have been better than Tarzan,' said Emma.

'Perhaps it is Mowgli . . .'

'He looks about forty-five.'

This made me think that Johnny Weismuller looked about forty-five when he was in fact twenty-five and that most male Hollywood stars prior to the 1960s looked mature in a way that nobody does today. At thirty Robert De Niro looked thirty, whereas Ronald Reagan at thirty looked like President Reagan.

The drum was a success with Mina and Manu who ignored the plastic drumsticks and played it like a *tabla*. Before long Llewelyn was copying them, banging on the drum with his palm.

That afternoon we visited the Calcutta Book Fair which is held annually towards the end of January. Apparently, the fair attracts over a million visitors each year. It is to Asia what the

Frankfurt Book Fair is to Europe. Publishers from all over India are represented, as well as a large international contingent. It all takes place on the Maidan, at the southern end near the Victoria Memorial, where 350,000 square feet are given over to tents and pavilions. The visitors trample the ground until it resembles a beach of dust. The ground is watered at intervals to keep the dust down; it turns to mud, then back to dust.

There were several stands selling tea, not in clay *handis* but in thin plastic cups because the Book Fair was a prestigious occasion. Here and there stood bins to receive the used cups but the bins were too small and too infrequently emptied so, everywhere, white plastic cups littered the showground.

There were food stands, run by SEWA, the Self-Employed Women's Association. A public address system blared garbled announcements or broadcast what sounded like stylophone music.

We found plenty of books in English although it seemed the majority were textbooks or technical manuals. These were surprisingly popular. I watched two men arguing over the last copy of a book about industrial refrigeration.

There were some interesting antiquarian stands, but most of the older books were in Indian languages. People were carrying jute bags stuffed with books, as if they were buying a year's supply at a time. Many of the publishers offered discounts.

Gangs of photographers stood about, like paparazzi awaiting celebrities. If there were celebrities in the crowd, we did not recognise them. We were astounded by the crowds; in some tents it was impossible to reach the books we wanted to look at. And, in just about every tent, we were regaled with cries of '*Baby's Day Out!*'

If any city in India should host a book fair, it is Calcutta. Books have been published in the city since the late eighteenth century. As soon as there were presses in the city, printers were not only using Roman fonts but fonts in Devanagri, Persian and Bengali as well.

By 1834, up the river at Serampore, Baptist missionaries were printing religious tracts in forty-seven different languages. The press at Serampore was by no means restricted to evangelical literature; they published popular Bengali editions of the *Ramayana* and the *Mahabharata*. Bookshops and circulating libraries flourished.

To begin with, reading was a pastime for the educated minority. The real surge towards mass readership happened when the Bengalis started to publish their own books, cheaply produced and flimsy, but sold at prices that anyone could afford. These books were called Bat-tala editions, after the district in north Calcutta where they were manufactured, and they catered to the poorest of the literate population: a Bat-tala *Ramayana*, for instance, cost the reader one rupee whereas the Serampore edition had cost twenty-four rupees.

The range of titles published in this format was immense. Popular fiction, often with erotic or sensational subject matter, flourished. Bat-tala books were illustrated with woodcuts, executed in a folk-art style similar to the Kalighat *pats*. In a way, Bat-tala books were themselves the literary equivalent of folk-art, or perhaps they should be regarded as penny dreadfuls. Their huge popularity created a taste for reading that is still a Calcuttan characteristic.

At the Penguin tent (really the best organised in the fair) I bought Pankaj Mishra's *Butter Chicken in Ludhiana*, a travel book about small towns in India. As we were leaving the tent, we met Subhra Chatterjee. She told us she had been working at the fair. We knew she worked for the Spastics Society and guessed that that was in a voluntary capacity; we hadn't heard her mention any other job. Emma asked if she was a publisher and Subhra replied that, in fact, she was a television presenter for an arts programme on satellite television. 'I'm so glad to see you have Jay's book there. I was just coming to see how it was selling . . .' I told her that I'd bought it a few days before at the Ritika Bookshop. I had started reading it and was enjoying it. I asked if she knew anything about *Butter Chicken in Ludhiana*. 'Yes, yes. We have all read it. It's a hoot . . .'

CHAPTER THIRTY-SEVEN

We held a little birthday party for Llewelyn, at teatime in the Fairlawn courtyard. We invited the Smiths, the Dents, Manish, Andy Devane and Catherine Berge. I had wanted to invite Albert Lyon but Emma felt that would enrage Violet.

We bought a large Madeira cake from Nahoum's, decorated with one candle and a festive garland. We also bought some chocolate brownies.

We arrived to find the hotel full of Americans. A banner reading *Fairlawn Warmly Welcomes The Mennonite Delegates To Calcutta* was hung across the Corinthian columns. The Smiths seemed in two minds about the Mennonites; glad to have a block booking but instinctively wary of missionary activity, especially American missionary activity – there were always one or two missionary types among their guests but to have them take over the place was a different matter.

The Mennonites were disappointing to look at; I was hoping to find them in black hats and puritan garb. If anything, they stood out only for their size, several being obese. Many of the women were dressed in *salwar kameez*, while the Indian women who acted as their guides all wore western clothes. The Mennonite men, religious farmers, wore T-shirts emblazoned with the names and dates of other conventions around the world. A few wore such voluminous jeans that it was necessary to hold them up with braces. Some wore tractor-driver's caps and some wore cowboy hats.

Calcutta is a magnet for religious nuisances, to whom it has great symbolic value as the most desperate city in the world. I don't know what the Mennonites thought they could do. 'They all come here,' said Ted, 'Mormons, Jehovah's Witnesses. We've had most of them over the years . . .'

One pink-faced Mennonite strolled over to Llewelyn who was playing around the loom chairs. 'Why, hello there, little fellow.' Llewelyn looked up at him disdainfully and continued to rearrange the cushions. The pink-faced man then turned to Emma and asked if we were 'ministering' in the city.

Andy Devane had a present for Llewelyn, a red and white gingham sunhat. Then Catherine appeared, dressed in saffron pyjamas with a pilgrim's orange scarf around her neck covered in script. She carried a painted wooden roundabout for Llewelyn.

The Dents came downstairs, Rosemary somewhat anxious about their flight back to England the next day, Harry carrying an enormous balloon for Llewelyn and wearing a thick Viyella shirt under a pullover. 'But aren't you hot?' asked Catherine, to which he answered 'Yes, warm enough, thank you.'

The last to arrive was Manish with a big surgical dressing on his forehead. He told us he had been delayed at Park Street station, arguing with a young Mennonite woman about rein-carnation. 'She was alarmingly stupid, quite unfit to express her ideas to intelligent people.'

'Did she attack you?' asked Ted, looking at the bandage.

'No, no.' Manish smiled. 'This is from the weekend. I was walking down a staircase that disintegrated beneath me. I wasn't badly hurt. It looks worse than it is . . .' He glanced up at the banner. 'Oh dear, I had not realised this was their head-quarters.'

Violet told him that although some of the Mennonites were staying with them, there were even more at the Great Eastern. Ted remarked that most of the Mennonites bore German surnames. This aroused his suspicions. 'What is a Mennonite? That's what I want to know . . .'

'I should keep well clear of them,' said Andy. 'Now, why don't I ask Jamal to bring us some tea?'

Catherine told us how hectic her last week had been. Hovering over everything was the presence of Ismail Merchant.

'You get on well, don't you?' I asked her.

'Yes, but he is such a powerful personality. I don't know if I can cope with him at this stage. It is a surprise. I was not even certain he was coming at all.'

Manish said, 'It says on your scarf that you have worshipped at the temple of Jagannath in Puri.'

Catherine held up her scarf. 'Ah, so that's what it means. I found it in New Market.'

Harry handed Llewelyn the balloon. 'You are a very lucky baby to have your first birthday in India.'

Violet laughed. 'Of course, he won't remember any of it. Never mind . . .'

I heard Andy telling Manish how much he admired the Calcuttan's ability to use what was to hand. He mentioned Satyajit Ray's films, the way some scenes were lit with car headlights, and an itinerant children's entertainer who had created a mobile roundabout from an old truck wheel. 'A few original thoughts making him a good living, that's the way it should be.'

The tea was laid out. There was a plate of bread and butter and another of digestive biscuits. We lit the candle on Llewelyn's cake and we all sang *Happy Birthday* to him. He looked rather taken aback. Then Manish and Harry sang it again in Bengali.

As I was cutting the cake, Laxmi came into the courtyard so, of course, I offered her a slice and asked her to take one for Osman as well. Violet gave a theatrical cough, caught my eye and shook her finger. 'Spoil servants and you lose their respect . . .'

We gave Abdul a slice. He was delighted. 'Anyways, Wahlen, happy number one birthday. Now you are old man like me . . .'

That evening, back at Lake Gardens, we learnt that, an hour or so after we had left the Book Fair, there had been a major fire there. Dr Bagchi told us the news. The blaze had started when a SEWA foodstand caught alight. The place had been evacuated and, although nobody was killed, many people were injured in the stampede for the exits.

'But many, many books have been lost,' said the doctor, 'the estimate is in crores, not lakhs . . .'

'Translate,' asked Emma quietly. I told her that a lakh is one hundred thousand and a crore is ten million.

'Many publishing businesses destroyed,' said the doctor, 'entire stocks – pshoot!'

The next morning we read all about the fire in *The Statesman*. It sounded like *The Day Of The Locust*.

CHAPTER THIRTY-EIGHT

I went with Jay Chatterjee to Metiabruz. Fortunately Subhra had left the fairground before the fire started. While Sukumar drove, Jay told me that the Indian publishing world was in a crisis because of the fire.

Metiabruz certainly no longer resembled Xanadu. There were warehouses and sheds, scruffy empty plots and black ponds choked with weeds. To the north we could see the cranes of the Garden Reach shipyards.

Jay stopped the car to buy three green coconuts and he asked the *daab*-wallah where we could find the Sibtainabad Imambara. In the Bangla Bazar, was the answer. The people in the bazaar were mainly Muslims, the men in prayer-caps and some of the women in *burqas*. There were hundreds of *derzis* bent over their sewing-machines all making the same garments, striped shirts with raised collars. Jay explained that they were contracted by export companies; it was cheaper to hire individual *derzis* than set up a factory.

Jay was telling me about a friend whose father had been an official of the South Eastern Railway. As a child, she had lived in a house that had been part of Wajid Ali Shah's palace. The house was haunted by the sound of ankle-bells.

We came to a whitewashed arched gateway emblazoned with the two mermaids that were the insignia of the Lucknow royal family. We walked from the car into a tidy courtyard, where we removed our shoes. The courtyard was paved with marble and cool underfoot. A group of young men were sitting listening to an elder. Behind them was the porticoed prayer hall where several glass chandeliers hung from the ceiling, all in different colours. An attendant came forward to show us around.

The *imambara* was built in 1866. An *imambara* is a symbolic structure representing the martyrdom of Hussein, the Prophet's grandson, at the battle of Karbala. Often an *imambara* houses the tomb of the Nawab who built it. The veneration of relics, shrines and tombs is largely a Shi'ite characteristic; Sunni Muslims regard such behaviour as superstitious. The Nawabs of Oudh were Shi'ite in a part of India where most Muslims were Sunni.

In later life, Wajid Ali Shah took comfort in his Shi'ite faith. During Muharram, the first month of the Muslim calendar, he would meditate in the prayer hall, seated on a platform. The king would be dressed in mourning clothes for Hussein. On the tenth day of Muharram, Wajid Ali Shah, riding a white horse, would lead a procession through the streets of Metiabruz. Some followers carried floats called *tazias*, large (usually flimsy) models of Hussein's tomb. Usually, nowadays, such *tazias* are made of silver foil but in Lucknow and Metiabruz there is a tradition of growing wheat on a bamboo frame, trimming each stalk until a topiary-like representation of the tomb is achieved. Other followers of the procession, in identification with their slain hero, would lacerate their chests and backs with hooked chains. The procession still takes place. The embroidered banners and alams (flat metal hands) were stored in the *imambara*.

Looking around, we noticed all sorts of Wajid Ali Shah memorabilia. His throne, a Koran written in his own hand, his shield and his sword. A portrait of the king in old age, looking stolid and respectable, dressed in a white *angarkha*, one hand on the hilt of a sword and the other resting on a table beside a vase of flowers. The tomb itself was draped with a faded golden cloth; a large silver *tazia* and a smaller golden one were placed on top of it. The attendant showed us an impression of the Prophet's footprint that looked implausibly big to us. 'I think it's a yeti,' whispered Jay.

There was another tomb in the *imambara*, that of the king's oldest son, Prince Birjiz Qadr. As Wajid Ali Shah had literally hundreds of *mutai* (temporary) wives, there must have been some dispute about succession. Jay said that the offspring of *mutai* marriages were categorised as 'harem descendants'. There were, doubtless, many still to be found in Metiabruz. Prince Birjiz Qadr was born of an official marriage. Above his tomb was another *tazia*, modelled in polystyrene.

The attendant told us that Wajid Ali Shah's great-grandson, Prince Anjum Quder, lived above the prayer hall. He was President of the All India Shia Conference. Jay asked if we could meet him. He was an old man, the attendant said, and very tired, having just returned from Delhi on the overnight train: nevertheless he would go upstairs and see if the Prince would receive us.

The Prince's quarters reminded me of rooms in a college. Dark solid furniture, every surface piled with books. I noticed the absence of glass in the windows, just shutters to block out the elements. The Prince wore a brown dressing-gown and sat upright in a high-backed wooden chair. He looked like Graham Sutherland's portrait of Somerset Maugham. He spoke to Jay in Urdu, quiet but welcoming, apologising for his tiredness. The train journey had been disturbed by *goondas*. Some of the passengers had been robbed. The Prince was not one of them. No doubt, he told Jay, the incident would be reported in the newspapers and the scoundrels would be described as terrorists. They were not terrorists, said the Prince, merely brigands.

He showed us a book that he had just received from London. It was a facsimile of the *Baburnama*, the illustrated memoirs of Babur, the sixteenth-century founder of the Mughal dynasty. The original was in the Queen's collection and had been displayed at Windsor Castle. The Prince asked if I was in contact with the Royal Family. I said I had no personal contact with them. Then he asked if they were generally approachable and I replied that, in theory, anyone could approach them, through the proper channels. The Prince nodded and told Jay that that was as it should be.

The attendant indicated that we should leave the old Prince to rest. We thanked him and said goodbye. Downstairs, I told Jay that I was surprised the Prince had not spoken English. Jay said that the Prince would certainly have been able to speak English but had spoken an old and pure form of Urdu instead.

CHAPTER THIRTY-NINE

While Catherine was staying at the Fairlawn, Albert Lyon steered clear of Sudder Street. I bumped into him at Classical Books on Middleton Row. He looked pale and haggard, clutching a book entitled *The Last Days of Netaji*.

We went to a café called the Drive-In for some tea. The café was run by a pair of brothers, very gung-ho and American in their approach to business, and their clientele (corporate types with mobile phones and button-down shirts) reflected the same longings. Everywhere you looked, there were advertisements for Coca-Cola. Only the name was American, Albert said, the food was standard *dhaba* fare, quite good and served promptly. He pointed out that it would be difficult to park in front of, let alone drive in to, the place.

'I hear you're a singer . . .'

'Oh, not really. I like folk songs. I try to pass them on. That's how folk music works.'

One of the proprietors came up and asked if we would like iced water.

'Is the ice made with filtered water?' asked Albert.

'It is latest refrigerator, boss.'

'I think we'll pass on the iced water,' said Albert.

'There are some marvellous folk songs,' I said. 'I think I prefer the sad ones.'

'Laments,' said Albert. Then he told me that, for fifteen years, he had organised a folk club in South-East London. He had tried to run something similar in Calcutta, 'With limited success, I'm afraid . . .'

He recommended a recent Bob Dylan album that featured traditional material, blues and ballads. I asked if that had been playing at his *adda* and he replied that it probably was, he listened to it all the time. I told him he looked like Bob Dylan. He laughed. 'When I was younger I did. In the 60s. It stood me in good stead. I even saw him on his 1966 tour . . .'

Could it have been Albert Lyon who shouted 'Judas!' when Dylan strapped on his electric guitar?

'I was just a little kid in the 1960s,' I said.

'Halcyon days,' said Albert but with a certain abruptness, as if their passing saddened him too much to discuss them. I have noticed that many people who eulogise that particular decade do not necessarily want to give details. Changing the subject, I asked if he had seen Lalitha recently.

'No. She has abandoned me. Completely. This seems to happen in India. The dialogue between men and women is strained. Pull too hard and it snaps. Just like that . . .'

'Oh dear.'

'Yes, it's disappointing. Very disappointing. I face a lonely old age.' Albert declared this so frankly I thought at first he was being ironic. Then I realised that he was not. Albert suddenly put his hand on top of mine. It was only embarrassing in that it was such an Ancient Mariner gesture. 'What's it all about, really? That's what I want to know . . .'

'You mean, Lalitha and Trish Crystal?'

Albert pulled his hand away. 'Certainly not! I don't care about them.'

'What's what about then?' I felt rather dim.

'Calcutta! Calcutta, of course . . .' Albert thumped the

[283]

metal table. This brought the proprietor over again, to see if we had changed our minds about the iced water.

'I don't know,' I said, 'it's a big place.'

'Yes. But don't you think you ought to be able to grasp it?'

'I don't see how one could.'

'Don't you want to? You can't look away! That's the point!' shouted Albert. 'You have to break down with it. That's the point.'

'Why?'

'Don't you understand a thing about Kali?'

'Seriously?'

'I am being serious. She is very powerful.'

'All the more reason to stay cool.' I lit a cigarette, to show how cool I was.

Albert drummed his fingers pensively, establishing a rhythm like a *bhajan* or devotional song. I wondered if he was about to sing. But he coughed instead, a nasty rattling, wheezing cough that left him looking even paler. His pale hands flapped my smoke away. The tea came, which restored his colour.

'Calcutta is Kali. The whole city is an expression of the Goddess. Don't you see that? She challenges you with images so ghastly you want to tear your eyes out. That's terrible for a poet.'

'Imagine what a doctor feels like . . .'

'I am talking as a poet. How can you put that into words? What good would words do? You have to answer that. How can a civilisation grow that contains such suffering?'

The rhythm he was tapping changed and suddenly Albert sang in an odd nasal voice that was more like Bernard Cribbins than Bob Dylan. He also closed his eyes and cupped a hand over his left ear, something I assumed folk-singers only did in comic turns.

'It's the song in the sigh of the weary,
Oh hard times, hard times, come again no more.
Many days you have lingered around my cabin door,
Oh hard times, come again no more.
While we seek mirth and beauty in music loud and gay,
There are frail forms gathering at the door.
Though their voices are silent, their bleeding lips will say,
Oh hard times, come again no more . . .'

Everyone at the Drive-In fell silent. When I was certain there was no second verse on its way, I asked, 'Is that a Dylan song?'

'He sings it. I think Stephen Foster wrote it . . .'

'Want a glass of water now, boss?' asked the waiter.

CHAPTER FORTY

Emma was having lots of clothes made. Her mother had sent her the latest issues of *Vogue Patterns*. She took these to Mr Akhlaque Ahmed at Shah'n Shah in Madge Lane. Emma had asked Violet for the name of a good tailor but Violet had said that all her own clothes were bought in London.

In the end Emma chose this particular tailor because it shared the name of a favourite album by Nusrat Fateh Ali Khan. The shop had a glass door that was heavy and stiff; you had to push it open with your shoulder.

Mr Ahmed was a portly, light-skinned man, usually dressed in pin-striped trousers and a businessman's shirt. We never saw him wear shoes and sometimes he was seated on the floor with the contents of a stainless-steel tiffin box spread before him like a picnic. As Emma discussed fabrics, asking where to find heavy silks and lining materials, he would toy with a chicken leg or shell a hard-boiled egg. Together they decided on blouses, skirts, a long pink *achkan* coat and a pair of trousers.

She found that he worked very slowly. Mr Ahmed explained that the spring held a concentration of Muslim festivals and that his regular clients celebrated these occasions by ordering new outfits. He was himself a religious man. Often Emma would visit the shop on the off-chance that a skirt was ready only to find it was closed for some holiday. There was no point in chivvying him; his attitude was that quality work took time. He knew exactly how long we were staying in Calcutta and promised 'Everything will be there.' And indeed everything was. Emma, who can sew competently herself, inspected all the details and was full of praise. I admired the buttons on the *achkan* coat, nine in three groups of three, covered with the fabric and fastened not with buttonholes but with Elizabethan-style loops.

Emma also had some shirts made for Llewelyn from checked cottons that caught her eye in New Market. For these, she went elsewhere, to Mr Ali who was less a tailor than a traditional *derzi*, working alone with a pedal-operated sewing machine just around the corner from the Fairlawn.

Every time Emma visited Mr Ali she noticed a young European sitting in the back of his shop, who said nothing but sat in a kind of trance and watched the *derzi* sew. Once Emma asked him if he was learning to make clothes. 'No,' the man replied in a French accent, 'I learn a lot from Mr Ali but not sewing . . .' Mr Ali was plainly embarrassed by this lugubrious presence on his tiny premises but too polite and kind-hearted to tell the Frenchman to go away.

Most of Mr Ali's customers were backpackers (whereas none of Mr Ahmed's were) so he was used to quick work and charged very little. She found him frustrating in other ways: asked to copy an existing shirt, he would change the shape of a collar or make the sleeves inches longer than they should have been. It took Mr Ali some time to grasp that he was dealing with a perfectionist. There were tense moments between them. Then Emma discovered Mr Ali's flair for *kurta* pyjamas and these, in plain white cotton, became Llewelyn's standard attire at home at Lake Gardens.

I waited for Emma and Llewelyn at the Fairlawn. I found the
fittings rather tedious (my opinion counted for little) so I sat
drinking a lime soda and reading Jay's novel. The Smiths were
upstairs still. It was just before noon. Various guests wandered
in and out.

A middle-aged Indian man was speaking to Patrash in
slow, deliberate Hindi. Patrash kept answering him in slow,
deliberate English. The man had a baggy body on a lean
frame. His hair was very black, with a giveaway tint of blue. He
wore a dove-grey safari outfit, a fanciful military affair with
multiple pockets, epaulettes, belt-loops and button-straps, so
that he appeared to be tied-up, slim trousers with a crisp flair,
white suede loafers. On one wrist was a heavy gold watch and
on the other a silver identity bracelet of the kind that mods
wore in the 1960s. Around his neck he wore a sky-blue nylon
cravat. He carried an attaché case. Sticking from his mouth was
a wooden toothpick.

Patrash said, 'I have spoken to them, sir. They are
coming.' The man nodded his thanks but his attention had
been caught by a tall Scandinavian girl who was buying a
bedspread from the salesman in the courtyard. The girl wore
a filmy sarong through which her long muscular legs were
plainly visible. As the man stared at her, the toothpick rose up
and down.

'Papa! Papa!'

Two young Indian girls rushed down the stairs to
embrace the man. At first glance the girls looked about fifteen
but a closer look revealed them to be in their early twenties.
The man beamed and spoke softly to them in Hindi. Both
sisters wore Levi's and Nike trainers. One had a pair of Ray-
Bans pushed up in her hair like an Alice band.

'Papa, you must see our room!'

'If it suits your requirements, then I am happy.'

'It's exactly how Hari described it. Very funky . . .'

'Funky?' said Papa, raising his shoulders. 'Funky is what I am paying for? What does funky mean, non-AC?'

He followed his daughters upstairs. When he came down again, on his own, he questioned Patrash extensively in Hindi. I worked out that he was asking about water. Patrash shook his head slowly and answered in his suave continental way. 'So far, I can say we are not having problems. It is a tube well . . .'

The man paid his daughters' bill in advance. He took a pile of bank notes from his attaché case and laid them on the counter. Some were dollars and some were sterling.

Later, at lunch, we shared a table with the two sisters, Bunty and Dixie Mashru. They had just arrived from Delhi. Bunty worked in an advertising agency and Dixie as a production assistant on various film projects. They spoke with the same faint American inflection that the presenters of *MTV Asia* use.

They were staying in Room Sixteen. We all joked about the photograph of the Duke and Duchess of York.

The sisters were in Calcutta for a family wedding. I asked if their family was Bengali. 'Papa's family is totally Delhi,' said Bunty, 'Mummy's side is originally Bengali but stationed in Assam since the 1800s. I suppose they are Assamese.'

'Assamese sounds too tribal,' said Dixie, wrinkling her nose.

'Why are you staying here?' asked Emma. She would have expected them to stay with relatives. Dixie explained that, although their parents were staying with relatives in the Salt Lake district, 'We told Papa we would only go to this gosh-awful wedding if we could stay here . . .'

Bunty said, 'Hari, he's my boss, told us it's funky . . .'

They both looked around for evidence of this assertion. There were few other lunchers that day: Andy Devane, a group of Swedes, an Australian couple and the Smiths. Whatever the sisters saw satisfied them, they smiled contentedly at one another.

Dixie said, 'Calcutta is much cooler than Delhi . . .'

'Hari says it's India's New York.'

'Delhi is too suburban . . .'

Bunty said, 'Calcutta is more sexed-up.' We heard them use this expression often, it simply meant glamorous.

'We love this hotel. Do you know, Ismail Merchant was staying here? Mrs Smith told us . . .'

'To think we just missed him . . .'

'And he's single,' declared Bunty, all wide-eyed.

The Smiths had been to a function for the British visitors at the Tollygunge Club. Violet described the Prime Minister as 'tall and distinguished, lovely clothes, a real gentleman . . .'

Ted was more guarded. 'I think the fellow's growing a moustache. Upper lip, not shaved properly. Looks a bit slapdash, On Her Majesty's business . . .'

'And did the Deputy High Commissioner dance?' asked Emma.

'Certainly not. Wouldn't have been at all appropriate.'

'Nice man, the High Commissioner, great fun,' said Violet.

'Where did John Major stay?'

Up went Ted's eyebrows. 'At the Taj. Funny choice. People always used to stay at the Grand.'

'Apparently it is easier to guard them at the Taj,' said Violet.

'He should have stayed here,' I said.

Ted sniffed. 'Couldn't have if he'd wanted to. We were full of Ammonites . . .'

GLOSSARY

Most of the words and phrases in Bengali and other Indian languages have been explained in the text. These are a few that, I felt, needed further explanation:

Acha – An expression used frequently in northern India to convey affirmation, approval, admiration, understanding etc. *Acha* is as all-encompassing as 'OK'.

Achkan – A tight-fitting knee-length coat with buttons down the front and a small upstanding collar. Sometimes it is called a *sherwani*. Traditionally Muslim gentlemen wear them in black cloth. Jawaharlal Nehru usually wore a white *achkan*.

Akhara – A centre for Bauls, but it also means a wrestling arena or a gym.

Almyrah – A lockable cupboard or wardrobe. The word, in Indian usage since the sixteenth century, is of Portuguese origin.

Alpana – Floor decoration, in coloured powders or flower petals, much the same as *rangoli*.

Angarkha – A long tunic worn by men, fastened at the left breast by Hindus, on the right by Muslims.

Baksheesh – A tip or hand-out.

Bekti – An estuarine fish, also called *bhetki*. It is a member of the Perch family (*Lates Calcarifer*). Of all the fish sold in Calcutta, its flavour is the closest to that of a North Atlantic fish. For that reason *bekti* was the favourite of the British who adapted European recipes around it and it remains popular in the Anglo-Indian cookery of old hotels and clubs.

Bhadralok – The old bourgeoisie of Calcutta. The common people were called the *chotalok*, or small people.

Bhang – A mildly intoxicating preparation of cannabis, often taken during the Spring festival of Holi.

Bhaji – Deep-fried vegetable snack.

Bhel puri – Savoury snack from street-vendor, consisting of small puffed breads and a variety of accompaniments. Especially popular in Bombay.

Bhon kattya – I've ripped you to shreds.

Busti – Slum area or shanty town.

Chai – Tea. *Chai* from a street-vendor is usually made from tea dust and boiled with milk, sugar and sometimes spices.

Chee-chee – Derisive term for Anglo-Indians, referring to their lilting singsong way of speaking.

Chillum – The bowl of a hookah or a straight clay pipe used for smoking tobacco or cannabis.

Daab – Green coconut.

Dal makhani – *Dal* is the generic name for all kinds of edible pulses. *Dal makhani* is a rich recipe, calling for plenty of *makhan* or butter.

Derzi – Neighbourhood tailor.

Dhaba – Inexpensive restaurant, usually run by Punjabis and specialising in 'non-vegetarian' dishes. In the countryside, *dhabas* serve as transport cafés.

Dholak – A double-headed drum used by folk musicians.

Dhoti – A traditional sarong or loincloth worn by Bengali

men, made of starched calico and arranged in careful folds or pleats.

Dosa – A pancake of fermented rice flour.

Dupatta – An elegant double sided scarf worn by women, especially students.

Durwan – A gatekeeper or doorman.

Ek dum – Imperative: 'On the double' or 'As quickly as possible'. Also used in agreement: 'Bang on' or 'Absolutely.'

Goonda – A ruffian or a violent criminal.

Gram – Chickpea.

Gulab jamun – 'Rosewater plum', in reality a type of sweet served in syrup.

Gully-gully – A kind of conjuror, originally from the Middle East. The *gully-gully* men who worked in India specialised in illusions of nature (fast-growing seeds, for example) and could make untrained birds perform tricks.

Gurdwara – Sikh temple.

Halal – Ritual method of slaughter by Muslim butchers.

Han – Yes.

Idli – Steamed cake of fermented rice. South Indian originally but popular across the subcontinent.

Jatra – Traditional folk theatre of Bengal.

Kabaadi – An ancient team-game, seven players in a team, similar to tag or 'prisoner's base', in which the catcher has to hold his breath while simultaneously repeating '*kabaadi, kabaadi*'.

Kathi roll – Kebab served in a rolled flat bread, comparable to a burrito.

Khus – Vetiver (*Andropogon squarrosus*), sweet-smelling grass used for screens and mats. It is also used as a culinary herb.

Kurta – Loose knee-length shirt worn over pyjama trousers.

Lingam – Phallus of Shiva.

Lunghi – Sarong or loincloth.

Mogra – The Arabian jasmine (*jasminum sambac*).

Nabob – Ostentatiously wealthy Briton in India. The word derives from *Nawab* (see below).

Namaskaar – A Hindu greeting, with bowed head and palms pressed together as if in prayer.

Nawab – Ruler of a province under the Moghul Emperor.

Nimki – Savoury snack mixture, similar to the 'Bombay Mix' sold in Britain. Sometimes anglicised as *namkins*.

Paan – Astringent combination of chopped areca nut, lime (the chemical, not the fruit), spices, aromatic jams and other ingredients, wrapped in a betel leaf. Sometimes taken as a digestive after a meal.

Pansari – Chemist, druggist, provider of patent medicines.

Pau bhaji – a street snack of curried vegetables served with a soft European-style bread roll called a *pau*, which apparently means a foot. The roll is vaguely foot-shaped. Others maintain that the dough was traditionally kneaded by foot. There is also a theory that *pau* is a corruption of the French *pain*.

Pitha – A sacred place. Also a sweetmeat made from rice flour or cream of wheat.

Prasad – Offering of food to a temple deity.

Puja – Hindu worship.

Pukka – Genuine, well-made.

Punkah – Old-fashioned ceiling fan, from the days before electricity, operated by a *punkah-wallah*.

Puri sabzi – Fried (puffed) bread with curried vegetables. Popular snack on railway journeys.

Qawwali – Rapturous singing by followers of Sufi saints. The greatest of recent *qawwali* singers was Nusrat Fateh Ali Khan.

Salaam – Muslim greeting.

Salwar, salwar kameez – Loose tunic and baggy trousers, worn by women.

Sanyassin – A Hindu who has renounced all worldly ties.

Sarod – A type of lute. There is a metal plate, similar to that of a dobro guitar, fitted across the gourd belly. Amjad Ali Khan is the contemporary master of the *sarod*.

Shabash – Well done! Bravo!

Shamiana – An awning or open-sided tent, often brightly coloured.

Shehnai – A type of oboe, related to the shawm of medieval Europe. It is used in folk celebrations as well as in classical music. It is supposed to sound auspicious. Bismilla Khan is the foremost virtuoso of the *shehnai*.

Singhara – Literally a water-chestnut (*Trapa bispinosa*) but in Bengal *singhara* refers to the samosas sold in sweetshops and foodstalls.

Sitar – Musical instrument, something like a guitar, with a gourd as its sound-box and five or seven strings, played with a plectrum. My favourite *sitar* player is the late Nikhil Bannerjee.

Sudra – The lowest of the four Hindu castes. Manual worker or menial.

Surbahar – A larger, thicker-stringed, heavier-fretted version of a *sitar*, with a deep, dignified tone. Imrat Khan is a master of the *surbahar*.

Tabla – The most popular percussion instrument in Hindustani classical music, consisting of a pair of drums, the *dayan* (treble) and the *bayan* (bass). Zakir Hussein is the great *tabla* soloist.

Tambura – A drone instrument, usually with four strings.

Thandai – Refreshing yoghurt drink. *Thandai* actually means 'coolness'. Sometimes it is laced with *bhang*.

Yaar – Friend. Commonly used in speech among males, like 'mate'.

Wada – Teatime savoury, generally vegetarian.

Zamindar – A major land-owner.

Zarda – Chewing tobacco; also any combination of herbs chewed to freshen the mouth.

SELECTED READING

By no means exhaustive, this list is made up of favourite books. Anyone searching for rare or out-of-print books about India (from all over the world) should contact Hugh Ashley Rayner, 4 Malvern Buildings, Fairfield Park, Bath BA1 6JX (telephone 01225 463552 or email hughrayner@indiabooks.co.uk).

P. Bandyopadhyay – *Bauls of Bengal* (Firma KLM Private Ltd, Calcutta 1989)

Chitrita Banerji – *Life And Food In Bengal* (Weidenfeld & Nicolson, London 1991)

Gautam Bhatia – *Punjabi Baroque* (Penguin India, Delhi 1994)

Jayabrato Chatterjee – *Last Train to Innocence* (Penguin Books, Delhi 1995)

Sukanta Chaudhuri (editor) – *Calcutta, The Living City*, vols I and II (Oxford University Press, Delhi 1990)

Minakshie Das Gupta, Bunny Gupta & Jaya Chaliha – *The Calcutta Cookbook* (Penguin Books India, Delhi 1995)

Desmond Doig – *Calcutta, An Artist's Impression* (The Statesman Ltd, Calcutta 1970s)

John Dowson – *A Classical Dictionary of Hindu Mythology and Religion* (Asia Publishing House, London 1989)

Krishna Dutta & Andrew Robinson (editors) – *Noon In Calcutta* (Bloomsbury, London 1992)

Balraj Khanna – *Kalighat: Indian Popular Painting* (Redstone, London 1993)

J.P. Losty – *Calcutta, City of Palaces* (The British Library, London 1990).

Ajit Mookerjee – *Kali, The Feminine Force* (Thames & Hudson, London 1988)

Geoffrey Moorhouse – *Calcutta, The City Revealed* (Weidenfeld & Nicolson, London 1971)

Pratapaditya Pal (editor) – *Changing Visions, Lasting Images: Calcutta through 300 years* (Marg Publications, Bombay 1990)

K. M. Sen – *Hinduism* (Penguin, London 1961)

Prabhas Sen – *Crafts of West Bengal* (Mapin, Ahmedabad 1994)

Herbert Stark – *Hostages to India* (Star, Calcutta 1926)

Raleigh Trevelyan – *The Golden Oriole* (Oxford University Press, Oxford 1987)

ACKNOWLEDGEMENTS

I should like to thank everyone who showed us such kindness and hospitality in Calcutta: those who appear in the book and those who don't. I must apologise for this catch-all arrangement; to list every name would take pages and pages and there would be the risk of forgetting someone.

At home, my thanks go to Mr Lakhanpal at the Government of India Tourist Office, Brian MacArthur at *The Times*, my agent Charles Walker and my editors Arpita Das, Renuka Chatterjee, Peter Carson and Nicky White. I would also like to express my gratitude to all the friends, in Britain and India, who read *Abdul's Taxi to Kalighat* in its formative stages and who gave me such vital support.